BESTSELLING BOOK SERIES

Asset Allocation For Dummies®

Cheat Sheet

Knowing What to Ask Your Financial Advisor

Don't be embarrassed to ask a financial advisor for investment help when you need it. Shop around: Meet with two or three potential advisors before you pick one. Visit them and meet the staff at their office. And don't be scared to ask the tough questions to gauge their investment expertise — the best financial advisors will welcome your questions and be proud to share their responses with you. Here are a few to get you started:

- ✔ **How did your clients do in the last down market?** Everyone's a genius in a bull market, but how did the advisor do when times got tough?

- ✔ **Can you describe your investing approach for me?** The answer will tell you the firm's investment philosophy. Don't hesitate to ask for details.

- ✔ **Are you sensitive to taxes?** You want an advisor who tries to maximize your after-tax results. It's not what you make, but what you keep, that counts.

- ✔ **What do you invest in?** Look for a firm that provides you the most choices and flexibility (a mix of assets like mutual funds, individual stocks, bonds, and exchange-traded funds).

- ✔ **Where will my assets reside, and how are they protected?** Most firms house their clients' assets with a custodian. Ask the firm if its custodian is a member of the Securities Investor Protection Corporation (SIPC), which provides limited protection for consumers if the custodian goes under, and if the firm and its custodian have other insurance, to provide additional protection.

Understanding Common Asset Allocation Terms

To make your way down the asset allocation highway without hitting too many bumps, here are some basic terms to guide you:

- ✔ **Total return:** Returns quoted in the press often focus strictly on growth (for example, "The S&P 500 is up 6 percent this year"). You want to know *total return*, which is the combination of income (interest from bonds or dividends from stocks) and growth.

- ✔ **Nominal returns:** Returns that aren't adjusted for inflation. Most returns presented are nominal returns.

- ✔ **Real returns:** Returns that are adjusted (downward) for inflation.

- ✔ **Standard deviation:** The most common measure of investment volatility; gauges how much an investment's return varies over time from its long-term average.

- ✔ **Risk drag:** Over realistic investment horizons (more than a year), an investment's volatility can eat away at its return. This effect is called *risk drag*, and it's a subtle but real phenomenon that you need to keep an eye on.

- ✔ **Perfect negative correlation:** This is the holy grail of investing: finding a set of investments whose returns fluctuate in opposite directions from each other, to exactly the same degree every time. You won't find it, but you can approach it, and it really will help reduce risk.

- ✔ **Efficient frontier:** If you can't improve a portfolio — in other words, it's impossible to find another one of similar risk with a better return, or one of similar return with lower risk — then that portfolio is on the *efficient frontier*. The efficient frontier is a great place to be.

- ✔ **Rebalancing:** Over time, your portfolio will drift away from its target allocation. *Rebalancing* is the process that brings it back into alignment. If you do it right, rebalancing can reduce the risk and increase the return of your portfolio.

For Dummies: Bestselling Book Series for Beginners

Asset Allocation For Dummies®

Deciding on Your Investment Strategy

Take these factors into consideration to decide on your investment strategy before determining your asset allocation:

- ✔ **Your investment horizon and long-term financial goals:** Your money needs to keep working for you far into the future, even if you're already retired. Do the work now to project your long-term cash flow.

- ✔ **Your return requirements:** What kind of return do you need from your portfolio? The answer will tell you how conservative or aggressive your investment strategy needs to be.

- ✔ **Your risk tolerance:** How far are you willing to go to get the return you need? The higher the return you'd like, the more risk you must take.

- ✔ **Your constraints:** Constraints are nonnegotiable, period. Maybe you won't consider certain investments for personal or moral reasons, for example. Maybe you won't even think about dropping a poorly performing stock from your portfolio because you inherited it from your Great-Aunt Jenny.

- ✔ **Your tax situation:** Tax-free, lower-yielding municipal bonds may be a good choice for you now — however, taxable, and higher-yielding, bonds may serve you better in retirement, if you end up in a lower tax bracket. (For more tax tips, see Chapter 14.)

Building a Successful Portfolio

Build a successful portfolio by following asset allocation's top-down, systematic approach:

1. **Decide on your investment strategy.** How conservative or aggressive should you be? Take the factors that we outline in this Cheat Sheet into consideration. For help, you may want to ask a financial advisor. Then commit to your strategy by writing it down, in an Investment Policy Statement (see Chapter 7).

2. **Figure out your asset allocation.** Your investment strategy informs your asset allocation. First decide on the asset classes and subclasses you want to use (your asset baskets), which include cash, fixed income, equities, and alternatives (such as real estate and commodities). Then determine how big each of these baskets should be.

3. **Fill your asset baskets.** Start filling your baskets with specific investments — stocks and stock funds, bonds and bond funds, cash equivalents, real estate investment trusts (REITs), and commodity index funds. While filling your baskets, put higher-taxed (tax-inefficient) investments in tax-deferred accounts and lower-taxed (tax-efficient) assets in taxable accounts.

4. **Rebalance opportunistically.** Rebalance when some of your asset allocation baskets begin to over-flow. Redistribute the excess to the baskets that have become underfilled. Systematically selling high and buying low will keep you true to your asset allocation and generate increased returns over the long haul.

For Dummies: Bestselling Book Series for Beginners

Asset Allocation
FOR
DUMMIES®

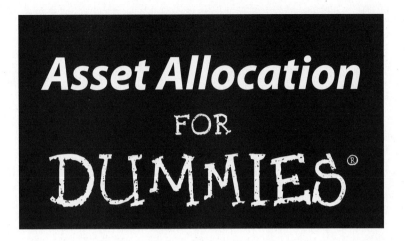

Asset Allocation FOR DUMMIES®

by Jerry A. Miccolis, CFA®, CFP®, FCAS, MAAA
Brinton Eaton Wealth Advisors

and Dorianne R. Perrucci
Financial writer

WILEY

Wiley Publishing, Inc.

Asset Allocation For Dummies®

Published by
Wiley Publishing, Inc.
111 River St.
Hoboken, NJ 07030-5774
www.wiley.com

Copyright © 2009 by Wiley Publishing, Inc., Indianapolis, Indiana

Published simultaneously in Canada

For general information on our other products and services, please contact our Customer Care Department within the U.S. at 877-762-2974, outside the U.S. at 317-572-3993, or fax 317-572-4002.

For technical support, please visit www.wiley.com/techsupport.

Wiley also publishes its books in a variety of electronic formats. Some content that appears in print may not be available in electronic books.

Library of Congress Control Number: 2009925030

ISBN: 978-0-470-40963-3

Manufactured in the United States of America

10 9 8 7 6 5 4 3 2 1

WILEY

About the Authors

Jerry A. Miccolis: Jerry's clients, colleagues, and friends were caught a bit off-guard when, in 2003, he decided to change careers, from enterprise risk management to personal wealth management. But, toward the end of his 30-year stint in the actuarial and risk-management fields (including 25 years with the international management consulting firm Towers Perrin, where he eventually led the global enterprise risk management practice), he had already nearly achieved the two most sought-after certifications of his chosen second career — Chartered Financial Analyst (CFA) and Certified Financial Planner (CFP). He's never been happier, helping real people secure their financial future. A senior financial advisor at, and co-owner of, Brinton Eaton Wealth Advisors in Madison, New Jersey, Jerry adds his CFA and CFP designations to his credentials as a fellow of the Casualty Actuarial Society (FCAS) and member of the American Academy of Actuaries (MAAA). Jerry, who is also a member of the Financial Planning Association (FPA) and the New York Society of Security Analysts (NYSSA), holds a BS in mathematics from Drexel University.

The coauthor of *Enterprise Risk Management: Trends and Emerging Practices* (The Institute of Internal Auditors Research Foundation) and *Enterprise Risk Management: An Analytic Approach* (Tillinghast-Towers Perrin), Jerry has chaired numerous professional committees and is a widely quoted author and speaker on the subject of strategic risk management, investment management, and their interrelationship. Jerry has been published in professional journals *(Strategy & Leadership, Operational Risk, Risk Management, Institutional Investor, CFO Magazine, Investment Advisor,* and *Financial Planning)* and in the mainstream media *(The New York Times, The Wall Street Journal, The Baltimore Sun,* MarketWatch, *MSN Money,* and Marketwire). He has appeared as an expert commentator on CBS Radio, ABC TV, and IRMI. com, the Web site of the International Risk Management Institute.

All of this, though, is what Jerry does between senior softball games, his real passion. There, Jerry plays third base and shortstop and bats much lower in the lineup than he thinks he should.

You can read more of his and his colleagues' investment advice at www. brintoneaton.com (click Research Corner) and about his softball addiction at www.casact.org/newsletter/index.cfm?fa=viewart&id=5639.

Jerry A. Miccolis, CFA, CFP, FCAS, is a principal of Brinton Eaton Associates, Inc., d/b/a Brinton Eaton Wealth Advisors, an investment adviser registered with the United States Securities and Exchange Commission. No reader should assume that the book content serves as the receipt of, or a substitute for, personalized advice from Mr. Miccolis, from Brinton Eaton Associates, Inc., or from any other investment professional. Please remember that different types of investments involve varying degrees of risk. Therefore, it should not be assumed that future performance of any specific investment or investment strategy (including the investments and/or investment strategies referenced in this book) will be profitable.

Dorianne R. Perrucci: Dorianne jokes that she's still looking for the 13¢ that caused her first checking account to bounce. Dorianne, who has written for *Newsweek, The New York Times, Mediaweek,* and TheStreet.com, began reporting about personal finance and investing in 1998 for Jane Bryant Quinn's *Washington Post* column. Previously, she reported for a daily newspaper, wrote a political column for a U.S. senator, and produced articles and books for several of the country's leading charities, including Covenant House, the Times Square shelter for homeless and runaway youth. She currently edits and collaborates on investing books, including: *The Demise of the Dollar . . . and Why It's Great for Your Investments,* by Addison Wiggin (Wiley Publishing); *I.O.U.S.A., One Nation, Under Stress, In Debt,* with Addison Wiggin and Kate Incontrera (Wiley Publishing); *The Ultimate Depression Survival Guide,* by Martin D. Weiss (Wiley Publishing); and the *AARP Crash Course in Creating Retirement Income,* by Julie Jason (Sterling Publishing).

Dorianne, a graduate of Marquette University's School of Journalism, is a member of the American Society of Journalists and Authors and the New York Financial Writers Association. When she isn't busy explaining the consumer's next investment challenge, she continues to search for that missing 13¢.

Dedication

To you, the average investor, who is curious enough to wonder if a *For Dummies* book can really help you get superior investment results, like the pros. Asset allocation, which begins with determining the right (and the right-size) baskets for your investment "eggs," isn't exactly a piece of cake, but we promise, if you're determined to learn the recipe, we'll make the process a very satisfying one for you.

Acknowledgments

It takes a village to write a book. Okay, not original, but true — you need a tribe of supporters to make it safely to the "efficient frontier" of investing.

Jerry Miccolis thanks his coauthor, Dorianne, for her contagious enthusiasm and offbeat sense of humor — and for constantly nagging him to "Keep it accessible!" Numerous editorial suggestions from his Brinton Eaton colleagues — Bob DiQuollo, Ben Jacoby, Jeremy Welther, Jerv Brinton, Nick Laverghetta, Ellen Clawans, and Abby Scandlen — vastly improved the final manuscript. Special mention to Marina Goodman, who seemed to take particular pleasure in offering blistering critiques of early drafts but also made excellent original contributions and helped prepare many of the exhibits and examples. They and the rest of the staff — Colleen Betzler, Dave Hill, Eric Mancini, Doris Merrick, Adrian Fedorkiw, Kim Dibenedetto, and Pam Trunfio — graciously picked up the slack for Jerry at the office. Most important, Jerry thanks Marcella, his wife and muse, for her unfailing support, encouragement, and understanding, during the nights and weekends he devoted to this book.

Dorianne Perrucci thanks Jerry, for his patience in explaining technical jargon and would like to ask him to explain *perfect negative correlation* one more time. She thanks her agent, Marilyn Allen, and the entire amazing *For Dummies* team, especially Acquisitions Editor Stacy Kennedy, who actually *wanted* to publish a book on asset allocation; Elizabeth Kuball, project editor extraordinaire; and Dummifier Brittain Phillips, whose mysterious ability to rework text works wonders. Dorianne is also grateful for her family and a host of colleagues and friends for continuing to cheer her on.

Publisher's Acknowledgments

We're proud of this book; please send us your comments through our Dummies online registration form located at `http://dummies.custhelp.com`. For other comments, please contact our Customer Care Department within the U.S. at 877-762-2974, outside the U.S. at 317-572-3993, or fax 317-572-4002.

Some of the people who helped bring this book to market include the following:

Acquisitions, Editorial, and Media Development

Project Editor: Elizabeth Kuball

Acquisitions Editor: Stacy Kennedy

Copy Editor: Elizabeth Kuball

Assistant Editor: Erin Calligan Mooney

Editorial Program Coordinator: Joe Niesen

Technical Editor:
Louis J. Schwarz, QFP, CFP, RFC

Senior Editorial Manager: Jennifer Ehrlich

Editorial Supervisor and Reprint Editor:
Carmen Krikorian

Editorial Assistants: Jennette ElNaggar, David Lutton

Cover Photos: © Yiap Lightbox/Alamy

Cartoons: Rich Tennant
(`www.the5thwave.com`)

Composition Services

Project Coordinator: Kristie Rees

Layout and Graphics: Carrie A. Cesavice, Reuben W. Davis, Melissa K. Smith, Christin Swinford

Proofreaders: Melissa Cossell, Jessica Kramer, Broccoli Information Management

Indexer: Potomac Indexing, LLC

Special Help: Brittain Phillips

177-6826

Publishing and Editorial for Consumer Dummies

    Diane Graves Steele, Vice President and Publisher, Consumer Dummies

    Kristin Ferguson-Wagstaffe, Product Development Director, Consumer Dummies

    Ensley Eikenburg, Associate Publisher, Travel

    Kelly Regan, Editorial Director, Travel

Publishing for Technology Dummies

    Andy Cummings, Vice President and Publisher, Dummies Technology/General User

Composition Services

    Gerry Fahey, Vice President of Production Services

    Debbie Stailey, Director of Composition Services

Contents at a Glance

Table of Contents

Introduction

$\mathcal{Y}$ ou don't need to be an expert analyst, a star stock-picker, or a rocket scientist to have better investment results than most other investors. You just need to allocate your assets in the right way, and have the conviction to stick with that allocation. Talk about empowering!

The big secret behind asset allocation — the secret that most sophisticated investors know and use to their benefit — is that it's really not all that hard to do.

If you follow asset allocation's systematic, top-down approach to investing, you'll be more likely to arrive at your financial destination safely, and with a lot more success and portfolio stability than if you try a bottom-up approach like the stock-pickers and market-timers employ (generally with lousy results). You'll reach your long-term goals more reliably — and that's a huge comfort during times of market volatility, when a charging bull market can turn overnight into a snarling bear market.

That's not to say that sticking with asset allocation is the easiest thing in the world. It can be challenging, and it requires discipline, courage, and a little humility. At times, you'll be bucking prevailing market trends and have to turn a deaf ear to pundits, friends, and family, who will think you're nuts when you sell off your winners and buy losers to balance your portfolio. That'll take some intestinal fortitude. Some of asset allocation's key concepts can seem counterintuitive in other ways, too — but if you stick with the program, you'll get more out of your money than you ever thought you could.

By following the asset allocation approach, you'll

- ✔ Help insulate your portfolio against market fluctuations, the overall economy, the effects of inflation, and more.
- ✔ Make smarter decisions than the vast majority of individual investors out there — and do better than most of them over the long term.
- ✔ Make fewer mistakes with your portfolio. Diversifying your investments, choosing assets that don't always move up or down at the same time, and rebalancing your portfolio opportunistically will make it harder for you to stumble.

In short, you'll be a winner in the only monetary game that counts — enabling your life's dreams by protecting your financial future.

About This Book

There are several books about asset allocation out there, most of which are written for investment experts. This isn't one of those books. Sure, Jerry is a wealth-management expert with tons of asset allocation experience and Dorianne is a financial journalist, but we pride ourselves on our love for explaining the mysteries of investing to average investors like you. In this book, we make the often overly technical information about asset allocation accessible, whether you're a beginner or you have a little investing experience under your belt. We had fun writing this book together, and we hope you have fun reading it and using its contents to help you reach your financial goals.

One of the ways that we make the information contained in this book easier for a beginning investor to digest is the use of plenty of charts and tables. When you encounter these helpful tools, take a moment to size them up. You'll be rewarded, and you may be surprised by how much information you pick up right away. These illustrations just may be the handle you need to get a nice, firm grip on asset allocation.

Conventions Used in This Book

To help you navigate your way through this book, we use the following conventions:

- ✔ We use *italics* when we define new terms that probably aren't familiar to you.

- ✔ We use `monofont` for Web addresses. Some Web addresses may need to break across two lines of text. If that happened when the book was printed, just type in exactly what you see in this book — we didn't add any extra characters (such as hyphens).

- ✔ We discuss several different types of investment returns throughout this book, and what they mean for you. But when we use the word *return* without further modification, we're referring to *total nominal return,* which combines income and growth unadjusted for inflation. (You can read all the details in Chapter 2.)

What You're Not to Read

This book is a reference, which means you don't have to read it from beginning to end (any more than you have to read a dictionary from beginning to end to get what you need from it). If you're in a hurry, you can even skip certain pieces of information and still get the gist of what you need. Here's what you can safely skip:

- ✔ **Anything marked with a Technical Stuff icon:** For more on this icon, see the "Icons Used in This Book" section, later in this Introduction.

- ✔ **Text in gray boxes, which are known as _sidebars:_** Sidebars contain interesting — but not essential — information.

- ✔ **The copyright page:** Sure, the publisher's attorneys' feelings will be hurt, but you can skip the fine print without losing out on anything important. Shh! We won't tell.

Foolish Assumptions

When we began writing this book, we started with a few assumptions about you, our esteemed reader:

- ✔ You have a good idea of what you want to accomplish financially, but you don't know exactly how to get there.

- ✔ You've done a bit of investing, but not a lot, and you'd like to benefit from what the experts know about asset allocation.

- ✔ You know there has to be a better, more reliable, route to investment success than listening to all the talking heads in the financial media or chasing the latest hot stock tip.

- ✔ You're wondering if it's possible for anyone to make this stuff easier to understand — or even fun.

How This Book Is Organized

This book discusses asset allocation in what we believe is a natural, logical order. You can read the chapters that way, if you want. But this also a true _For Dummies_ book, so feel free to bounce around and read a little here and a little there, depending on what you're interested in and what you want to understand first.

Part 1: Discovering the Not-So-Secret Recipe for Asset Allocation

In Part I, we lay out the basics behind the asset allocation recipe, which begins with diversifying the assets you choose for your portfolio. But diversification isn't all there is to asset allocation. In order for you to figure out your ideal asset allocation, you need to assess the level of risk you're comfortable taking in exchange for the return you're seeking. In other words, how much are you looking to make, and how much risk are you willing to take on?

We also look at the many types of asset classes you can choose, ranging from standard choices (cash, fixed income, equities) to alternative choices (such as real estate and commodities). After you've got a grip on the various types of asset classes, then you're ready to make some specific choices like stocks, bonds, mutual funds, exchange-traded funds, and the like.

We tell you how you can avoid costly mistakes, and protect your portfolio from volatility, by choosing investments that don't always move up or down at the same time. Finally, we fill you in on portfolio rebalancing, which is overlooked by most investors but embraced by the pros, who know it can be used to control risk and generate extra return.

Part 11: Getting Started

You need to nail down your own personal investment strategy, and in this part we walk you through an exercise that helps to define your parameters. Those parameters include your investment horizon, risk tolerance, portfolio constraints (for example, for religious or personal reasons, you may not want to buy stocks that invest in alcohol or gambling), tax situation, and special circumstances, such as protecting your assets from creditors or your estate from taxes.

Then you're ready to develop your investment strategy and figure out what you need to sustain your lifetime cash flow. We know it sounds like a lot of big decisions, but we break it all down for you. If you're going to need $50,000 a year (in today's dollars), starting in five years, and you have $350,000 now, how are you going to get from here to there? Do you know your current assets and liabilities? Your current and future sources of income and expenses? And finally, how do you tie all this information together in a meaningful and useful framework, leading to the asset allocation that's just right for you? We answer those questions, and many more, in this part. We also give a kick-start to establishing your own unique asset allocation by looking at some valuable sample allocations.

Part III: Building and Maintaining Your Portfolio

This part shows you how to fill your asset allocation baskets with specific investments of various types. Wondering what specific investments you should buy? We tell you. Don't know how to buy those specific investments? We fill you in. Worried about the many types of fees and expenses that can creep up on you? We let you know how and where to look for them.

Because most investors have several accounts (one or more taxable accounts, individual retirement accounts for husband and wife, and so on), we also match the right investments with the right accounts, to exploit the tax characteristics of the different accounts and avoid creating unnecessary tax bites. Then we get into the details of portfolio rebalancing (introduced in Part I) so you can get extra return if you rebalance faithfully. Finally, we explain how to measure your results and compare your portfolio's performance with the appropriate external benchmarks, so you know how well you're doing.

Part IV: Going beyond the Basics

In this part, we take a close look at alternative investments (real estate and commodities, for example) and the wonderful things they can do for your portfolio. Then we point out how you can gain the kind of tax knowledge that'll help you keep more of your well-deserved gains. After all, there's no sense in giving away too much of your money in taxes when it can be avoided with some savvy planning. We also identify the situations that should prompt you to revisit — and validate or revise — your long-term asset allocation plan.

If you need help figuring out some (or all) of the asset allocation process, we help you look over the choices of financial advisors available, and tell you the importance of paying attention to their credentials. (**Hint:** Some of those credentials are meaningless and/or misleading!) We also discuss how much these experts get paid — and by whom — and how to make sure they're working in your best interests, not their own.

Part V: The Part of Tens

If you like top-ten lists, this part is for you! The three chapters in this part help you jump-start your asset allocation with easy-to-digest (and interesting) information. Our list of ten important asset classes with their historical rates of return is a valuable reference you can use on its own, or as a tool to come back to time and again as you read other chapters. We also point out ten common mistakes that prevent investors from becoming good asset allocators. When it comes to bang for your buck, this part scores, well, a perfect ten.

Icons Used in This Book

Throughout this book, we use *icons* (little pictures in the margin) to draw your attention to certain kinds of information. Here's what the icons mean:

When you see a Tip icon, read it to find a nugget of asset allocation wisdom that you can apply as you carry out your investing strategy.

Anything flagged with a Remember icon is especially important to your understanding of one of asset allocation's many facets. This is the stuff you don't want to forget.

The Warning icon flags a potential problem or pitfall that could give you fits if you weren't aware of it. If you're into dodging bullets, stay on the lookout for Warning icons.

The Technical Stuff icon appears next to material that can be a bit tricky. You may not be able to pick up on it right away, and it may not be absolutely critical to your understanding of the topic being explained, but if you can manage to tackle the information, it'll give you an even firmer grasp of asset allocation . . . or at least impress your friends.

Where to Go from Here

You can tackle this book in several ways. If you're a beginner, you may want to read Chapter 1 to get the big picture, and then scan through the beginnings of the other chapters to find the inroad that interests you the most. If you really want to know what makes asset allocation such a great strategy, check out the chapters in Part I. There you'll find some of the background material that'll help you to understand why asset allocation makes so much sense. Or maybe you've heard a little bit about all the different types of assets out there, but you want to read a lot more. If that's the case, flip to Part III. There you can find out what's on offer and what makes the most sense for your portfolio.

If you've already wrapped your brain around investment and asset allocation basics, it may be time for you to turn to Part IV, where we discuss a few
more-advanced topics like alternative investments and tax strategies. This
part also includes a very helpful chapter that tells you how to find the best
financial advisor for you.

No matter where you start, don't feel compelled to read this book straight
through, from beginning to end. We wrote the book so you could start anywhere, and we provide lots of cross-references to point you to other places in
the book where you can find information you may need to better understand
what we're talking about. Whichever way makes sense to you — dig in, you
(and your portfolio) will reap the rewards!

Part I

Discovering the Not-So-Secret Recipe for Asset Allocation

The 5th Wave   By Rich Tennant

"When you asked me to advise you on investing your nest egg, I assumed you were speaking figuratively, Mr. Bunter."

In this part . . .

We start by looking at the big picture of asset allocation — from what seems like 30,000 feet. But as we talk about risk and return, and review the various asset classes and how to mix them together in the right proportions, you begin to focus in and see how getting that mix right is the single most important investment decision you can make. We also introduce portfolio rebalancing, which is a process overlooked by most investors but championed by the pros, to control risk and generate extra return.

Chapter 1

Understanding Asset Allocation

In This Chapter

▶ Appreciating the importance of asset allocation

▶ Discovering how to apply asset allocation to your portfolio

▶ Getting started with building your portfolio

▶ Going beyond the basics to get the most out of asset allocation

*P*sst! Want to know the trick to making a killing in investments? One that offers fat financial returns with little or no risk? Sadly (and as you'd probably guess), there's no such thing.

Want to know how you can score great long-term investment results while minimizing unnecessary risk and costs? In that case, you've come to the right place! With the right asset allocation, you can enjoy substantial investment returns with the lowest possible amounts of risk and cost.

Asset allocation, in simplest terms, is deciding how to divvy up your invest-ment dollars among various types of assets. More fully, it's a comprehensive, coherent, top-down, strategic approach to investing that has well-established science and years of real-life superior investment results to back it up. In other words, it's bona fide, and when it comes to investing, nothing consis-tently beats it.

In this chapter (and throughout this book), we show you how and why asset allocation works and, perhaps more important, how it can work for you. We take you step by step through the time-tested approach to investing that the most successful professionals use. We explain how you can reap the benefits of rebalancing, which is the closest thing to a free lunch you'll ever find in investing. And we show you how to do all this and save on your taxes, too!

In true *For Dummies* fashion, Chapter 1 is a microcosm of the book that fol-lows. Think of this chapter as a bird's-eye view of asset allocation. We hit all the high points, and, as we go, we point you to the chapters you can visit to get a more detailed treatment of each topic.

Figuring Out Why Asset Allocation Is So Important

When it comes to your investments, what's more important than asset allocation? In our opinion — and in the opinion of most every reputable investment expert — nothing.

In this section, we clue you in on why asset allocation is so important, using a couple different perspectives. First, we use the infamous story of Enron to show you the terrific power of diversification, which is one of several fundamental aspects of asset allocation. Then, to give you a feel for asset allocation's other key aspects, we use the rest of the section to take a broader view, exploring what independent studies have to say about the role of asset allocation in driving investment success.

Encapsulating the Enron story

Here's the short version of the Enron story: Beginning in the early 1930s as a modest oil pipeline company, Enron grew over the years, through mergers and acquisitions of other energy companies. By the late 1990s, it was very aggressive in energy trading and other complicated financial engineering ventures. (Don't worry about the details — it was really, really complex stuff.) Enron had, in fact, become an industry leader and business-school case study in the creative use of these sophisticated financial arrangements. By early 2001, Enron had grown to be the seventh largest company in the United States based on revenue and had been named America's Most Innovative Company for the sixth year in a row by *Fortune* magazine. It was also on *Fortune*'s 100 Best Companies to Work for in America list in 2000.

Then the bottom fell out. Before the end of 2001, Enron was bankrupt. The cause was accounting fraud. The lengths to which Enron's executives went to conceal their illegal activities were epic in their ingenuity and complexity. That's the white-collar-crime part of the story that was splashed all over news headlines for months. But that's not the worst part.

The worst part — and the part most relevant to you, the average investor — was this: Even while the Enron executives were perpetrating their fraud, they were encouraging their own employees to stake their financial futures on the company. In addition to offering an employee stock ownership plan (ESOP), Enron urged its employees to invest in company stock in their retirement plans. The company's matching contributions to its employees' 401(k) plans were made exclusively in Enron stock. And, in the fall of 2001, as its fraudulent financials were unraveling, Enron made it impossible for its employees to switch out of Enron stock in their retirement plans.

It was a real tragedy for thousands of Enron employees, who watched help-lessly as their retirement funds and personal financial futures evaporated. Sadly, it happened because Enron led them to violate one of the immutable laws of sound investing: Never, *ever* put too many of your eggs in one basket.

Keep your investments diversified! Don't invest too much in any one security, especially your employer's stock. (Enough of your financial future is already tied to the company's well being.) As a general rule, don't invest more than 5 percent of your invested assets in any one stock.

So that's the enduring lesson of Enron for investors: Diversify, diversify, diversify! Asset allocation begins with portfolio diversification, but as we describe later, it goes much further.

Exploiting the 90 percent solution

Quick — what decision will have the biggest impact on your investment results? It's not *stock picking* (chasing so-called "hot" tips on individual securi-ties, usually without regard to a coherent portfolio strategy) or *market timing* (trying to beat the market by timing when to get in and get out of it). The lion's share of your performance will be determined by your asset allocation — how you divide your money among various types of assets.

According to several well-regarded academic studies over the years, over 90 percent of the difference in returns among various investment portfolios is explained by one thing: asset allocation. That fact alone should lead you to a profound revelation: You should spend the vast majority of your investing time and effort on getting your asset allocation right. Nothing else matters nearly as much.

Separately, study after study has shown that investors who take other approaches, such as market timing or stock picking, consistently underper-form the market averages over the long term.

But if those types of dubious investment strategies have been shown to fizzle out in the long term, why do you see so much newsprint and radio and TV airtime devoted to them? Why are most of the stories about market timing and stock picking instead of asset allocation? Because those other things are sexy. They're exciting. And they play to our baser instincts — our desire to jump into the next great low-effort, get-rich-quick scheme. By contrast, asset allocation is a steady and reliable approach that takes some thought and consideration. In other words, it's relatively unexciting. But it's the investing approach the pros have used for decades to get better long-term results than those other guys. (Check out the "Appreciating the science of asset alloca-tion" sidebar in this chapter to find out why.) Asset allocation gives you a much better chance of ending up with more money in the long run. How's that for unexciting?

Appreciating the science of asset allocation

Sometimes, asset allocation and its associated activities seem counterintuitive. It may make you uncomfortable, particularly when those around you are doing the opposite of what you're doing (buying when you're selling, selling when you're buying, avoiding investments you're embracing, and so on). At those times, reassure yourself with some knowledge of the science behind what makes asset allocation work.

One of the principles of asset allocation is the reduction of portfolio volatility. Excessive volatility can cost you real dollars because of a phenomenon called *risk drag*. As we explain

in Chapter 2, risk drag eats away at your investment return over time. By combining the right investments in the right proportions, you can tame risk drag.

Finding those investments and determining those proportions is also a matter of some science. The trick is to find investments that don't *correlate* very well with each other (meaning, they don't all go up or down at the same time). Investments like that may seem unappealing to new investors, but those in the know realize that they can use them to create real portfolio magic, as we show you in Chapter 4.

And here's the best news of all: You don't have to be a financial genius or fork over a huge wad of cash to a world-class broker or an elite hedge-fund manager to reap the rewards of asset allocation. You just need to understand the basics and figure out how to apply those basics to your personal investment situation.

The rest of this chapter shows you how to do just that.

Uncovering the Basics of Asset Allocation

Successful asset allocation involves a few basic concepts. These main components, which form the centerpiece of Part I, are as follows:

- ✔ Understanding the fundamental relationship and trade-off between investment risk and return
- ✔ Selecting the asset classes that are right for you
- ✔ Determining the right mix of those asset classes to achieve your objectives
- ✔ Rebalancing your portfolio periodically to maintain your desired mix

We take you step by step through these basics in this section.

The complete asset allocation picture contains other less basic features (developing your investment strategy in the context of your long-term financial plan, filling your portfolio with the right securities, putting those securities into the right accounts to get the best after-tax results, measuring your performance, and so on), which we cover a little later in this chapter.

Balancing risk and return

Risk and return are the two central concepts underlying all of investing. To enjoy a return on your investments, you have to take some risk. Although *return* (your percentage gain) can be measured with objective precision, risk is a very personal, subjective concept. Whether you define your own concept of risk as uncertainty, instability, the chance of losing money, lack of peace of mind, or in some other manner, one thing is generally true: The more return you want, the more risk you have to accept. As you consider the length of time over which you'll be investing, your ideas about risk and return may change in surprising ways. You can read all about these concepts, including the all-important trade-off between risk and return, in Chapter 2.

The risk-return trade-off has been the subject of much academic study. One of the really useful tools that has emerged from all that study is the *efficient frontier*. It might sound a little cold and complicated, but it's really a simple visual device that'll help you reach a deep understanding of asset allocation's core concepts and guide you toward the asset allocation that's right for you. We show you how to use the efficient frontier in Chapter 2.

Selecting your asset classes

An early step in asset allocation is determining the *asset classes* (groups of investments with similar characteristics) that you want in your portfolio. In Chapter 3, we take you on a tour of the asset classes at your disposal. There are traditional classes, such as cash, fixed-income investments (including bonds and bond funds), and equities (including stocks and stock funds). We cover issues such as maturity, creditworthiness, and taxability of the various types of fixed-income investments, as well as the size, style, and sector of your equity investment choices.

We also dig into so-called *alternative investments,* which can help stabilize your portfolio. These include real estate, hard assets (such as commodities), and hedge funds. And we discuss going global with international investments in all these areas.

Many of the asset classes you can invest in may have unique and important roles to play in your portfolio, so it's wise for you to get to know them as well as you can.

Determining your asset mix

In addition to knowing what kinds of assets are available for you to include in your portfolio, you also need to understand how to mix those assets in the right proportions.

To best appreciate how the right mix works for you, and to help you find your ideal mix, you really need to understand *correlation* (the way your various asset classes behave in relation to each other). We can't stress the importance of correlation enough, and you can dive into the details in Chapter 4.

The holy grail of investing is a set of asset classes that have perfect *negative correlation* with each other, meaning that one zigs when the other zags (that is, if one moves up, the other moves down by the same amount, at the same time). Asset classes like that can be combined to create a portfolio that has absolutely no risk! But, as you may imagine, perfect negative correlation — like perfection of any kind — is impossible to find in real life (with the exception of chocolate peanut butter ice cream), so you try to get as close as you can. You can reduce risk drag (see Chapter 2) considerably, and thereby improve your portfolio's return, just by properly mixing assets that have positive, but weak, correlation. In Chapter 4, we show you how to let these ideas guide your decisions on asset mix.

In determining how much of an asset class to include in your portfolio, keep in mind that the characteristics and behavior of any one asset class on its own are irrelevant. What really counts is the behavior of the *entire* portfolio when that asset class is added to it. This is a guiding principle of asset allocation. (We cover how to put this principle to practical use in Chapter 8.)

Rebalancing your asset mix

Setting up your asset mix isn't the end of asset allocation. The financial markets, where investors buy and sell securities, will see to it that different asset classes inside your portfolio will grow at different rates. Over time, your portfolio will, therefore, drift away from the mix you set up so carefully. When that happens, you'll need to occasionally buy and sell assets to get your portfolio back to your target allocation. That process is called *rebalancing*.

Rebalancing on the right schedule will do more than keep your portfolio faithful to its asset allocation. It'll help you rein in risk. More surprisingly, it'll also help you generate extra return seemingly out of thin air! That's what we mean when we say that rebalancing is the closest thing to a free lunch you'll ever find in investing.

Rebalancing sounds great, right? It really is, and you can read up on the details in Chapter 5. Rebalancing forces you to buy low and sell high. It allows you to exploit a phenomenon called *volatility pumping* to get you that extra return. But you have to have the fortitude to do it correctly, because it'll require you to do things at times that are contrary to what others around you who haven't read up on asset allocation are doing. But the payoff is worth it: Rebalancing will reduce your risk and ramp up your long-term returns.

Getting Started with Your Investment Strategy

As you can read in the previous section, Part I of this book is all about understanding the basic tenets of asset allocation. That's crucial stuff, and it's tough to do much with asset allocation if you don't have a grasp on the basics. But when you've wrapped your brain around them, how do you make those basics work for you? The next step is developing a well-considered investment strategy, and that's what you can discover in Part II.

As we outline in Chapter 6, your strategy should lay out the following parameters:

- ✔ **Your investment horizon:** This is the length of time you expect to be invested. It's critically important to get this right, and here's a big clue: It may be longer than you think.

- ✔ **Your return objectives:** This isn't the return you want, but the return you need. We help you determine your return objectives when we discuss your long-term financial plan, later in this section.

- ✔ **Your risk tolerance:** However you define your subjective concept of risk, there's likely a point — a limit — beyond which you're just not comfortable going. We show you how to use this tolerance level to find your best-performing asset allocation.

- ✔ **Your portfolio constraints:** You may have certain investments, or even whole asset classes, that you just won't consider for personal reasons (for example, maybe you won't invest in a tobacco company because your father died of lung cancer, or you won't invest in a beer company because drinking is against your religious beliefs) or certain holdings that you just won't let go of (maybe you just can't bring yourself to sell the stock your grandma left to you). We explain how to deal with these limitations.

✓ **Your tax situation:** Your tax bracket may lead you to consider certain asset classes that wouldn't make sense for you otherwise. We discuss how you can exploit this situation.

✓ **Your special circumstances:** If you have an unusual exposure to lawsuits (due to your profession, perhaps) or an overriding desire to protect your assets from estate taxes, we describe how you might make certain adjustments to your portfolio.

You should set these investment strategy parameters after looking at your long-term financial plan. We show how to do that in Chapter 7, where we introduce another useful tool, your Lifetime Cash-flow Projection (LCP). We're not going to lie: Developing your LCP is the most work we ask you to do in this book. Compared to some of the other tasks, it can feel like heavy lifting. You don't have to do it if you don't want. We're not saying you can't get yourself a decent asset allocation without an LCP, but we really don't think you should cut corners when it comes to your financial future. In addition to helping you derive the asset allocation that's just right for you, your LCP also allows you to test any number of critical "what if" scenarios as you go through life. We also advise you to document your investment in an Investment Policy Statement, just as the pros do.

Speaking of the pros, in Chapter 8, we show you how they would use all this information to derive an ideal asset allocation for you. We show you what you can learn from them to do it yourself. We also give you a head start by showing some sample asset allocations and taking you step by step through an example with a fictional couple, John and Jane Doe.

Building Your Portfolio and Keeping It True to Your Long-Term Goal

After you've settled on your asset allocation (you've assigned target percentages to all the asset classes you want in your portfolio), then what do you do? That's when it's time to do some shopping. You have to buy securities to put in your portfolio to achieve the allocation you decided on. When you do that, you have to figure out in which of your various investment accounts to buy the securities. (You keep your securities in accounts, and determining which accounts should hold which securities is an important process.)

But if you're smart, you won't stop there. You'll diligently monitor your portfolio, so that, among other things, you'll know when you need to rebalance. And finally, you'll want to measure your portfolio's results in a meaningful way to gauge whether all this is working the way you want. We cover all these things, in turn, in this section and throughout Part III.

Selecting securities

Within each of the asset classes we outline in Chapter 3, there are scads of securities you can buy to represent the asset class. With thousands of possibilities, how do you choose? In Chapter 9, we take you on a tour of the securities available to you. There are stocks and bonds, of course. There are also mutual funds and exchange-traded funds, and we explain why we generally prefer the latter over the former. We also discuss index funds and actively managed funds, annuities, options, structured notes, exchange-traded notes, and others.

To keep your asset allocation in ship shape, you'll want to buy different securities in different circumstances. Sounds logical enough, but what's the best way for you to actually *buy* securities? You have a couple of broad choices: You can buy them on your own or buy them through a broker. There are advantages and disadvantages to each approach, and we cover all the relevant information in Chapter 9. You can also, if you dare, use shorting and/or leverage to expand your opportunities. We're not crazy about the prospects of those techniques for new investors, but we know you'll hear about them as you continue to grow as an investor, so we fill you in on the details.

Any security you buy carries a cost. Some of those costs — like trading commissions — are explicit; others — 401(k) management fees, for example — aren't. Some can be quite large. We provide a very complete catalog of fees and expenses that you may encounter and tell you how to uncover and compare them.

Mastering asset location

That's right — we said "location," not "allocation." *Asset location* is the tactic of matching your securities with your accounts in an optimal way to exploit all the tax advantages you can. If you choose the location of your assets wisely, you can save a bundle in taxes. (Flip to Chapter 10 to read more.)

Throughout the book, we advise you to do your asset allocation on a holistic basis (that is, across all your investment accounts in the aggregate). Those accounts may include an individual taxable account for you and, if you're married, one for your spouse. Maybe the two of you have a joint account or two. And then there are IRAs, 401(k)s, health savings accounts, and more. When you really sit down and think about it, you may be surprised by just how many accounts you have. You should consider them all in total when you apply your asset allocation.

That doesn't mean that you apply the same allocation percentages to each of the accounts — quite the contrary. The reason? Taxes. Each of the securities you may want to buy has its own income-tax characteristics, and some are more tax-friendly than others. And each of the accounts you own has specific tax features. Some are fully taxable, some are tax deferred, and some may be tax free. You can save a lot of taxes by being clever about which securities you locate in which accounts. In Chapter 10, we take you through a detailed example, using the Does (a fictional couple we introduce in Chapter 8), to show you how to be tax smart at the account level while achieving your desired asset allocation at the portfolio level.

Monitoring your portfolio to stay on target

The rebalancing that we talk about earlier (and in depth in Chapter 5) can provide you substantial benefits. (Remember that rebalancing is what we call the closest thing to a free lunch you'll ever find in investing.) But to get those benefits, you have to rebalance at the right times.

The "right time" to rebalance can't be scheduled in advance. These times aren't specific calendar dates; they occur when your portfolio drifts away from its target asset allocations by a sufficient amount. So, you need to keep tabs on your portfolio to make sure you don't miss those rebalancing opportunities.

In Chapter 11, we go through this rebalancing exercise with the Does. As we also discuss in that chapter, there are additional reasons to diligently monitor your portfolio. The individual securities you own may suddenly go sour and start losing value. Or, after a good run, they may simply run out of steam. When you add a security to your portfolio, you should set guidelines around its market price. Those guideline prices will act as useful triggers, to let you know when you should review the security and possibly remove it from your portfolio.

You also want to monitor your portfolio to be on top of opportunities to take advantage of certain tax-saving tactics, such as tax loss harvesting, which we discuss in more detail in the "Tackling taxes" section, later in this chapter.

Measuring your results

You may have heard the old saw "You can't manage what you can't measure." When it comes to investing, that nugget is a golden one. So it's certainly worth knowing how to measure your investment results the right way.

In Chapter 12, we outline the following five key elements for understanding your investment results and putting them in meaningful context:

- ✔ **Principal:** The amount you invested
- ✔ **Term:** The length of time over which you're measuring your results
- ✔ **Risk:** The degree of safety built into your investment
- ✔ **Opportunity cost:** The results you could've gotten for a typical alternative investment with similar risk over the same term
- ✔ **Suitability:** The degree to which this investment is in step with your financial plan

We show you how to express your results as a return, to address the first two elements — principal and term. Then, to cover the next two elements — risk and opportunity cost — we explain how to derive, and compare your return against, relevant benchmarks. Finally, we revisit your LCP, which we discuss earlier in this chapter and in Chapter 7, to help you determine the suitability of your investment and to track future progress.

Reaching Past the Asset Allocation Basics

If you establish the best asset allocation for your situation, pick your investments carefully, mix them together in the right proportions, rebalance them when appropriate, and do all the other things we describe in this chapter, you can become a savvy investor with a consistent, successful portfolio. And as your investing knowledge and experience continue to grow, you can add some other ideas and techniques to your asset allocation arsenal. These beyond-the-basics items are the focal point of Part IV.

Adding alternatives

Alternatives are those investments that go beyond the traditional asset classes of cash, fixed income, and equities. In Chapter 13, we examine a wide range of alternative investments — from pork bellies to property — and tell you how you can buy them. We also review what the right alternatives can do for your portfolio by allowing you to exploit their poor correlation — their tendency to zig in the market when your other investments zag.

Tackling taxes

It's not what you make, but what you keep, that counts. In Chapter 14, we share some tactics that the pros use to minimize their income taxes. We look at tax-smart selling, we revisit asset location, and we expand on tax-loss harvesting, which is a way that you can take lemons (in this case, losses) and make lemonade (tax breaks). But we also warn you against going too far. The best investors recognize that the real goal is not minimizing taxes, but maximizing after-tax results.

Don't let saving taxes get in the way of intelligent investing.

Altering your allocation

You also want to be alert to revisiting your asset allocation over the years. Although your asset allocation is designed for the long haul, you don't want to be blind to changes — in your own situation and in the environment around you — that should trigger a return visit to the assumptions you relied on to establish your allocation. We explore these changes, and your appropriate responses, in Chapter 15.

Embracing expert help

Even the most talented do-it-yourselfer needs the support of an expert now and again. You can be an asset allocation ace and still need to call on a professional financial advisor for help on a specific challenge or with a particular facet of your investment strategy (or even for the whole ball of wax).

Chapter 16 is devoted to helping you determine just what kind of assistance you may need and where to find it. We guide you through the labyrinth of professional designations and tell you which ones are the most meaningful and relevant for your needs. We give you a set of probing questions to ask potential advisors, so you can separate the wheat from the chaff. And we explain advisors' various means of getting paid, so you can be sure that their incentives are in line with your own.

Chapter 2

Weighing Risk and Return

- -

In This Chapter

▶ Measuring the return on your investments

▶ Understanding risk

▶ Evaluating the risk-return tradeoff

- -

*T*he two most fundamental concepts in investing are risk and return. It's difficult to achieve any degree of success with your investments without a firm grasp of these two notions. What are risk and return? What do they mean? How do you measure them? And how do they interact with each other? In Chapter 2, we present answers to these questions, and help get you comfortable with these two critical facets of investing.

Return is the good stuff. Everybody wants an appetizing return. It's like the delectable flavor in an excellent dish. Risk is the bad stuff — the nasty saturated fat in the recipe. But, alas, the best-tasting foods also tend to contain the most nasty stuff. That's the trade-off — in cooking, and in investing. You have to take the bad with the good. The art (really, the science) is in striking the right balance. Whenever you invest, the challenge is to find the most profitable balance of risk and return.

In this chapter, we take a close look at return and the various ways to measure it. It's easy to get confused by all the different types of returns you may see published daily in the stock tables of newspapers and financial Web sites, but we'll help you see through the clutter. We also examine risk, a much less intuitive concept, but one that actually holds the key for unlocking successful investing. In essence, risk is subjective, but we show you how to measure it in a meaningful way. We clue you in on how risk depends heavily on the period of time you intend to invest, which is an important concept to grasp as you strive to make the most of your investments.

Finally, we introduce the idea of the *efficient frontier,* a very powerful visual aid that brings risk and return together quite naturally. We show you how to use the efficient frontier to minimize risk and maximize return — so you can have your cake and eat it, too.

Measuring Return

You can't tell how well your investments are doing unless you're able to measure results. The generally accepted way for you to do that is by expressing your investment gains (or losses) during an investment period as a percentage of the amount you invested. This percentage, which can be positive or negative, is called an investment *return.*

For example, if you invest $100 at the beginning of a period — a period can be any length of time — and it grows to $110 by the end, the result for you is a $10 gain. That $10 is 10 percent of your original $100 investment (10 ÷ 100 = 0.10), so your investment yielded a 10 percent return. But if, instead, you end the period with $95, your $5 loss — 5 percent of your original $100 investment (5 ÷ 100 = 0.05) — would represent a –5 percent return.

Are those results good? Well, it depends on what you were trying to accomplish, how much risk you took, and what the general investment environment was like during that period. For example, a –5 percent return for an aggressive portfolio during the extended bear market of 2000 to 2002 might be considered a fairly nice return indeed. (A *bear market* is one in which securities decline in value.) A 10 percent return for the same portfolio during the bull market of 2003 would've been disappointing. (Securities generally increase in value during a bull market.) In Chapter 12, we dig into the gory details of measuring investment results, but in this chapter we provide you with the basics so you can build a solid foundation of understanding.

In this section, we cover the different types of returns you'll see, and what they measure. Investment returns are expressed as *growth, income,* and *total return* (a combination of growth and income), and are either adjusted for inflation *(real return)* or not *(nominal return).* We'll work a few examples together, calculating time-weighted and dollar-weighted returns, and simple and compound average returns. Finally, we discuss the fees, expenses, and taxes that affect the return you receive.

Total return and its components

Two main components make up investment return:

- ✔ **Income:** Income generally takes the form of interest (in the case of bonds) or dividends (in the case of stocks). Income cannot be negative.
- ✔ **Growth:** Growth, also called *market appreciation,* is the change in market value of your investment from the beginning of your investment period to the end. Growth can be positive or negative.

The combination of income and growth — expressed as a percentage of the amount invested — is called *total return*.

If you invest $100 in a stock at the beginning of a period, receive a dividend during the period of $5, and at the end of the period, the market value of your stock is $110, then your income is $5, your growth is $10, and your total return is $15 ($5 + $10) divided by $100, or 15 percent.

If, instead, the ending market value is $90, and everything else is the same, then your income is still $5, your growth is –$10, and your total return is –$5 ($5 – $10) divided by $100, or –5 percent.

Both income and growth are important to you, which is why you want to focus on total return.

Be careful when reading about returns in the press. You may read, "The S&P 500 Stock Index was up 10 percent over the last 12 months." When quoted that way, it usually refers only to growth, omitting income. If you read, "The total return for the S&P 500 Stock Index over the last 12 months was 10 percent," then you know that both growth and income have been included.

Nominal return versus real return

Sometimes it's useful to know if your portfolio is keeping ahead of inflation. If your return one year was 2 percent, and inflation was 3 percent, you've lost ground (your portfolio lost purchasing power). To measure return against inflation, the term *real return* was developed.

Real return is simply your return minus inflation. In this example, your real return was –1 percent (2 percent – 3 percent). Your unadjusted return of 2 percent is called your *nominal return*. If, in the same year, your friend's nominal return was 10 percent, her real return was 7 percent (10 percent – 3 percent).

Nominal returns aren't adjusted for inflation; real returns are.

Whether you're talking about total return or its components (income and growth), those returns can be expressed as either a nominal return or a real return. When we use the word *return* in this book, unless we specifically indicate otherwise we're referring to total nominal return (income and growth combined, unadjusted for inflation).

Unless specifically referred to as a real return, any mention of returns you encounter (in the media, on the Internet, and so on) will likely be referring to a nominal return, which is a return that isn't adjusted for inflation.

Understanding time-weighted return versus dollar-weighted return

All the returns mentioned so far in this chapter assume a single beginning-of-period investment and no further deposits or withdrawals to or from the account. When there are mid-period deposits or withdrawals, which will be a frequent occurrence, you need to do a little more arithmetic to properly calculate your return. Let's assume that at the beginning of the period, you invested $100, and at mid-period, you added another $100 to your investment. Let's further assume that the return on your investment in the first half of the period was 10 percent, and the return in the second half was –5 percent.

What was your return for the whole period? There are actually two answers: The *time-weighted return* was roughly 5 percent and the *dollar-weighted return* was roughly 0 percent. (We use the word *roughly* because those percentages aren't completely precise due to compounding, which we discuss in a few pages.) What's the difference between time-weighted return and dollar-weighted return? Which return is correct? It all depends on how you like your information served:

- ✔ **Time-weighted return:** The time-weighted return reflects the fact that, for half the investment period, the return was 10 percent, and for the other half it was –5 percent. The two parts of the period are the same length, so they're equally weighted, resulting in a full-period return of roughly 5 percent.

    Why is the time-weighted return particularly helpful? If you're trying to do a fair comparison of your investment to others available at the same time, or to an industry benchmark return, then the time-weighted return is a great way to do so.

- ✔ **Dollar-weighted return:** The dollar-weighted return, as you'd guess, places more emphasis on the dollar amounts involved in the investment. Sticking with the same example, your investment during the second half was twice the dollar amount of your investment during the first half; therefore, the second-half return should get twice the weight, resulting in a full-period return of roughly 0 percent.

    What makes the dollar-weighted return so useful? If you're looking for an accurate historical depiction of what happened to your wealth, it's tough to beat the dollar-weighted return. To see why the dollar-weighted return gives you an accurate historical depiction of what happened to your wealth, think about how your wealth actually changed in this example.

    During the first half of the period, you gained $10 ($100 × 0.10). As the second half began, you added to your accumulated $110 (your original $100 investment plus your $10 gain) the second deposit of $100, for a total mid-period investment of $210. During the second half, you lost roughly \$10 (\$210 × 0.05). Your second-half loss of roughly \$10 almost exactly offset your first-half gain of \$10, so your investment gain for the whole period was roughly \$0.

Thus, the roughly 0 percent dollar-weighted return calculation has real meaning to you — it accurately depicts the change in your actual wealth.

Here's how you can remember the distinction between time-weighted and dollar-weighted returns:

✔ If you want to know how *you* did — how your wealth changed over the life of the investment — use dollar-weighted return.

✔ If you want to know how *the investment itself* did (perhaps to compare it to other investment choices your friends may have made, or to benchmark returns you see in the newspaper), use time-weighted return.

Again, one measure is not necessarily better than the other; it just depends on what information you'd like to know.

The only fair way to compare investment choices — undistorted by mid-period deposits and withdrawals — is to use a time-weighted return. That's why financial firms routinely calculate investment returns based on this measure.

If you tend to make lots of deposits and withdrawals, then computing either time-weighted or dollar-weighted returns can be quite complex and cumbersome. In that case, it's best to have an investment advisor do it for you. If you don't have an investment advisor and need one, see Chapter 16.

Annualizing multiyear returns

When you've been investing for several years, it's useful to express your investment return on an annualized basis, because it's common to think of and compare returns over a 12-month period. There are two ways to do this: simple average and compound average.

The *simple average* method is very basic, and the calculations involved might take you back to math class in grade school, when the closest thing you had to an investment was a baseball-card collection. To figure out a simple average for the return on an investment you have as an adult (the kind of investment that probably didn't come with a stick of gum), just add up your return percentages for a certain number of years, and then divide by that number of years. For example, let's assume that over a five-year period, your annual returns are 10 percent, 5 percent, 7 percent, –5 percent, and 13 percent. The simple, or arithmetic, average return is the sum of the five returns (10 percent + 5 percent + 7 percent – 5 percent + 13 percent = 30 percent) divided by 5. The simple average, then, is 6 percent.

Using the same five-year returns as above, the *compound average* return is 5.8 percent. This is also referred to as the *compound annual growth rate* (CAGR).

How do you calculate it?

1. **Convert each year's return to decimal form and add the decimal to 1.**

   For this example, that would mean 0.10 + 1 = 1.10; 0.05 + 1 = 1.05; 0.07 + 1 = 1.07; –0.05 + 1 = 0.95; and 0.13 + 1 = 1.13.

2. **Multiply the resulting numbers — which each correspond to an individual year — together.**

   In this example that would be $1.10 \times 1.05 \times 1.07 \times 0.95 \times 1.13 = 1.3267$.

3. **Take the root of the product equal to the number of years you're working with.**

   This example includes five years, so you would take the fifth root of the product you came up with in Step 2: $1.3267^{1/5} = 1.058$.

   Use an Excel spreadsheet, or the root key on your calculator, to do this calculation for you.

4. **Subtract 1, and express the result as a percentage.**

   So, 1.058 – 1 = 0.058 or 5.8 percent.

Compound average returns are more meaningful than simple average returns, because they better reflect the real world. This can be seen by taking a more extreme example.

Suppose you made a two-year investment. Your return in the first year was 100 percent (your investment doubled), and in the second year it was –50 percent (your investment dropped by half). If you started with $100, your investment grew to $200 in year 1 (double $100), and shrank back to $100 in year 2 (half $200). The simple average return is (100 percent – 50 percent) ÷ 2 = 0.25, or 25 percent . To calculate the compound average return, you follow these steps:

1. **Convert each year's return to decimal form and add the decimal to 1.**

   So, 1 + 1 = 2 and –0.5 + 1 = 0.5.

2. **Multiply the resulting numbers — which each correspond to an individual year — together.**

   So, $2 \times 0.5 = 1$.

3. **Take the root of the product equal to the number of years you're working with.**

   So, $1^{1/2} = 1$.

4. **Subtract 1, and express the result as a percentage.**

   So, 1 – 1 = 0, or 0 percent.

Which calculation offers a more realistic result? You ended up with exactly what you started with ($100), so your actual return was 0 percent, no question, and it remains 0 percent when annualized. The simple average return clearly overstates the performance of this investment. Generally, it always will.

The compound average return is always the better measure. Don't use the simple average just because it's easier to calculate — it can give you questionable answers. But you need to understand this type of measure, because sometimes that's how returns are presented.

The compound average return will always be less than or equal to the simple average return. This is because of *risk drag*, a subtle but very real phenomenon explained a little later in the "Understanding how volatility erodes return: Risk drag" section. In fact, the only time the two averages will be equal is when the individual years' returns are all the same. Since this is very unlikely, it's almost always the case that the simple average will be less realistic than the compound average return.

Don't trust simple average returns. When you're presented with an investment's annualized return, make sure you know which averaging method was used. If you have to, do the math yourself to get your hands on the compound average return.

Accounting for taxes, fees, and expenses

You also need to be aware of the costs that can reduce your return. The biggest factors that erode returns are taxes, fees, and expenses. We explain all three in this section.

Considering the taxes that affect your investment returns

Your gains are subject to income tax. Interest income and *short-term realized capital gains* (gains made on investments you own for a year or less) are generally taxed at your ordinary income tax rates. In addition, in many states you'll pay state income taxes, which vary depending on where you live. Dividends and *long-term realized capital gains* (investment gains that result after owning the investment for more than a year) are usually taxed at lower rates.

Although tax rates, as well as the relative treatment of different types of gain, change over time, the fact is that taxes are bound to take a bite out of your return. Even if the gains occur within a tax-deferred account — an IRA or 401(k) for example — though they aren't taxed at the time they're received or realized, they are taxed, along with your principal, at your ordinary income tax rates when you pull that money out of the account. Because taxes are very specific to each individual, and because they're usually levied well after the time gains occur, returns are almost always expressed on a pre-tax basis.

There's nothing inappropriate about this, but recognize that, in general, not all your return is ultimately yours to keep. It's as certain as death and — well, you know the rest.

Understanding fees and expenses

In addition to taxes, various fees and expenses can nibble away at your return. These include *transaction fees* (commissions charged by a stockbroker for trading securities, for example), *margin expenses* (expenses incurred if you borrow against your account), dividend adjustments, custodial fees, and fund management fees. (For more information on specific fees, turn to Chapter 9.)

Mutual funds levy fund management fees, which lower the return you would otherwise receive. So do exchange-traded funds (ETFs), which trade throughout the day like a stock and contain a basket of securities like a mutual fund. Compared to mutual funds, ETF charges are generally low. Mutual fund and ETF charges are calculated as a percentage of assets and are disclosed in the fund prospectus. Additionally, if you engage an investment advisor, advisory fees can be deducted directly from your account or invoiced separately. In employer-sponsored qualified plans such as 401(k)s, there are management fees that aren't explicitly shown or disclosed but that reduce your return. These can be substantial (often exceeding the fees charged by investment advisory firms), and they depend on the amount of revenue-sharing negotiated between your employer and the plan administrator.

The often large and hidden nature of 401(k) fees is one very good reason that it's generally smart for you to roll over your 401(k) into your IRA at your earliest opportunity.

When you review your investment performance statements, make sure you know whether the returns you're looking at are gross or net of fees and expenses. Reputable firms will clearly disclose this information.

Measuring Risk

Any discussion of return is incomplete without a discussion of risk.

As all the investment brochures and prospectuses say, "Past performance is no guarantee of future results." This lack of certainty about future returns is essentially what is meant by risk. It's an inherent part of the investment experience.

One way to express risk is the short-term fluctuation in the value of your portfolio. The short-term investor who checks his account status several times a month will see, and measure, his investment risk in this way. For him, risk might be expressed by the day-to-day or week-to-week fluctuations in his return. A return that fluctuates from 2 percent one week to –2 percent the next might represent an intolerable amount of risk for this investor.

For some other investors, losing money in the short term may not matter all that much. For the longer-term investor who's mostly concerned with the size of her account several years down the road, risk may be expressed as the chance that her portfolio may not stay sufficiently ahead of inflation over that period.

So you can see from these two examples that risk is very specific to each investor. In this section, we explain how to distinguish between risk and volatility — a difference that confuses some investors. We also tell you how to measure risk and how to take special care to incorporate a very important factor into your understanding of risk: your time horizon.

Differentiating between volatility and risk

Sometimes, *volatility* (of return) is used interchangeably with *risk*. But volatility and risk aren't the same thing. First of all, volatility is an objective concept, intrinsic to the investment itself, and it can be explicitly measured. You won't find shades of gray in measurements of volatility. Risk, on the other hand, is quite subjective, and unique to each investor — including you! Allow us to elaborate with a rather extreme example.

Consider the following two "investments": playing the roulette wheel and buying a Treasury bill. Clearly, the wheel is quite a bit more volatile than the Treasury bill, because the probability of losing your entire investment is significant.

But which investment is more of a risk? It depends on who's making the investment. Take, for example, the unfortunate soul who needs to come up with a payment in the next 30 days to an unforgiving creditor, in an amount exactly twice the assets he currently has available. To this investor, the Treasury bill represents a much riskier proposition than the roulette wheel. The extremely remote chance that the Treasury bill is going to provide a big enough return in such a small amount of time make it a risky investment in this case. This investor needs as much volatility as he can find to minimize his risk of coming up short in a month. The roulette wheel presents at least the *possibility* of doubling his investment in the short term; with Treasury bills, the investor is virtually guaranteed to fail. In this example, Treasury bills are the less volatile, but more risky, alternative. (We told you this example was extreme. Of course, we aren't recommending gambling as a prudent investment strategy, unless your investment goals include scoring two free coupons for the steak and lobster buffet and getting comped for an upgrade to a room with a hot tub!)

Volatility is an objective measure that is clearly identifiable. Risk, on the other hand, is subjective and exists totally in the eye of the beholder. It's important that you carefully consider and clearly articulate what level of risk causes you discomfort — what keeps you awake at night — with regard to your investments.

Understanding how volatility erodes return: Risk drag

There is another very important aspect of the interplay between volatility and return to understand, and it's known as *risk drag*. Over realistic investment horizons (for example, greater than a single year), volatility can actually decrease your return. The example in Table 2-1 illustrates this phenomenon.

Table 2-1	An Illustration of Risk Drag			
	Portfolio A		Portfolio B	
Year	*Annual Return*	*Account Balance*	*Annual Return*	*Account Balance*
		$100		$100
1	8%	$108	23%	$123
2	8%	$117	−14%	$106
3	8%	$126	−7%	$98
4	8%	$136	20%	$118
5	8%	$147	16%	$137
6	8%	$159	14%	$156
7	8%	$171	−18%	$127
8	8%	$185	27%	$162
9	8%	$200	−2%	$158
10	8%	$216	32%	$208
Average Return	8%		9%	
Standard Deviation	0%		18%	
Ending Balance		$216		$208

Source: Brinton Eaton Wealth Advisors.

As you review Table 2-1, ask yourself this question: If you're an investor with a ten-year investment horizon, which portfolio would you rather hold? Portfolio A has a simple average annual return of 8 percent, and Portfolio B has a simple average annual return of 9 percent. What's it going to be?

Without the benefit of Table 2-1, Portfolio B would seem like the clear winner. But if Portfolio B has a *standard deviation* (a measure of volatility — see "Standard deviation," later in this chapter) of 18 percent and Portfolio A has a standard deviation of 0 percent, should that change your mind? The table indicates that, indeed, it should. Depending on its volatility, a higher-returning portfolio may not result in greater wealth.

In fact, any asset with volatility greater than zero will see its multiyear return eroded —the more volatility, the more erosion. This phenomenon is called *risk drag.* It's subtle but real, and it's one reason you should never be satisfied with a display of only a single year's results for any investment.

Another way to describe the result in Table 2-1 is to note that the compound annual average return for Portfolio A is the same as its simple average return of 8 percent. However, for Portfolio B the compound average return is 7.6 percent, which is much less than its simple average return of 9 percent. In fact, the volatility of this portfolio's return is so high that its compound average return is even less than Portfolio A's simple average return. And as you can read in "Annualizing multiyear returns," earlier in this chapter, it's the compound average return that matters to you.

Using statistical measures for risk

When it comes to measuring risk, you can do it yourself by using some tools from the field of probability and statistics. If the sight of those two words takes you back to your school days and makes your palms sweat and eyes start to glaze over, fear not! We explain the details of how to measure risk — in layman's terms — in this section.

Range

Range is certainly one of the most straightforward risk measures — it's simply the spread of results from lowest to highest. For an example, we'll reuse the five-year series of annual returns that we analyze earlier in this chapter: 10 percent, 5 percent, 7 percent, –5 percent, and 13 percent. The lowest return is –5 percent; the highest, 13 percent. The range over the five-year period is the difference between the two, or 18 percent.

In general, the wider the range, the greater the volatility, or fluctuations, in returns.

Standard deviation

One of the most common measures of risk in investment circles is *standard deviation,* which is a measure of departure from an average. In other words, the more an investment's return varies from an average, the greater the standard deviation.

For an example of how to calculate standard deviation, we'll look back to the five-year series of annual returns that we use throughout this chapter: namely, 10 percent, 5 percent, 7 percent, –5 percent, and 13 percent. The simple average return for this series is 6 percent. (For an explanation of how to find a simple average return, turn back to "Annualizing multiyear returns.") The standard deviation of this series of returns is calculated using this simple average of 6 percent:

1. **Take the difference between each year's return and the simple average return percentage.**

   Here's how this would look in our example:

   - Year 1: 10 percent – 6 percent = 4 percent
   - Year 2: 5 percent – 6 percent = –1 percent
   - Year 3: 7 percent – 6 percent = 1 percent
   - Year 4: –5 percent – 6 percent = –11 percent
   - Year 5: 13 percent – 6 percent = 7 percent

2. **Square each of these differences.**

   Again, here's how this would look:

   - Year 1: $4 \times 4 = 16$
   - Year 2: $-1 \times -1 = 1$
   - Year 3: $1 \times 1 = 1$
   - Year 4: $-11 \times -11 = 121$
   - Year 5: $7 \times 7 = 49$

3. **Add up the differences.**

   In this example, that means you add $16 + 1 + 1 + 121 + 49 = 188$.

4. **Divide by the total number of annual returns minus 1.**

   In this case, the total number of annual returns is 5. Subtract 1 and you get 4. So, you have $188 \div 4 = 47$.

5. **Take the square root of the result.**

   The square root of 47 is 6.86, and for this example that's your standard deviation.

   Use a calculator to get the square root of a number.

One reason standard deviation is a more popular measure of risk than range is that standard deviation provides more contextual information. Generally, for any sufficiently large group of values, about two-thirds will lie within one standard deviation of the group's simple average. Even more — about 95 percent — will fall within two standard deviations.

Catching up on the downside

Are you an investor with a long-term view? Are you willing to ride the frequent fluctuations of a more volatile investment, and are you mostly concerned about beating inflation over several years? If you answered yes to all those questions, you may want to consider paying attention to a less common risk measure called *downside risk.* Downside risk is a measure of the probability that a set of annual returns, or a multiyear compound return, will fail to exceed some minimum objective. If, for example, your objective

is to simply beat inflation, then the probability of your *real return* (your nominal return minus inflation — see "Nominal return versus real return," earlier in this chapter) failing to exceed 0 would be a suitable risk measure for you.

Calculating downside risk is beyond the scope of most individual investors, and it isn't typically calculated or published by financial firms. A qualified expert (see Chapter 16) could calculate it for you if you're interested.

One way this information is used in investing is to note that, if an investment's expected return is 8 percent and its standard deviation is 4 percent, then the probability of next year's return being between 4 percent and 12 percent (within one standard deviation on either side of 8 percent) is about two-thirds. And the probability of the return being between 0 percent and 16 percent (within two standard deviations on either side of 8 percent) is about 95 percent.

Standard deviation tends to be the commonly used risk measure for most investment purposes. Keeping an eye on an investment's standard deviation will help you monitor the period-to-period fluctuation of your return over time.

Generally speaking, the larger the standard deviation, the greater the volatility.

If you're a short-term, worrywart investor, standard deviation provides a helpful measure for you because it measures period-to-period volatility.

Candidly assess what causes you anxiety. Only then can you decide on a risk measure (or collection of measures) that's right for you — and only then can you meaningfully compare any two investment choices with each other.

Factoring in your time horizon

You can't fully understand investment risk without considering your investment horizon. What may be risky to some investors with a short timeline may not be risky at all to investors who have the luxury of being patient. It all depends on the time that you have to invest.

To illustrate this point, consider the effect of the investment horizon on three broad asset classes: Treasury bills (T-bills), intermediate government bonds, and large-company stocks. In Figure 2-1, we show the historical range of compound average annual returns (see "Annualizing multiyear returns," earlier in this chapter) for these three assets, assuming different holding periods.

As expected, for short holding periods (such as one year), the range of returns for stocks is much greater than for bonds, which, in turn, is greater than for T-bills. Specifically, for T-bills, the worst one-year return was 1 percent, and the best was 15 percent, for a range of 14 percentage points. Meanwhile, for large-company stocks, the worst one-year return was –26 percent, and the best was 53 percent, for a range of 79 percentage points.

Over longer holding periods, these ranges narrow considerably. For example, over a ten-year holding period, the worst compound average annual return for T-bills was 0 percent, and the best was 9 percent, for a range of 9 percentage points. For stocks, the range narrowed all the way down to 18 percentage points (worst was 1 percent; best was 19 percent). As you can see, the longer the holding period, the smaller the difference in ranges across all three asset classes. In fact, over a ten-year investment horizon, the range of returns for stocks would actually be preferred to that for bonds and T-bills by most investors, because the worst return for stocks (1 percent) was actually better than the worst return for T-bills (0 percent).

Figure 2-1:
A range of compound average annual returns over different holding periods.

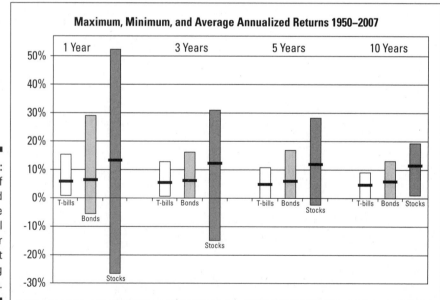

Maximum, Minimum, and Average Annualized Returns 1950–2007

Sources: The U.S. 30-Day Treasury Bill Index. Barclays Capital U.S. Aggregate Bond Index. © Barclays Capital, Inc. Used with permission. Standard & Poor's data. Standard & Poor's, S&P, S&P 500, and S&P GSCI are registered trademarks of the McGraw-Hill Companies, Inc. Used with permission of Standard & Poor's. All rights reserved. Brinton Eaton Wealth Advisors analysis of data, compiled using Morningstar EnCorr.

In fact, there hasn't been a ten-year period since 1950 during which the worst returns for stocks wasn't positive. That can't be said of T-bills or bonds. Meanwhile, the average return for stocks was always much better than that for T-bills and bonds, across all holding periods.

In essence, given enough time, *risk spreading* across time occurs — the good years and the bad years tend to offset each other.

You can see that the length of your investment horizon will have an impact on the mix of assets in your portfolio. As an example, the longer your horizon, the more comfortable you can be considering equities. We discuss that situation, and many more concerns relating to time horizons, in Chapter 6.

Evaluating the Trade-Off between Risk and Return

When you have a pretty good understanding of risk and return (which you can gain by working your way through the first two sections of this chapter), you're ready to start applying that knowledge to your investment choices.

If you're feeling a little risk averse, don't worry! Many investors imagine that there's a perfect portfolio out there somewhere that can generate ridiculously high returns with little — or even no — risk. Unfortunately, no such portfolio exists. What you can do is apply a concept that's been used successfully since the early 1950s, when its creators won a Nobel Prize for their insights. Called *Modern Portfolio Theory* (known popularly as the theory of "Not Putting All Your Eggs in One Basket)," the theory suggests that investors just like you, who don't like risk, can maximize the returns in their portfolio, through *diversification,* the strategy of choosing from more than one investment.

Keep the following two sections in mind, and you, too, can figure out how to sort through and find the right combination of "baskets" (asset classes — see Chapter 3) among which to distribute your eggs.

Recognizing that there's (usually) no such thing as a free lunch

In general, if you want more return, you'll have to accept more risk. However you measure risk, higher-returning investments typically carry more risk. Stated another way, higher-risk investments typically reward you with greater returns; that's the payoff for accepting the higher risk. After all, if higher-risk investments returned the same as lower-risk investments, who would choose the former?

As we discuss in Chapter 5, the closest thing to a free lunch that you'll find in investing is rebalancing. Done right, it can actually get you more return with no additional risk.

Heading for the efficient frontier

One very good way to evaluate the trade-off between risk and return in your investment strategy is to decide on a standard measurement for risk and one for return, and then compare investment possibilities based on the relationships between your risk and return measures.

Say, for example, that you've decided on using expected one-year nominal return as a measure for an investment's return, and you picked standard deviation of the one-year return as your measurement for risk. You have thousands of investment options to choose from. For this example, just imagine that you know both of your chosen measures (expected one-year nominal return for return and standard deviation of the one-year return for risk) for every single investment option that's available to you.

If you wanted a very straightforward visual representation of how the risk compares with the return for those investment options, you could plot each option on a graph that uses measures of standard deviation for the horizontal axis and expected return for the vertical axis. In case you don't have your graph paper handy, we've provided an example in Figure 2-2.

Look at investment choice A. It has an expected return of 8 percent and a standard deviation of 6 percent. Investment choice B occupies a different location on the graph because it has an expected return of 12 percent and a standard deviation of 10 percent.

With a handy graph like this, it's apparent that certain investment choices are clearly inferior to others. To see what we mean, have a look at investment choice X on Figure 2-3, which is the same graph from Figure 2-2 but with a new feature called the efficient frontier.

Investment choice X is one of several investment options that don't offer a good return in relation to their risk level. In other words, there are a number of other investments that, for no greater risk, will give you a higher return. These better choices lie in the sector bounded by choices X, Y, and Z on the map.

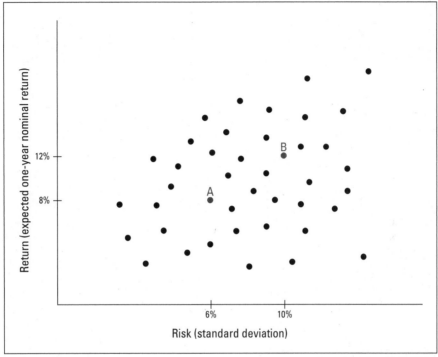

Source: Brinton Eaton Wealth Advisors.

Figure 2-2:
A graph of
investment
choices
that plots
risk against
return.

Against these other, more appealing alternatives, investment X is considered inefficient. It can, therefore, be removed from consideration. In fact, you can also throw out the majority of the investment choices on this graph. Once you remove all these inefficient choices, you're left with a set of investments that lie on a curve sloping from lower left to upper right. These are the efficient investments, so named because for any one of them, it's not possible to find another investment that has lower risk for the same level of return, or higher return for the same level of risk. The curve that these efficient investments lie on is called the *efficient frontier*. There are no investment possibilities to be found northwest of the efficient frontier, and you know that the best investment choices for you lie along the frontier. The efficient frontier is a very powerful concept — one we discuss throughout this book.

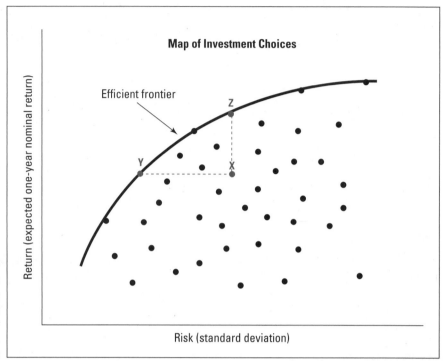

Source: Brinton Eaton Wealth Advisors.

Figure 2-3:
Determining
the efficient
frontier for
investments.

After you've figured out which investment options have the highest potential for return coupled with the lowest risk, how do you choose among them? There is no objective right answer to this question. It depends on your own subjective opinion. But there's a simple way to get to the answer that's right for you.

For an illustration of how you can find your ideal investment along an efficient frontier, consider Figure 2-4. If you take the time to apply this information, you can put this theory to work for you very effectively.

Because all the investments along the frontier are equivalently efficient, the only way to increase your return is by increasing the degree of risk you're willing to take (that is, by moving northeast along the frontier). So, because any rational investor would want to maximize his return — assuming the associated level of risk was tolerable — the only thing he needs to do is determine how much risk is too much for him. That tells him how far east he dare go, and because he wants to stay on the frontier, it also tells him how far north he can go. This process, thus, uniquely determines the investment choice he should make.

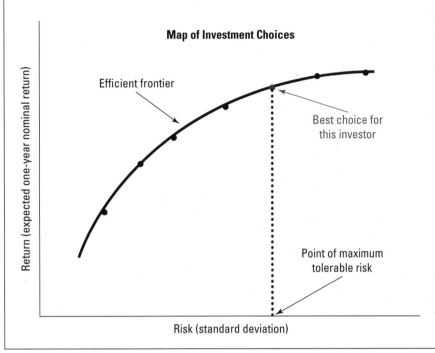

Figure 2-4:
Using your
risk toler-
ance to
make your
investment
choice.

Chapter 3

Making Sense of Asset Classes

In This Chapter

▶ Knowing the basic asset classes to consider in your portfolio

▶ Understanding alternative investments

▶ Expanding your horizons to include international exposure

*J*ust as in gourmet cooking, in asset allocation an essential early step is identifying the proper ingredients. The best chefs realize that each ingredient has a specific role to play when creating a delicious dish. Likewise, the best investors identify a wide variety of investment types and incorporate them in an efficient, profitable portfolio. Put in too much stock, or too much stock from a small company, and you may end up with too much of a good thing. Similarly, mix in too many low-risk, low-interest-bearing cash equivalents or bonds, and your portfolio may get weighed down and fall flat.

In this chapter, we discuss the specific features of the individual components (the asset classes and subclasses) that go into creating a successful investment portfolio. There are conventional classes that all financial professionals agree you should own (fixed income and equities), but you need to consider a number of other asset classes, too: international investments as well as alternative investments such as real estate, commodities, and hedge funds. We help you get to know the full menu of asset classes, and explore their many features. Finally, you discover how to weigh the options available among these investments, so that you know how to add them to your portfolio's asset allocation mix.

Identifying the Traditional Classes

There are three main, or traditional, asset classes that you should consider when putting together your portfolio:

> ✔ **Stocks:** You can include stocks, or equities, through which you own a piece of a company and receive a slice of its profits. This asset class promises the highest returns, but it also carries the most risk. (Flip back to Chapter 2 for a helpful discussion of risk and return.) Equities make sense in the right proportion, and especially if you have a long time horizon.

✔ **Bonds:** You can also mix in a number of fixed-income investments like bonds, which are a less-risky asset class. Bonds pay a fixed rate of return in exchange for the money you lend to a company, municipality, or government agency. They help balance the risk in your portfolio.

✔ **Cash:** You can always incorporate cash and cash equivalents in your portfolio. These short-term investments include certificates of deposit (CDs), money-market deposit accounts, and money-market mutual funds. They carry the least risk of all, but they also promise the least return. Because these investments are your *safe money* (money you expect to use in the near future to pay for an important goal, such as education or a new home), the relatively low returns are acceptable.

Want to know more about these traditional asset classes, and how you can use them to your advantage? This section is loaded with all that information.

Embracing equities: Stocks and stock funds

One asset class that you'll definitely want to consider is equities, which include stocks and stock funds. Owning a share of stock in a corporation means that you literally own a piece of the corporation. As an owner, you're entitled to your proportionate share of the profits, or earnings, of the corporation. These earnings are returned to you in the form of a *dividend* (a cash payment to shareholders declared periodically by the corporation's board of directors) and/or in the form of stock price appreciation.

There are two basic types of stock:

✔ **Common stock:** Owning common stock means you have the right to vote at shareholder meetings and receive dividends.

✔ **Preferred stock:** When you own a preferred stock, you forgo voting rights in exchange for a higher claim on assets than is held by investors who own common shares, if the company becomes insolvent. Preferred stocks are really fixed-income investments (see "Considering other types of fixed-income investments," later in this chapter, for more information).

Stocks are the foundation of most investors' portfolios for the simple reason that stocks have outperformed most other investments over the long haul, as you can see in Figure 3-1. You can see — from the solid black horizontal line about midway through each bar on the graph — that the average annual return for stocks over the last 50-plus years (since 1950) is in excess of 10 percent, about twice the average return from bonds, and more than twice the average return from Treasury bills.

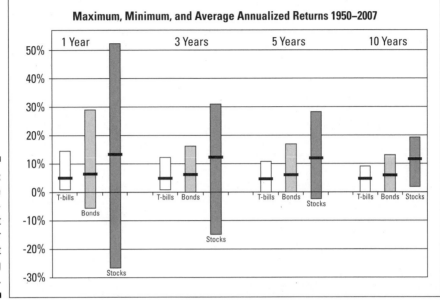

Figure 3-1:
Performance
of differ-
ent asset
classes over
different
holding
periods.

Like bond mutual funds (see "Getting familiar with bond mutual funds," later in this chapter), stock mutual funds offer liquidity, stability, income, and diversification, which make these funds a very desirable choice. Here are some of their benefits:

✔ **Stock mutual funds are probably the easiest way for an investor to purchase an equity investment.** They can be bought and sold just like any mutual fund, instead of through stockbrokers. Also, they can be bought and sold in any amount, whereas stocks are best purchased in large, even lots.

✔ **Stock funds contain a basket of individual stocks, so you're not overly exposed to the market risk of any individual stock.**

✔ **Different types of stock funds allow you to narrow your focus to the part of the stock market you're most interested in.** For example, you can buy a fund of small-cap U.S. equities or large-cap energy companies. (We explain the difference between small-cap and large-cap stocks in the "Size" section.)

The big upside to stock mutual funds: diversification and ease of buying and selling. The big downside: management fees inside the mutual fund, which aren't present when buying or selling a stock directly.

When you're considering a stock for your portfolio, there are three features you should be familiar with: size, style, and sector.

Size

Stocks are often categorized by size, called *market capitalization* (or *market cap* for short). Market cap is simply the current market value of a share of the stock (the stock price) multiplied by the total number of shares outstanding. For example, if a company has 50 million shares of its stock outstanding, and each share has a market value of $100, then the company's market cap is 50 million × $100 = $5 billion.

Stock size ranges may vary among brokerages, but here are the general breaking points between large-cap, mid-cap, and small-cap stocks:

- ✔ **Large cap:** Companies with a market cap of more than $10 billion
- ✔ **Mid cap:** Companies with a market cap of $2 billion to $10 billion
- ✔ **Small cap:** Companies with a market cap under $2 billion

The small-cap category is sometimes split further, with *micro cap* representing the lower end of the small-cap range (between $50 million and $300 million). Micro cap sounds miniscule, but there's a still smaller classification: *Nano-cap* companies have a market cap of less than $50 million.

Generally, the larger the market cap, the more stable the stock price over time and the lower the expected long-term return. Similarly, the smaller the market cap, the more volatile the stock price over time and the higher the expected long-term return. Although these relationships don't always hold up over short time periods, they're reasonable expectations for the long run. These size characteristics come into play when you set your asset allocation percentages (see Chapter 8).

Sector

A stock's *sector* is determined by the industry of its issuing company. Standard & Poor's divides stocks into the following ten major industry sectors listed here (along with specific examples of each, to help you understand what's what):

- ✔ **Basic materials:** Alcoa, Dow Chemical, Weyerhaeuser
- ✔ **Consumer discretionary:** Amazon.com, Home Depot, Starbucks
- ✔ **Consumer staples:** Campbell Soup Company, Procter & Gamble, Wal-Mart
- ✔ **Energy:** Chevron, Halliburton, Schlumberger
- ✔ **Financials:** Allstate, MetLife, Bank of America

- ✔ **Healthcare:** Aetna, Johnson & Johnson, Medtronic
- ✔ **Industrials:** 3M, General Electric, Southwest Airlines
- ✔ **Information technology:** Apple, Microsoft, Yahoo!
- ✔ **Telecommunications:** AT&T, Qwest, Verizon
- ✔ **Utilities:** Consolidated Edison, Duke Energy, Southern Company

Dow Jones & Company divides stocks into ten comparable groups.

During different phases of the economic cycle, some sectors tend to perform better than others do. For example, during periods of economic expansion, consumer discretionary stocks tend to do well; during periods of contraction, healthcare and consumer staples (also known as the *defensive sectors,* because they provide relatively stable earnings regardless of the health of the economy) tend to be the relative winners. Trying to take advantage of these tendencies by tactically tilting your portfolio accordingly is called *sector rotation.* The trick, of course, is to know when the turning points in the economy will occur before the majority of other investors do. Roughly half the investors who try to do this will get it right at any given time.

The best strategy is to have a good mix of industry sectors in your portfolio, and to be mindful of whether the economy is expanding or contracting when you do so. For more information, turn to Chapter 8.

Style

Stocks also tend to be characterized by their style, and they fall into one of two style classes: *growth stocks* or *value stocks.* There are no official definitions of which is which, but the idea is that value stocks are underpriced, whereas growth stocks aren't underpriced but are felt to have solid prospects. One measure that's used to help determine whether a stock is over- or underpriced is the *price-to-earnings ratio (P/E ratio,* for short). If, compared to companies of similar size and sector, a company's stock price is low relative to the company's earnings, then it has a low P/E ratio and it's considered a value stock.

Some investors like value stocks, because they feel that these stocks, the earnings of which are high relative to their price, are simply not fully appreciated yet by the stock market and their time will soon come. Other investors like growth stocks, because the companies are generally strong, and this strength is reflected in the price that the stock market gives the company's stock; the thinking is that the company's strength will continue to drive its stock price even higher. Then there are those investors who say they are growth at a reasonable price (GARP) investors — in our view, those are people who really can't make up their minds between growth and value!

As you can see, the style of a stock has less to do with the inherent qualities of the company than it does with how the company's stock is currently priced by the stock market. So who's right: the value investors or the growth investors? Well, growth stocks and value stocks take turns falling in and out of favor, depending on which style offers the higher total returns at the time. Some pundits have made careers out of trying to predict these turning points, and they tend to be right about half the time. It's fairly safe to say, though, that over the long term, value stocks tend to perform more favorably.

In our opinion, style is less important than size or sector.

Getting a handle on fixed-income investments: Bonds, bond funds, and more

Another asset type for you to consider is the *fixed-income investment*. As its name states, a fixed-income investment, which includes bonds and bond funds, pays you a fixed rate of return, in exchange for the money that you loan to a company, a municipality, or a government agency.

Who doesn't love a good bond? Unlike stocks, bonds promise you regular interest payments. Bonds are also less volatile than stocks (meaning, they tend to hold their value), while stock prices can fluctuate significantly. And if you hold a bond to maturity, you know exactly how much you're going to get back at maturity: the *par value* (face value) of the bond.

So why would you want to invest in anything but bonds? Well, one good reason is that while the interest payments and par value are promised, they aren't guaranteed — bond issuers have been known to *default* (fail to pay all their promised interest and/or principal payments). The more important reason is that, over the long term, the total return (see Chapter 2) on bonds is generally inferior to that of most other asset classes.

If you want to reach for extra return with your portfolio, don't plan to do it with bonds. You buy this type of fixed-income security primarily for stability, not for return.

Understanding how bonds work

The fixed periodic income you get on your bond is determined by its *coupon rate,* which is basically a predetermined interest rate. For example, you may buy a bond with an annual coupon rate of 4 percent, payable quarterly. The periodic income, or *coupon payment,* is simply the par value times the coupon rate. So, if the 4 percent bond you purchased had a par value of $1,000, you'd receive an annual income of $40 a year, payable in quarterly installments of $10 each.

When you buy a bond, its *market value* (price) will be higher or lower than its par value, depending on whether prevailing market interest rates are lower or higher than its coupon rate. If the purchase price is greater than the par value, you buy the bond at a *premium;* if it's less, you buy it at a *discount;* if it's the same, you buy the bond *at par.*

For example, let's say your 4 percent, $1,000 bond is a ten-year bond. Let's also assume that the prevailing interest rates out in the market for ten-year obligations are 3 percent. In that case, your 4 percent bond might cost you something like $1,085, or an $85 premium over its $1,000 par value. Does buying a bond at a premium sound crazy — a bum deal? No, it's simply the market making a natural adjustment to the price of the bond to make its quarterly $10 payments equate to the prevailing interest rate (in this case, 3 percent). It makes sense for this bond to be worth more than its par value, because its coupon rate (4 percent) is high relative to interest rates prevailing out there in the general market for similar bonds (3 percent). If, instead, the prevailing interest rates are 5 percent, then this 4 percent bond could probably be bought for around $923, or a $77 discount under its $1,000 par value. If the prevailing interest rates are 4 percent, then your bond would cost close to $1,000 — its par value.

Now, whether you bought a bond at a premium, at a discount, or at par, after you buy the bond, its market value will continue to increase or decrease relative to its purchase price, depending on whether prevailing market interest rates move lower or higher, respectively, than they were at the time of purchase. So, using the case of our premium 4 percent bond that we bought for $1,085 (because prevailing rates were 3 percent at the time of purchase), let's assume that, five years into the bond's ten-year term, prevailing market interest rates move down to 2.5 percent. By then, the market value of your bond exceeds the $1,085 you paid for it. If prevailing rates had moved up — say, to 3.5 percent — then the market value of your bond would be less than $1,085 (but still greater than the $1,000 par value, since 3.5 percent is still less than the bond's 4 percent coupon rate.)

As the bond approaches maturity, its market value will converge to its par value. Therefore, at expiration, all bonds will be worth their par value (excluding any unfortunate default situations). So, if you buy a bond and fully expect to hold it until maturity, you really don't care about how its market value changes over the life of the bond — you're in for the long haul. Note that, while this convergence is true of individual bonds, it isn't true of bond mutual funds (see "Getting familiar with bond mutual funds," later in this chapter), since these funds will always be holding some bonds that have not yet matured.

Some bonds carry a coupon rate of 0 percent — these are called, naturally enough, *zero-coupon bonds.* Although they produce no coupon payments during their life, these bonds are sold at a discount deep enough to make them attractive, commensurate with coupon-paying bonds of similar maturity. For example, in an environment where prevailing market interest rates are 4 percent, a ten-year $1,000 bond might cost around $675, or a discount of $325. Investors don't receive any periodic interest payments over the course of a zero-coupon bond's maturity, but these bonds, which are issued at a fraction of par value, increase gradually in value as the bond approaches maturity.

Zero-coupon bonds are useful if you're saving to achieve a long-term goal, such as college tuition, and you don't need a regular payout.

Be wary about buying a bond with a *callable option* (meaning, the issuer can call the bond for redemption and pay you back early). You may lose interest and be faced with a lower interest rate on a replacement bond.

Exploring the three major types of bonds

There are three principal issuers of bonds: the U.S. government, individual states and municipalities, and corporations. Each type of bond has slightly different characteristics you need to know about to work with them wisely.

U.S. government bonds

Also called *Treasuries,* these bonds are the safest, because they're backed by "the full faith and credit of the United States government," meaning that, by law, they must be paid ahead of the government's other obligations. Income generated by Treasuries is free of state and local income taxes (but *not* federal income tax).

There are three types of Treasuries, and each matures after a different amount of time:

- ✔ **Bills:** 90 days to 1 year
- ✔ **Notes:** 2 to 10 years
- ✔ **Bonds:** 10 to 30 years

The big upside on Treasuries: safety. The big downside: inflation risk, which can eat away at the relatively low interest rates these investments pay.

Municipal bonds

When you buy a *municipal* (or *muni*) bond, your money goes to work for public projects. The big upside on munis: They're free of local, state, *and* federal taxes. The big downside: usually a lower yield than taxable bonds.

Generally, munis are best for investors in high tax brackets, who can benefit from the triple-tax-free nature of these bonds. Although munis carry the risk of default (that is, the risk that the issuer cannot pay you back), this risk is generally very low. The risk is lowest for *general obligation bonds* (or *GO bonds*), which are fully backed by the state or municipality itself. More risky are *revenue bonds,* which are issued by an agency, commission, or authority created by legislation in order to construct a facility, such as a toll bridge, turnpike, hospital, university dormitory, or port. The fees, taxes, or tolls charged for use of the facility ultimately pay off the debt. But regardless of the type of muni bond, they're generally much less risky than corporate bonds (see the next section).

Corporate bonds

When a new business venture needs the money to get going, or an existing company is looking for the funds to expand, it turns to the private sector — you! — for help. There are literally dozens of types of corporate bonds, many featuring a *convertible feature:* The bond can be converted in shares of common stock or a *call provision* (the issuer can pay you back before the bond reaches maturity) like some of the other asset types we describe later in this chapter.

Although corporate bonds are generally the most lucrative of bonds, they're also the riskiest — they're backed only by the issuing corporation's promise to pay. You can find corporate bonds with one-year terms, but terms can range up to 15 years or more.

The big upside on corporate bonds: usually higher yields than municipal bonds. The big downsides: the default risk — no company is completely insulated against failure — and the fact that the interest payments on corporate bonds are taxable at all levels, from local to federal.

Getting familiar with bond mutual funds

Bond mutual funds (or *bond funds* for short) pay out periodic income by investing in bonds and other debt securities. They offer liquidity, stability, income, and diversification, which make these funds a very desirable choice among fixed-income investments. Usually, bond mutual funds pay out dividends more frequently than individual bonds, and they pay higher dividends than money-market and savings accounts. Approximately 2,000 bond mutual funds are available.

Bond mutual funds are probably the easiest way for an investor to purchase a fixed-income investment — you can buy and sell them just like any mutual fund, instead of having to go through specialized bond dealers. You can also buy and sell them in any amount, whereas bonds are best purchased in large, even lots. Bond funds contain a basket of individual bonds, so you're not overly exposed to the default risk of any one bond. And different types of bond funds allow you to narrow your focus to the part of the bond market you're most interested in (for example, you can buy a fund of short-term New York State munis or long-term, high-rated corporates).

The big upside on bond mutual funds: diversification and ease of buying and selling. The big downside: no guaranteed payback at maturity, because bond funds have no maturity date.

Considering other types of fixed-income investments

There are a number of other types of fixed-income investments that you should be familiar with, because they're so widely talked about.

Unless you're an experienced investor, avoid these investments.

Mortgage-backed securities

A mortgage-backed security (MBS) is so named because the interest and principal payments from an underlying pool of mortgages are packaged and paid out as income to investors in the MBS. These securities are tantalizing with their promises of high returns — the riskier the mortgages financed, the higher the interest rewarded — but approach them with great caution because of their extreme sensitivity to mortgage rate fluctuations.

You may recall the credit crisis that erupted in 2007 and the ensuing wave of home foreclosures. The Government National Mortgage Association (Ginnie Mae), the Federal National Mortgage Association (Fannie Mae), and the Federal Home Loan Mortgage Corporation (Freddie Mac) issue most MBSs.

Ginnie Mae bonds are the most widely held and traded MBSs. Upsides to MBSs include guaranteed monthly payments and higher yields than Treasury investments with comparable maturities and liquidity. The big downside: prepayment risk. If mortgages are prepaid in full, you get back your investment prematurely, which may have to be reinvested at a lower rate.

Collateralized debt obligations

Collateralized debt obligations (CDOs) are investment- or high-grade securities backed by a pool of bonds, loans, and other assets. These investments aren't for the faint of heart. CDOs are sliced into levels of different types of debt and credit risk called *tranches,* and each tranche represents a different maturity and level of risk. So the higher the risk, the more CDOs pay. Because of losses linked to subprime home loans, demand for CDOs fell by as much as 50 percent in 2008.

The upside: potentially higher returns than traditional bonds. The downside: considerable risk of loss.

Preferred stocks

Preferred stocks share characteristics of both debt and equity. The upside: a fixed dividend and priority over common stockholders in the event the company goes bankrupt. The downside: You don't have voting rights as a shareholder, and there's less potential for capital appreciation.

Convertible bonds

As their name indicates, *convertible bonds,* which have been described as a bond with a stock option wrapped inside, can be converted into equity in the issuing company. Some types of convertible bonds can be converted at the option of the buyer; other types are converted by the seller automatically, when the underlying stock price reaches a certain value.

The upside: If the underlying value of the company stock increases sufficiently, bondholders can cash in their bonds and make a quick profit on the sale of the stock they receive in exchange. The downside: Because of their hybrid characteristics, these bonds yield less than their issuer's normal bonds.

Checking up on a bond issuer's credit

When it comes to bonds, the ones that offer more safety also tend to offer lower yields. If you want to reach for higher returns from your bonds, you'll most likely have to accept a higher risk of default.

Before buying a bond, be sure to check the bond issuer's credit rating. It'll give you an indication of the issuer's ability to pay you back. We let you know how to conduct those checks in this section.

Keep in mind that all bonds carry some risk. There are two major types of risk associated with bonds, as follows:

- ✔ **Interest rate risk** is the risk that the bond's value will vary because of changes in prevailing interest rates. This risk is of more concern to some investors than to others — investors who don't intend to sell their bonds before maturity don't care about market value fluctuations during the life of the bond.

- ✔ **Default risk** is the risk that the bond issuer may not make good on its promised coupon payments and/or payment of par value at maturity. All bondholders should be concerned at varying levels about default risk. Some bonds carry less default risk than others. U.S. government bonds (Treasuries), for example, are backed by the full faith and credit of the U.S. government and are considered the safest bonds in the world. General obligation municipal bonds are next in default risk safety, or creditworthiness.

In order to fully understand the default risk of a bond, you need to be able to recognize the letters you'll see behind a bond investment before you buy. Letters signify credit ratings, indicating the quality of an issuing entity's financial health — in other words, the issuer's ability to pay you back. Bond ratings help you find out how risky it is for you to lend the issuer your money. Think of them as an institutional credit score.

More than half a dozen companies assess the financial strength of bond issuers, but three — Standard & Poor's, Moody's, and Fitch's — represent 90 percent or more of the ratings market.

The higher the letter, or rating — the greater the possibility that you'll get your money back. As a general guideline, long-term credit ratings get a triple A (AAA) for the highest credit quality, and a C or D for the lowest or "junk" quality. Within these parameters, there are different degrees. Table 3-1 presents rating symbols issued by Standard & Poor's and Moody's.

Table 3-1	Bond Rating Examples		
Bond Rating		**Grade**	**Risk**
Standard & Poor's	**Moody's**		
AAA	Aaa	Investment	Lowest risk
AA	Aa	Investment	Low risk
A	A	Investment	Low risk
BBB	Baa	Investment	Moderate risk
BB or B	Ba or B	Junk	High risk
CCC or CC or C	Caa or Ca or C	Junk	Highest risk
D	C	Junk	In default

Source: Brinton Eaton Wealth Advisors.

Don't gamble with the bonds in your portfolio. Play it safe and select investment-grade bonds with a credit rating of BBB to AAA.

Check the ratings of your bonds during the course of their terms. An upgrade or a downgrade can indicate changes in the issuer's ability to pay and can significantly change the bond's market price, which will directly affect the money you'll get if you sell the bond before maturity.

Laddering by maturity

Most of the time, the longer the term of a bond (the further out the maturity date), the higher the yield. To understand how interest rates compare, do what the financial experts do and look at the shape of the *yield curve,* which plots interest rates of bonds with equal credit quality, but differing maturity dates.

In a *normal yield curve* (see Figure 3-2), longer-term maturity bonds will have a higher yield.

In an *inverted yield curve* (see Figure 3-3), the situation switches, and shorter-term yields are higher. This happens only occasionally, usually when the bond market anticipates that yields are heading downward for the foreseeable future. (Some pundits see an inverted yield curve as an early warning signal that the economy is headed into a recession.)

A *flat yield curve* (also called a *hump curve;* see Figure 3-4) shows shorter-and longer-term yields very close to each other.

The bigger the slope, the bigger the gap between short- and long-term rates. Regardless of the slope of the yield curve, longer-term bonds are subject to more risk — both interest rate risk and default risk.

One way to minimize these risks, as well as to get a range of yields, is to purchase bonds (and/or bond funds) throughout the maturity spectrum, from short-term to long-term. This is called *bond laddering*.

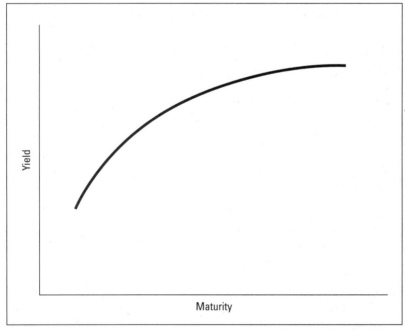

Figure 3-2:
A normal
yield curve.

Source: Brinton Eaton Wealth Advisors.

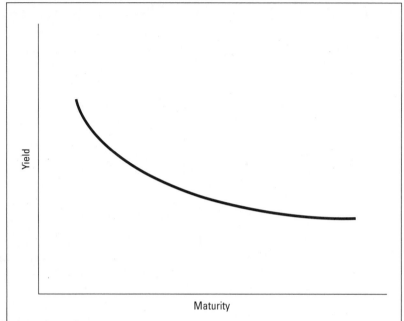

Figure 3-3:
An inverted
yield curve.

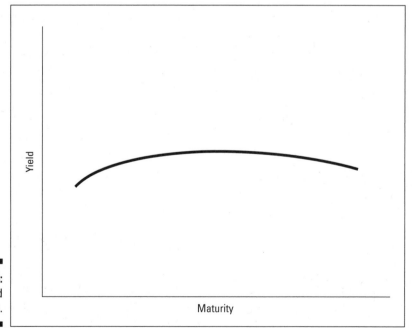

Source: Brinton Eaton Wealth Advisors.

Figure 3-4:
A flat yield
curve.

Capitalizing on cash and cash equivalents

Cash is legal tender that you can use to pay for goods or services, or to pay off debt. People hold cash and cash equivalents (more on those in a moment) in their portfolios for two main reasons:

- ✔ **Instant liquidity:** Instant liquidity is the ability to pay for goods or services quickly. You can access cash immediately from a checking or savings account, or from an investment account that also doubles as your checking account, without having to sell a stock, bond, or other security.

- ✔ **Stability:** Unlike other asset classes such as stocks and bonds, cash is always worth its face value. You don't have to worry about the market value of cash varying from its original value. If you have a $20 bill in your pocket in the morning, even if the stock market completely tanks that day, your $20 bill is still worth $20 at the end of the day — and a little more, too, if you put your cash in an account that earns interest. Stability can be very reassuring, especially during *bear markets* (when the market value of stocks is declining).

In our view, instant liquidity is the more compelling reason to hold cash in your portfolio, but only if you intend to make frequent withdrawals from your account. Stability is better served by short-term fixed-income investments, because fixed-income investments, such as bonds and bond funds, have a better chance of keeping up with inflation. (For more on fixed-income investments, see the "Getting a handle on fixed-income investments: Bonds, bond funds, and more" section, earlier in this chapter.)

Regardless of what we think, lots of investors hold cash in their portfolios for purposes of stability. Just remember that if you do, you need to be prepared to watch the true economic value of your cash erode over time as inflation nibbles away at its purchasing power, eating away at the ability of your cash to buy ever-more-expensive goods and services.

Cash equivalents are investments that mature in very short order (within a year, or even days or weeks or months) and can be easily converted into cash, without losing much money. Cash equivalents can include certificates of deposit (CDs), money-market deposit accounts, and money-market mutual funds. (Some people include short-term Treasury bills and notes as a form of cash equivalents, but we consider all Treasuries to be fixed-income investments.)

You don't want to hold too much money in cash or cash equivalents, because money in these investments loses buying power over the long term as inflation eats away at precious principal. Think about money invested in cash equivalents as savings you expect to use in the near future.

Certificates of deposit

Certificates of deposit (CDs) are offered by banks and other types of financial institutions, including credit unions, brokerage firms, and insurance companies. CDs pay you a rate of interest in return for holding your cash for a specified period of time. They typically pay slightly higher interest rates than savings or money-market deposit accounts, but they aren't as flexible as those accounts — you pay a penalty for early withdrawal.

Short-term CDs are offered from one month to one year. (CD terms can last for five years, but terms greater than one year aren't really considered cashequivalent.) Because they tie up your cash for a specified period of time, CDs are slightly less useful than cash in terms of instant liquidity but they're often a better provider of stability, because the rates of interest they pay can provide good inflation protection.

When you're shopping around for CDs, think twice before buying a *callable CD.* With a callable CD, the seller can terminate (call) the investment before the maturity date. If that happens, you'll be repaid in full for what you invested, but you won't earn the interest you were expecting, and you may be faced with a lower interest rate on a replacement CD.

If you buy a CD through a brokerage firm, ask if the bank issuing the CD to the broker has Federal Deposit Insurance Corporation (FDIC) insurance. If it doesn't, the Securities Investor Protection Corporation (SIPC), a private insurer of the securities industry, will provide some insurance, but not at the level the FDIC guarantees.

To take advantage of a longer-term CD's higher interest rate, split up your money and buy CDs with different due dates. This strategy, known as *laddering,* will give you higher yields (as longer-term CDs generally pay higher interest than shorter-term CDs), while ensuring some access to your cash as shorter-term CDs come due. (We explain laddering in more detail in the "Laddering by maturity" section, earlier in this chapter.)

Money-market deposit accounts

Money-market deposit accounts get their name from the fact that a record of your deposits and withdrawals are kept by the banking institution where you opened the account. Money-market accounts pay interest, like a savings account, but they limit your check-writing privileges.

These accounts are FDIC-protected, pay a higher interest rate than a regular bank savings account, and may offer rates that are competitive with CDs. Typically you must maintain an account balance above a certain minimum to qualify for the higher rates.

You may be able to link this account to your checking or savings account to lower your fees. Be sure to ask the bank where you have your checking or savings account about their money-market accounts.

Money-market mutual funds

You open *money-market mutual funds* directly with a mutual fund company, or through a bank or a brokerage firm. This is probably the most popular form of cash equivalent among serious investors, because the money-market mutual fund is tied to your investments at the same broker or mutual fund company. This way, dividend and interest payments from your other investments can be automatically swept into the money-market fund, as can proceeds from the sales of your other assets, and the funds can be used to quickly buy other investments through a phone call or online transaction.

Money-market mutual funds provide agility. Note that these funds, like all mutual funds, carry fees and expenses (but these are usually very modest). Also, there's no FDIC insurance, because your money is invested in a mutual fund, not held at a bank.

You can protect yourself from the risk of losing money in a bank or savings association by taking two simple steps:

- ✔ **Make sure that the FDIC insures the institution.** To check whether your bank or savings association is insured, call the FDIC at 877-275-3342, go to www.fdic.gov/deposit/index.html and click Bank Find, or look for the agency's official logo where deposits are received.

- ✔ **Make sure that your deposits don't exceed the limits of federal deposit insurance.** Basic insurance is $100,000 for an individual account, per depositor, per bank. (***Note:*** In 2008, Congress temporarily raised the limits to $250,000 through December 31, 2009.) The FDIC provides separate coverage for accounts held in other categories (certain retirement, joint, and revocable trust). For more information on limits, contact the FDIC at 877-275-3342 or calculate your coverage using the agency's Electronic Deposit Insurance Estimator (www2.fdic.gov/edie).

Understanding Alternative Investments

Although cash, fixed income, and equity investments are the big three, other options do exist. Taken together, these other asset types are called *alternative investments*. We describe them in more detail in Chapter 13, but this section is a brief introduction to complete our discussion of asset classes. At the end of this section, we also offer some insight into when you'll want to include these asset alternatives in your portfolio.

Looking at your options for alternative investments

A number of investment options are characterized as *alternative investments*. Some are quite exotic and are for very seasoned and sophisticated investors only. In this section, we focus on three groups of alternative investments that most investors can easily access: real estate, hard assets, and hedge funds.

Investment real estate

Most investors with a sizeable investment portfolio will own at least a portion of their primary residence. If you own your primary residence, that means it's a *use asset,* because you own it for purposes of using it (to live in) rather than to simply hold it. Although the equity in your home is an important part of your overall net worth, most experts agree that use assets shouldn't be considered part of your investment portfolio.

However, *invested real estate assets* can be part of your portfolio, and these include such things as rental property, apartment complexes, office buildings, warehouses, storage facilities, retail malls, and vacant lots. The most efficient way to own this type of property is through real estate investment trusts (REITs). If you want to get your hands on more information about REITs right away, turn to Chapter 13, where we discuss alternative investments in a lot more detail.

Hard assets (commodities)

Most of what you find in a portfolio are financial assets, represented by pieces of paper of one sort or another, such as stocks and bonds. There are other assets, called *hard assets* that include such items as oil, gas, metals, textiles, foodstuffs, and livestock.

Although it's possible to own these hard assets directly, most investors buy *futures* (a financial contract under which a buyer or seller agrees to buy or sell the underlying hard assets at an agreed-upon future date and price). Futures allow the investor's fortunes to rise and fall with the value of the hard asset, without taking possession of the asset itself — which is a good thing, because if you're like most investors, you don't really have room to store oil, gold, or pork bellies. (You'd need a pretty big freezer to hold pork bellies in your portfolio the old-fashioned way.) Thus, hard assets are commonly held as financial assets after all, even though they behave much differently than most other financial assets. (For more information on hard assets, check out Chapter 13.)

Hedge funds

Hedge funds are actively managed portfolios of investments typically set up as private investment partnerships. Originally, they were designed for very sophisticated investors as a way to make bets that *hedged* (reduced the risk) of the positions they held in the rest of their portfolios (hence, their name). Over time, however, the limited purpose and defensive nature of these investments evolved, and now there's a wide array of exotic alternatives — some quite aggressive and speculative — that has become available to the average investor.

Hedge funds fall into a number of categories called *strategies,* such as long/short, global macro, distressed debt, and convertible arbitrage. We discuss hedge funds in more detail in Chapter 13.

Knowing when to add alternative investments to your portfolio

Want to know when you should consider adding alternative investments to your investment portfolio? The timing will be right when the following are true:

- ✓ **You have the stomach to tolerate their unusual behavior.** You have to be able to go with the flow and ride the emotional roller coaster ride that accompanies the thrill of owning these less-than-orthodox investments.

- ✓ **You know you'll have the time to vigilantly monitor them.** The market value of these investments can change abruptly, and you (or your advisor) will need to be quick on your feet to be able to exploit the opportunities that this volatility creates.

By themselves, commodities, hedge funds, and other types of alternative investments can scare the heck out of you. But, paradoxically, when added to a portfolio in the right proportions, they can make a portfolio not only better, but safer. Turn to Chapter 4 to understand how something that looks as if it can break you will actually help improve your portfolio, when included in the right proportions. If you want to really get the ball rolling on alternative investment opportunities, check out Chapter 13.

Going Global with International Investments

We operate in a truly global economy. The values of assets in the United States are inextricably tied to what's going on in the rest of the world. The demand for raw materials in burgeoning economies such as India and China influences the supply and the pricing of those materials in virtually every other economy, including the U.S. The desire for U.S. Treasuries by central banks in many other countries influences the pricing and, thus, the yield of those securities here at home. The international connections go on and on. In light of these interrelationships, it seems natural to include internationally flavored assets in your portfolio.

In earlier times, before the economies around the world became as inter-twined as they now are, owning international equities (stocks and stock funds) was a way to add diversification to a portfolio. Now, however, these equities tend to rise and fall with domestic equities, all but eliminating their diversification value. But they remain advisable investments because their value is often denominated in foreign currency and so they provide a hedge against the value of the dollar. (This is a large part of the reason international equities did so well in the early years of the 21st century.) Regardless of your feelings about the direction of the dollar, you should consider international investments simply because there's no reason, in today's global economy, to confine yourself to purely domestic investments.

International investments are usually characterized by whether they're located in countries that are considered developed or emerging:

✔ **Investing in developed countries:** Developed countries represent relatively advanced economies. Most of Western Europe and Japan (the
so-called EAFA — Europe, Asia, and the Far East — countries) are developed countries with sophisticated economies. The equity investments
in companies of these countries are closely correlated to those in the
United States, and they're less volatile than their counterparts in less
developed countries. For these reasons, they're only a minor step in the
direction of going more global.

✔ **Investing in emerging markets:** Sometimes also called developing countries, *emerging markets* can be found in countries with less advanced economies than what you find in the developed part of the world. Emerging markets include those in Latin America and Asia (the so-called BRIC countries — Brazil, Russia, India, and China). Equity investments here are less correlated to the U.S., but they're becoming more so every day. These equities can be quite volatile. If you have the stomach for their erratic ride and you can handle the associated risk, they represent the more emphatic way to expand beyond domestic borders.

You have various vehicles to choose from if you want to invest internationally. You can invest in the equities of foreign companies directly, either by buying their stock on foreign exchanges or through American Depository Receipts (ADRs) issued on U.S. stock exchanges. The latter is much safer than the former, because foreign exchanges are not yet as liquid or as deep (in terms of number of participants) as domestic markets. You buy ADRs the same way you buy regular stocks.

In some emerging markets, there's also the risk of the government nationalizing the assets on their own exchanges, in which case you could lose your entire investment. You can mitigate this risk and still participate in the growth opportunities in such countries as India and China indirectly, through investing in U.S.-based multinational companies with big growth plans in those developing countries. These plans are usually spelled out in the annual reports of those companies, which you can find on the companies' Web sites.

You can invest in overseas real estate through international REITs (see the "Investment real estate" section earlier or check out Chapter 13 for more information on REITs).

And you can invest in mutual funds and exchange traded funds (ETFs — see Chapter 9) that track country-specific or region-specific indexes (for example, EAFA, BRIC, or emerging markets). Some of these funds can be quite narrowly defined, allowing you, for example, to invest in certain industry sectors in certain regions.

All in all, there is a multitude of ways to invest globally, and the choices are becoming more plentiful every day. Through some combination of these global investment opportunities, you ought to have a healthy dose of non-U.S. exposure in your portfolio. For conservative investors, the percentage may be 10 percent to 15 percent; for aggressive investors, 30 percent to 50 percent. Talk to your advisor or broker for more information on how to go global.

Chapter 4

Determining the Right Proportions: Your Asset Mix

. . . .

. . . .

*I*n this chapter, we explain why asset allocation — selecting your assets and mixing them together correctly — is the single most important thing you can do in investing. And we introduce what we call our guiding principle of asset allocation, to help direct your actions as you build your portfolio.

We address diversification — but also make clear that diversification alone isn't enough. We go further in this chapter to help you uncover and use the secret of *negative correlation* to your benefit. Negative correlation is considered the holy grail of investing — it's hard to find, but it can produce almost mystical qualities in a portfolio. If you can identify assets with good long-term growth potential, but whose short-term up-and-down movements essentially cancel each other out, then you may be able to create a portfolio that will outperform each of the assets within it!

Throughout this chapter, we reveal the underlying concepts of asset allocation. Without a solid understanding of asset allocation fundamentals and why they work, you may be tempted to make an unwise move with your portfolio — chasing a "hot" stock tip or following the lead of a friend who doesn't understand the big picture, for example.

You don't need to be an expert to have better investment results than most other investors. You simply need to start with a reasonably informed asset allocation and have the discipline to stick with it. So read on to empower yourself with the knowledge of the pros!

Putting the 90 Percent Solution to Work for You

Lots of forces and factors can influence how well your investment portfolio performs. Here are just a few of the most significant possibilities:

- ✔ **The state of the U.S. economy:** Is it expanding? Contracting? In recession? In recovery? Changes in the broader global economy are also important.

- ✔ **The activities and decisions of the Federal Reserve Board:** The Federal Reserve Board is responsible for setting the country's economic policy and managing the U.S. money supply — not what you'd call a minor role.

- ✔ **The growth — or lack thereof — of corporate earnings:** Corporate earnings are tricky because the real bottom line can be easily masked with a lot of the wrong information.

- ✔ **The health of the bond and equity markets:** These markets move in unpredictable ways — sometimes together and sometimes not.

And there are several other additional influencing factors:

- ✔ The condition of the domestic and international real-estate markets

- ✔ The cost of energy — oil, gas, and emerging substitutes

- ✔ The level of inflation and its trend

- ✔ The income-tax code and changes in it

- ✔ The quality of the individual securities you select for your portfolio

Which factor matters the most in determining the performance of your portfolio? It's a trick question. All the factors on this list have some impact, but the most critical factor isn't on the list at all.

According to a 1986 study by Gary Brinson, L. Randolph Hood, and Gilbert Beebower (the so-called BHB Study) and much subsequent corroborating research, there's only one short answer to what explains the vast majority — over 90 percent — of the difference in returns among various portfolios: asset allocation. Asset allocation, in essence, is selecting the right asset classes for your portfolio, and mixing them together in the right proportions.

With the right asset allocation, you can help insulate your portfolio against the fluctuations of most of the outside factors in the preceding lists. With the right asset allocation, you can even overcome some bad stock picks that you may have made (as long as you didn't make too many of them), so you can worry just a little bit less about those 200 shares of the glow-in-the-dark sunglasses company you bought in the late '90s. With the right asset allocation, you're already 90 percent of the way home.

Understanding asset allocation will make it harder for you to make mistakes down the road. But when you dig into asset allocation, you have to commit to the approach, even though it may seem counterintuitive to you and contrarian to your friends. Asset allocation will make you savvier than the vast majority of individual investors out there. And, if decades and decades of history is any indication, asset allocation will help you do better than most of those investors over the long term.

Keeping your eye on the important 90 percent: Allocating your assets

By far the most important thing you can do to achieve success in investing is to get your portfolio's asset allocation mix right. This is the top-down approach — the approach that we advocate throughout this book. It starts with an overall investment strategy, which we discuss in more detail in Chapter 7.

A well-put-together investment strategy connects with your long-term financial objectives, your return requirements, your tolerance for risk, your cash-flow needs, your tax situation, your constraints, and any special considerations you may have (see Chapter 6). This overall strategy then dictates your asset allocation. This approach is scientific, well reasoned, time tested, and coherent. By comparison, the bottom-up stock-picking approach (see the next section) is almost as bad as gambling. It's far less reliable than the asset allocation path.

Avoiding focusing on the other 10 percent

Would you spend most of your time and effort chasing something that may get you 10 percent of the way to your goal? Of course not! But that's what many novice investors do when they expend massive amounts of effort to build a portfolio based on stock picking. They focus on that one tantalizing aspect of investing when there is a much superior and more comprehensive strategy to consider.

What makes people focus on stock picking — that measly 10 percent of investing? It's simple: They can make money — a lot of money. If you were fortunate enough to buy into a fledgling software company named Microsoft back in the mid-'80s, by now you'd probably be a die-hard supporter of stock picking. But there are many more stories of failure and loss on the stock markets that you never hear about, and that's one reason that the stigma surrounding stock picking hasn't grown larger over time.

Building a portfolio by picking stocks and/or other securities without regard to the asset allocation that's created when you're done is a losing proposition. This is often called the bottom-up approach to investing. It's not guided by an overarching strategy. It's merely a collection of individual ideas with little or no consideration of how the pieces relate to each other. Investors who subscribe to the bottom-up approach consistently underperform the market averages over the long term.

Embracing asset allocation's guiding principle

As you begin (or continue) to make your decisions about asset mix, always keep in mind the following guiding principle of asset allocation:

> The characteristics and behavior of any single asset in isolation are inconsequential. What really matters is the asset's effect on your portfolio in its entirety.

To make sure you're really getting the most out of the asset allocation approach to investing, ask yourself the following question when you're considering an investment: Is my portfolio better or worse with this asset in it? Don't just think about the quality of the investment by itself — consider it alongside the other investments in your portfolio.

Figuring out which assets will be productive in your portfolio and which ones will be poison can be a tricky task. To check out a few examples of how that works, flip ahead to Chapter 8.

Laying the Foundation for Successful Asset Allocation

The secret behind asset allocation begins with diversification, which means that you don't put all your investment eggs into one basket. But that isn't all there is to it. It's not enough to simply avoid being concentrated in too few holdings. You have to spread your eggs around — and pick your baskets — with a broader strategy in mind.

In this section, we explain the interconnectedness of investments and how you can build a more sound portfolio if you strive to avoid those connections. We help you to think about how you can select your investments in a way that insulates your portfolio from problems and tumultuous changes in the U.S. and global economies.

Understanding correlation

To help us illustrate how the relationships between investments can have a major influence on the success of your portfolio, we'll start with an example. Say you decided to get into investing, but you never came across a wonderful book called *Asset Allocation For Dummies.* You hear that a friend of a friend has made a killing on the stock market in the last year or so — with little or no previous experience — and you guess that you could probably do the same. So you study up for a week or so, and you decide that Apache, Baker Hughes, Chevron, and Exxon are promising stocks, and you buy shares of each. Then you come across some reliable research saying that a mutual fund that tracks a commodity index is a wonderful opportunity. (*Tracking* means that the mutual fund moves in the same direction, by the same amount, at the same time, as the index.) So you fill out your portfolio with this fund and sit back and wait for the stacks of money to start rolling in.

To a casual observer, your portfolio looks diversified. But to the practiced eye, your portfolio has a terrible asset allocation. Why? Because if the price of oil declines, your entire portfolio will be in deep trouble. All your holdings are extremely sensitive to oil prices and you have absolutely nothing in place to offset this overdependence.

To achieve balance in your portfolio — that is, to minimize risk and maximize return — you need to embrace the concept of *correlation,* which, simply defined, is the way that investments in a portfolio relate to each other. More precisely, correlation is a measure that indicates the strength and direction of the linear relationship between two sets of values.

Correlation is measured by the *correlation coefficient,* though this measure is often referred to simply as correlation. (The formula used to determine correlation coefficients is beyond the scope of this book, but you can find it in *Statistics For Dummies,* by Deborah Rumsey, PhD [Wiley], if you find yourself with a hankering for that sort of thing.) Correlation coefficients range along a continuum from 1 to –1, with 1 (at one extreme) indicating perfect positive correlation, –1 (at the other extreme) indicating perfect negative correlation, and 0 (in the middle) indicating no correlation at all.

Here's an example of perfect positive correlation: When you're sitting at your computer and you move your mouse, the cursor on your screen moves in the same direction. Move the mouse right, the cursor moves right; move it left, the cursor moves left; move it a short distance, the cursor moves a little; move it more, the cursor moves farther. The movement of the mouse and the movement of the cursor have a perfect positive correlation of 1 with each other, because the motion of the second exactly corresponds, in magnitude and direction, to the motion of the first. There's an exact, and positive, linear relationship between the two; in other words, they move in lockstep with each other, in the same direction at the same time.

For an example of *perfect negative correlation,* pretend that you're playing a game of coin toss with your friend and the stakes are a penny a toss — heads, you win a penny from him; tails, he wins one from you. If you were to examine your wealth and his after each coin toss, you'd find that they have a perfect negative correlation of –1 — whenever you're up, he's down the exact amount at the same time, without fail. There's an exact, and negative, linear relationship between your respective states of wealth; in other words, as one value moves up or down, the other value moves by an equal amount in the opposite direction.

For our final example, if two sets of values have absolutely no connection with each other — stock market returns and your uncle's waistline, say — then you can expect their correlation to be zero.

But how does this correlation business apply to asset allocation? It's simple: You want to populate your portfolio with assets that have low — close to 0, or even negative — correlation with each other. That's how you unleash the power of asset allocation, as we discuss in the following sections.

Discovering the appeal of non-correlated assets

As you can tell by the example of the oil-dependent portfolio we use earlier in this chapter, having a selection of investments in your portfolio that are highly positively correlated with each other doesn't do you any good. In fact, too many of these investments can be very dangerous.

The solution? Select holdings that have poor correlation with one another — in fact, the poorer, the better. These assets won't move in the same direction at the same time. Sure, one may be down at a certain point in time, but chances are, the others will be steady or even up.

Strive for poor correlation when selecting your investments, and you'll go a long way toward spreading your risk and increasing the likelihood of a steady portfolio return.

Understanding non-correlated assets

Say you have a portfolio with a sizeable amount of equity investments (stocks and/or stock funds — see Chapter 3 for more information). Consider for a moment what may cause your equity investments to hit a rough spot — what may cause their value to decline. One possibility is an unexpected rise in inflation. Higher-than-anticipated inflation is bad news for just about everybody. Companies' earnings may be hit hard due to the rise in the cost of their raw materials, and they may not be able to pass along their higher costs to their customers. The companies' customers may buy less of what the companies are selling, because inflation in the other things they have to buy has eaten away at their budget. And potential investors in the companies will discount the companies' future earnings and dividend stream because those future payments will have less purchasing power than originally anticipated. This kind of inflation spike can wreak havoc on equity investments of all sizes, styles, and sectors, making it hard to find a safe haven. So, what can you do?

First, take a step back and review the broader landscape. What is inflation? What does it measure? In large part, it basically measures the change in cost of a basket of raw materials (commodities). When inflation spikes, it means the cost of that commodity basket spiked up. Wouldn't it have been nice to have had something in your portfolio that spiked up when inflation did, to offset the drop in the value of your equity investments?

You're in luck! Such a thing exists — you can invest in a fund that tracks the cost of a broad basket of commodities, which can include oil, gas, precious metals, textiles, foodstuffs, livestock, and so on. (Chapter 13 gives you more information about commodity index funds.) Such an investment will tend to rise in value when inflation does, almost by definition. It's an investment with very poor, even negative, correlation with your equity investments. In times of unexpected inflation spikes, it will help protect your equity-heavy portfolio from harm. This is one example of how assets with poor correlation can be a real boon for your portfolio.

Finding non-correlated assets

So, how do you find assets that have poor correlation with each other?

- ✔ You can look at the pattern of their returns over time (see, for example, the graphs of the returns for selected asset classes in Chapter 17). Assets with returns that tend to rise when others fall, and vice versa, are clear candidates.

- ✔ You can calculate the correlation of an asset with any other asset by using a financial calculator or the CORREL function in Microsoft Excel. Ask your financial advisor (see Chapter 16) for help if you need it. (For help with Excel, check out the edition of *Excel For Dummies* [Wiley] that corresponds to your version of Excel.)

To give you a head start, in Chapter 8, we illustrate some sample portfolios containing assets that are collectively poorly correlated with each other. For example, most portfolios should have a mix of bonds, stocks, real estate, and commodities.

Be wary of combining certain asset classes that are sometimes touted as having poor correlation with each other but are actually strongly correlated, such as:

- Growth stocks and value stocks
- Large-cap stocks and mid-cap stocks
- U.S. stocks and international stocks

You can read more about all these types of investments in Chapter 3.

Focusing on correlation, and looking for assets with poor correlation, is wonderfully effective — it works! A portfolio composed of poorly correlated assets (those with a low positive, or even negative, correlation with each other) will have considerable stability. All else being equal, such a portfolio will have much lower volatility — and higher long-term return — than one composed of highly correlated assets. Again, turn to Chapter 2 if you need to brush up on concepts like risk, return, and volatility, but keep reading in this chapter if you want to know more about the virtue of stability and the cost of volatility.

Realizing how 2 + 2 can equal 5 in your portfolio

One of the best parts about asset allocation is the way you can make your portfolio better than the sum of its parts. To help you understand how, take a look at Figure 4-1, which shows you the actual performance of two very common assets — stocks and real estate — over a recent 30-year period. These two assets are far from having perfect negative correlation with each other. (Flip back to the "Understanding correlation" section in this chapter for more information if you need it.) In fact, they're slightly positively correlated; their correlation coefficient is 0.13 over this period. The important point is that, like a number of assets encountered in real life, they are not *perfectly* positively correlated — they don't move in lockstep.

You'll see that stocks are represented in Figure 4-1 by the S&P 500 Stock Index and real estate is represented by the FTSE NAREIT All REIT Index, a collection of *real estate investment trusts* (REITs), companies that own and typically operate income-producing real estate. Return is calculated as the 30-year compound annual growth rate (assuming reinvestment of dividends); risk, as the annual standard deviation in the individual annual returns. (Refer to Chapter 2 for an explanation of risk and return.) The asset labeled "Combined" is a simple portfolio consisting of a 50/50 allocation to stocks and real estate, rebalanced annually (see Chapter 5 for a discussion of rebalancing).

The figure plots each of these three assets on the risk/return map, which you can read about in Chapter 2. If you don't want to flip back to that chapter right now, just keep in mind that, on the risk/return map, the best assets are those that appear farthest northwest because they have high return and low risk.

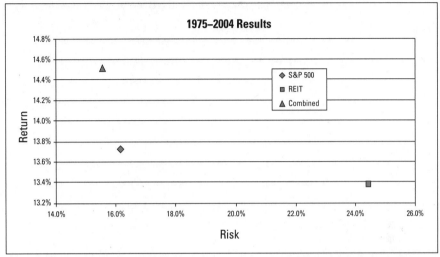

Figure 4-1:
How 2 + 2
can equal 5.

This simple two-asset example portfolio illustrates a truly remarkable phenomenon: By combining assets with less-than-perfect positive correlation, you can get a portfolio with less risk than you would achieve with any one of the assets alone. Specifically, stocks have a standard deviation in excess of 16 percent; REITs, in excess of 24 percent. But the combined portfolio's standard deviation is less than 16 percent. Nice, you're saying, but is it really remarkable? Here's the remarkable part: By combining these assets (and regularly rebalancing), you get a return for the portfolio that is greater than the return for any single asset within it! Although the return for stocks is about 13.7 percent over this period, and the return for REITs is about 13.4 percent, the return for the combined portfolio is 14.5 percent!

Is this result a fluke of this particular 30-year period and these two particular assets? No. Similar phenomena have been reproduced through simulation analyses, and in Chapter 5 we further explore the reasons behind this phenomenon. It doesn't always happen, though. Determining the right assets to put into a portfolio, and the proper allocations among them, is a matter of considerable art and science. But we give you some guidelines on identifying the magic ingredients in the "Recognizing the Most Important Features of an Asset" section at the end of this chapter.

Making Rudolph the Red-Nosed Reindeer work for your portfolio

A favorite Christmas tale tells the story of poor little Rudolph the Red-Nosed Reindeer. His nose is so bright, the rest of the herd snickers and laughs behind his back. But the very quality that makes him an outsider vaults him into a position of honor when Santa chooses him to guide his sleigh one especially foggy Christmas Eve.

It's not likely that Rudolph's story was created to provide a useful example for adult investors, but it just so happens that you can take quite a bit from the tale of the reindeer with the crimson schnoz. Rudolph's oddball nose seemed like a liability until the context changed, and then all of a sudden it was a godsend. The same can be true for some assets. Sometimes a seemingly inferior asset can do wonders for your portfolio, if the context is right.

If, for example, your existing portfolio enjoys a return of 14 percent and a risk (standard deviation) of 16-plus percent, would it make sense to add an asset whose return (13 percent) is worse, and whose risk is a whopping 24-plus percent? Well, the earlier example from Figure 4-1 provides the answer. (In fact, it's from this example that the just-cited risk/return percentages are taken!) Take as the existing portfolio the single-asset portfolio consisting of stocks. Take as the inferior asset real estate. Plainly, adding the inferior (REIT) asset to the (stock) portfolio improves it considerably. The portfolio's risk went down to below 16 percent, and its return went up to well above 14 percent.

This is no isolated peculiarity. Examples abound of cases where an asset, itself no stellar performer, can improve both the risk and the return of the portfolio it's added to.

Finding the holy grail of asset allocation: Perfect negative correlation

What's even better than poor correlation among the investments in your portfolio? Perfect negative correlation, that's what. If you can find two assets with a correlation of –1, then it doesn't matter how volatile each one is. You can eliminate the volatility completely, at the portfolio level, simply by putting both assets in your portfolio. Their volatilities cancel each other out; zero volatility is the result — and zero volatility is a very good thing indeed. As a practical matter, finding two assets with perfect negative correlation is next to impossible, but it's important for you to come as close as you can.

For a visual representation of what we're talking about, take a look at Table 4-1.

Consider two assets, A and B, each with a simple average annual return of 8 percent over ten years. (Check out Chapter 2 for more information on simple average returns.) As is typical of most assets, Asset A and Asset B don't come with a guaranteed 8 percent each year — the actual return is subject to quite a bit of variation from year to year.

Table 4-1   The Effect of Negative Correlation

	Asset A			Asset B				
	Annual Return	Account Balance	Rebalanced Amount	Annual Return	Account Balance	Rebalanced Amount	Portfolio Balance (A + B)	Portfolio Return
		$200	$200		$100	$100	$300	8%
Year 1	13%	$226	$216	−2%	$98	$108	$324	8%
Year 2	18%	$255	$233	−12%	$95	$117	$350	8%
Year 3	1%	$236	$252	22%	$142	$126	$378	8%
Year 4	16%	$292	$272	−8%	$116	$136	$408	8%
Year 5	3%	$280	$294	18%	$161	$147	$441	8%
Year 6	11%	$326	$317	2%	$150	$159	$476	8%
Year 7	11%	$352	$343	2%	$162	$171	$514	8%
Year 8	−7%	$319	$370	38%	$237	$185	$555	8%
Year 9	8%	$400	$400	8%	$200	$200	$600	8%
Year 10	6%	$424		12%	$224		$648	8%
Simple Average Return	8%			8%				8%
Standard Deviation	7.5%			15.1%				0%
Compound Average Return	7.8%			7.1%				8%

Source: Brinton Eaton Wealth Advisors

Asset B has twice as much volatility (measured by standard deviation, as defined in Chapter 2) as Asset A. You can see the damaging effect of volatility on your return if you note that the compound average return (the return that matters — see Chapter 2) is less than the simple average return for both assets. For Asset A, the compound average annual return is 7.8 percent; for Asset B, it's 7.1 percent. Both are less than their simple average returns of 8 percent, due to risk drag (another topic covered in Chapter 2).

If there existed an "ideal portfolio" that did return a guaranteed 8 percent each year, it would be much preferred to either Asset A or Asset B in Table 4-1. In addition to the comfort of knowing that you could count on your 8 percent return every year, you would actually be wealthier at the end of ten years with this ideal portfolio! (See the discussion of risk drag in Chapter 2 to better understand this result.)

You may be asking yourself, "Where can I get one of those ideal portfolios?" If you stare hard at Table 4-1, you'll realize that it's right under your nose. Hypothetically speaking, if Asset A and Asset B happen to be perfectly negatively correlated with each other, the portfolio in Table 4-1 could be an ideal portfolio. In fact, you can construct this ideal portfolio by simply putting two-thirds of your investment in Asset A and one-third in Asset B (in inverse relationship to their standard deviations — recall that Asset B's standard deviation is twice Asset A's, so it gets half the allocation). If you maintain this two-thirds/one-third asset allocation each year through rebalancing (see Chapter 5), your return will be exactly 8 percent, each and every year, guaranteed. That would mean that your compound average return and simple average return would be equal, and your portfolio's overall compound average return would be greater than that of either asset within it!

In all truthfulness, it's highly unlikely that two assets with perfect negative correlation with each other will ever be found in the real world, but it's not necessary for the relationship to be perfectly negative for there to be beneficial effects in combining assets. You should be thrilled if you encounter investments that have negative correlations of –0.35 or so. Even positive correlations below 0.2 are good.

Seeking stability and vanquishing volatility

As you work your way toward a successful system of asset allocation with your investment portfolio, you should always keep in mind that a high level of stability — or, equivalently, a low level of volatility — is an important characteristic to seek out in a portfolio. Building a stable portfolio will provide you with solid, consistent returns (who doesn't love that?), and cutting down on volatility will help you dodge the nasty effects of risk drag (see the preceding section and Chapter 2 for more on risk drag). In this section, we dig a little deeper into the importance of accentuating stability and cutting down on volatility.

Appreciating the virtue of stability

By *stability*, we mean steadiness in the return that your portfolio achieves from period to period. A nice stable return on your portfolio is a wonderful thing. For one thing, it saves you the aggravation of watching your investments behave erratically. It allows you to sleep better at night, slumbering peacefully while your portfolio earns you a steady, reliable return. The benefits of such a well-behaved portfolio can't be overstated; after all, your mental health is at least as important as your financial wealth. The last thing you want to see happen to your hard-earned assets is to have their market value ride an uncontrolled roller coaster up and down over the years.

But, in addition to helping you avoid a straightjacket, stability of return over time can also make you wealthier.

A stable return puts more money in your pocket over the long haul than a portfolio with returns that are way up one moment but way down the next.

You can see the benefits of a stable return in Table 4-1 and Table 4-2. In Table 4-1, which we discuss in the "Finding the holy grail of asset allocation: Perfect negative correlation" section, we increased the compound average return from less than 8 percent (7.8 percent in the case of Asset A; 7.1 percent in the case of Asset B) to 8 percent by increasing stability through a clever combination of assets. In that case, stability — all by itself — created wealth.

In Table 4-2, you can see that Portfolio A, which is much more stable than Portfolio B, outperformed Portfolio B. This happened even though Portfolio A had a simple average return (8 percent) less than that of Portfolio B (9 percent).

Table 4-2	Proof That Stable Portfolios Yield Greater Returns			
	Portfolio A		**Portfolio B**	
	Annual Return	**Account Balance**	**Annual Return**	**Account Balance**
		$100		$100
Year 1	8%	$108	23%	$123

(continued)

Table 4-2 *(continued)*

	Portfolio A		Portfolio B	
	Annual Return	*Account Balance*	*Annual Return*	*Account Balance*
Year 2	8%	$117	−14%	$106
Year 3	8%	$126	−7%	$98
Year 4	8%	$136	20%	$118
Year 5	8%	$147	16%	$137
Year 6	8%	$159	14%	$156
Year 7	8%	$171	−18%	$127
Year 8	8%	$185	27%	$162
Year 9	8%	$200	−2%	$158
Year 10	8%	$216	32%	$208
Average Return	8%		9%	
Standard Deviation	0%		18%	
Ending Balance		$216		$208

Source: Brinton Eaton Wealth Advisors

Avoiding the cost of volatility

When it comes to your portfolio, stability is like love — you really can't get too much of it. Volatility, on the other hand, is like a sunburn — even a little bit in your overall portfolio can really hurt! A portfolio with a very erratic return can cost you.

Look again at Table 4-2. Portfolio B could've been a winner. It had a simple average return of 9 percent, easily besting the 8 percent return of Portfolio A. But volatility did it in. The volatility of Portfolio B was so severe that its 9 percent simple average return was savagely eroded. All those ups and downs eventually took their toll. In fact, its compound average return (not shown on the table, but easily calculated from the annual returns per the instructions in Chapter 2) is a lowly 7.6 percent, a mere shadow of the 9 percent it could've been. In contrast, Portfolio A's simple average return of 8 percent wasn't eroded at all — its stability allowed its compound average return (again, the one that really matters) to stay strong at 8 percent.

So, finding ways to reduce the volatility of your portfolio, while not sacrificing its return, is a very worthwhile effort.

A portfolio should have a broad mix of investments. Make sure you include stocks, bonds, commodities, and real estate, because those asset classes generally don't move in the same direction at the same time. That strategy will help protect you from volatility.

Recognizing the Most Important Features of an Asset

So, what kind of assets do you really want in your portfolio? These choices are important, and you want to make sure you're getting the most bang for your investment buck.

The assets you choose should have three things going for them:

✔ **Healthy expected returns over the long haul.**

✔ **Sizeable volatilities:** If you read the earlier sections in this chapter, the idea of striving for high volatility may shock you. But remember, it's the volatility of the *overall portfolio* that you want to keep at a minimum, not necessarily the volatility of individual assets. If an individual asset has high volatility, it's more likely to have a high expected return, as we point out in Chapter 2. Furthermore, if an individual asset has high volatility, it's more likely that rebalancing (see Chapter 5) will have an additional, material, beneficial impact.

✔ **Poor or even negative correlation with the other assets in your portfolio:** You can read all about correlation in the "Understanding correlation," "Discovering the appeal of non-correlated assets," and "Finding the holy grail of asset allocation: Perfect negative correlation" sections, earlier in this chapter.

How do you find assets that have all three qualities? And how do you identify these properties for each asset? For any investment you consider, historical average returns and standard deviations (a good indicator of volatility) are typically included in the prospectus and other marketing material. Often, correlations with common indexes are also presented, but here the information is far from complete. Your advisor can help you on that front — ask her to share her correlation analyses with you. (If she hasn't done any, you may rightly ask what her recommended allocations are based on!) You can also refer to Chapter 8 for more on our take on some assets that have these desirable properties.

When deciding which assets to add to your portfolio, and in what proportions, don't forget our guiding principle of asset allocation: The characteristics and behavior of any single asset in isolation are inconsequential — what really matters is the asset's effect on your portfolio in its entirety. (Here again, Chapter 8 gives you a head start.)

Chapter 5

Stirring the Mix: Portfolio Rebalancing

A sset allocation has an important partner called portfolio rebalancing. Rebalancing takes asset allocation to the next level, unlocking additional power that helps make your portfolio more profitable and less volatile.

In this chapter, we look closely at rebalancing. We explain that rebalancing supports the underlying intent of asset allocation; it doesn't rethink it. In addition to helping you stay true to your asset allocation, rebalancing actually delivers better risk/return performance than a lazy buy-and-hold strategy.

You'll find that it takes some intestinal fortitude to be a rebalancer. It requires going against your intuition and making changes to your portfolio that may seem nonsensical to your friends and counter to what the pundits on TV urge you to do. But you'll see that it's worth it. You'll discover that, through rebalancing, you'll be able to finally enjoy that free lunch you've been looking for all these years.

Understanding how to successfully rebalance your portfolio will enable you to exploit the power of the periodic table — the investment periodic table, not the one above the chalkboard in your high school chemistry class — and put the principle of volatility pumping to work for you. We cover both of these concepts in this chapter. And after you read all about them, it'll be much easier for you to take on a contrarian mindset, which will then make it much easier for you to stick to the rebalancing process for increased returns over the long haul.

To finish up the chapter, we also provide a section that fills you in on exactly when you should look to rebalance your portfolio. Rebalancing correctly, and on the right schedule, will make sure you get all the benefit you can from your carefully considered asset allocation.

Getting Your Free Lunch with Rebalancing

Because rebalancing offers huge benefits with little to no additional risk, we like to say that it's the closest you'll ever come to a free lunch in investing. Start rebalancing and belly up to the free-lunch counter!

To better understand what we mean, take a look at Figure 5-1. We start with two assets: stocks and real estate (specifically, real estate investment trusts, or REITs). Stocks are represented by the S&P 500 Stock Index; REITs, by the FTSE NAREIT All REIT Index. (We plot each of these two assets on the risk/reward map introduced in Chapter 2, which is worth a look if you're a little unsure of the relationship between risk and return.) Here, the return measure is the compound average annual return; risk is measured by the annual standard deviation of those returns. The data used for each index is for the 30-year period from 1975 through 2004.

You can see that stocks had a return of about 13.7 percent and a standard deviation of a bit over 16 percent. REITs had a return of 13.4 percent and a standard deviation of roughly 24.5 percent. If you constructed a portfolio made up of a 50/50 weighting of stocks and real estate, and you held it for the entire 30-year period without rebalancing, you would've gotten a return halfway between the return of the two assets we started with (a little over 13.5 percent), as you may expect. But the standard deviation of the combined portfolio turns out to be much less than midway between the standard deviations of the two original assets. In fact, the standard deviation of 16 percent is slightly less than the standard deviation of stocks, and much less than that of REITs. This is due to the diversification benefit that we explain in Chapter 4.

Now, suppose that, instead of simply holding the 50/50 portfolio for 30 years, you rebalanced it every year. In other words, at the end of each year, if your portfolio had drifted away from its 50/50 weighting (which it typically did), you adjusted it back. If stocks grew faster than REITs one year, you sold enough stocks — and bought REITs with proceeds — to bring the weightings back to 50/50 (and vice versa, if REITs outgrew stocks in any year).

As you can see, the rebalanced portfolio ended up with a return of 14.5 percent and a standard deviation of about 15.5 percent. This is vastly superior to the portfolio that was not rebalanced — it has a lower standard deviation and a considerably higher return.

You may be wondering how a difference of about 1 percent a year in return — 14.5 percent versus 13.5 percent — can be termed *considerable?* Well, don't forget the power of compounding. Over those 30 years, an original investment of $1,000 growing at 13.5 percent a year ends up being $44,656; the same $1,000 growing at 14.5 percent a year becomes $58,098. That's an extra $13,442 for every $1,000 invested! Not too shabby.

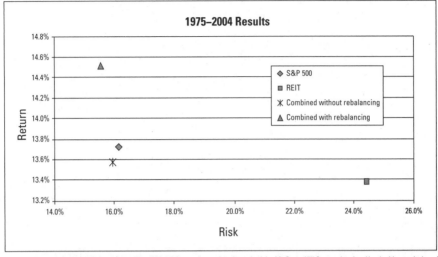

Figure 5-1:
Getting a
free lunch
through
rebalancing.

Not only is the return for the rebalanced portfolio higher than the combined return of the two assets without rebalancing, but it's also higher than either asset alone. The rebalanced portfolio has a higher return than any of the assets within it. (And, don't forget, the risk is lower, too.) This approach creates something from nothing. It's alchemy. It's finally getting that free lunch!

Understanding the Power of Rebalancing

Before we explain the ins and outs of rebalancing it's important that we define the term, because there are some common misperceptions out there about rebalancing.

Rebalancing involves the buying and selling of various investments within your portfolio to achieve a certain allocation by asset class. Does this represent a change in your investment strategy, or a rethinking of your long-term asset allocation? No, and no again! In fact, it's just the opposite.

First, as we discuss in detail in Chapter 4, you establish your investment portfolio according to an overall strategic allocation to three broad asset classes (fixed-income, equity, and alternative investments). Within each of those broad classes, you then adhere to a more refined allocation scheme that establishes, for example, how fixed-income investments should be spread among various maturities, and how equity investments should be spread among various industry sectors.

After you set up your portfolio, you'll find that your actual allocation on any given day thereafter is subject to the ups and downs of the market. Your allocation changes when some investments increase or decrease in value more or less than the others in your portfolio. Over time, your allocation may drift quite far away from what you originally intended. When that happens, it's time to restore order. Rebalancing is what you do to get your portfolio back in order — back to its target asset allocation.

This section tells you all you need to know about how rebalancing works and how you can make it work for you!

Rebalancing doesn't mean reallocating. It means resetting your portfolio back to its target asset allocation, which can actually increase your portfolio's return. If you diligently rebalance, you can actually increase your portfolio's return to a point higher than the return of any asset within it.

Left unattended, your portfolio will virtually always drift away from your target allocations — the market will see to that, as not everything in your portfolio will grow at the same rate. You need to be alert to this phenomenon and restore order by rebalancing. If you aren't sufficiently vigilant and let your portfolio bubble away without paying attention, you'll find that your investment mix will be not only different from what you intended, but also most likely riskier.

Why would an unattended portfolio end up riskier than you intended? Riskier investments tend to have higher returns (as we cover in Chapter 2). Assuming those returns are in the form of market appreciation, or are otherwise reinvested back into the investments that produced them, those riskier investments will tend to outgrow the lower-risk/lower-return investments in your portfolio. Over time, this will result in too much of these higher-risk/higher-return investments in your portfolio. Why is that such a bad thing? Why would having too much high-return investments be something to avoid? Because, if you wanted the associated higher level of risk in your portfolio, there are better ways to achieve it. That is, you could have constructed a higher-risk portfolio in the first place that would likely produce a better return than one you arrived at purely by accident.

How rebalancing works: Unlocking the energy of the periodic table

To help you get a feel for how rebalancing works, start by taking a look at Figure 5-2, which is often referred to in investing circles as the *periodic table*. It does bear a resemblance to the chemists' periodic table of the elements, but don't strain your eyes looking for the symbol for tungsten or the atomic weight of argon. This periodic table is different, and the direct relationship to periodic behavior (in investment terms) will become clearer in a moment.

Each column in Figure 5-2 represents a single calendar year. Within each column, several popular asset classes (bonds of varying maturities, real estate, commodities, and various equity sectors) are shown. For each asset class, you can see the total return (see Chapter 2) that that asset class delivered in each year. The asset classes are sorted from highest return to lowest return within each year. For example, in 1993, the total return for the technology equity sector was 21.7 percent; for commodities, it was –12.3 percent. In 2007, the total return for the energy sector was 34.4 percent; for the financial sector, –18.6 percent. Each of the asset classes is shaded so you can more easily track an asset class's ranking from year to year.

Even after only a quick glance, you can see that there's a substantial amount of random movement within the list. No asset class maintains its spot in the rankings for very long, and there's no discernable pattern to how any one class moves up or down the list from year to year. (You can't see it here, but at more frequent intervals than annual, the random movement is even more pronounced.) There's simply a lot of volatility among asset classes in the market, and this movement is, in large part, unpredictable. All you can say for sure is that the leaders eventually become laggards, and vice versa.

This is due to a well-researched statistical phenomenon called *reversion to the mean* that you may have heard about. In short, it means that things can't behave far above or below their long-term average level for very long; at some point, the hot (or cold) streak has to end and a period of underperformance (or overperformance) follows. The long-term average remains intact. This is true of every hitter in baseball, and it's true in investing.

Some people (particularly those in the active-investing or market-timing school) try to predict the turning points for these asset classes and invest accordingly. You have to be incredibly smart — or just darned lucky — to get this timing right. Here's a poorly kept secret: Nobody is that smart. But that hasn't stopped people from trying. They tend to do better than average a little less than half the time, according to study after study. In other words, over any reasonable length of time, they underperform the market averages. Don't buy into the market-timing hype. With regular rebalancing, you don't have to predict the timing. And, over the long term, you'll beat the active investing crowd.

What are the mechanics of rebalancing? You sell enough of the overweighted assets in your portfolio to bring them down to their target allocations, and use the proceeds to buy enough of the underweighted assets to bring them up to their targets. The custodian that holds your assets probably has an online rebalancing tool that you can use. You input your target allocations and it shows you how much you need to buy and sell of each asset class.

Figure 5-2: The periodic table illustrates the inherent volatility among asset-class returns.

Rank	1993	1994	1995	1996	1997	1998	1999	2000	2001	2002	2003	2004	2005	2006	2007
1	Technology 21.7%	Technology 19.9%	Healthcare 58.0%	Technology 43.9%	Financials 48.2%	Technology 78.1%	Technology 78.7%	Utilities 57.2%	Real Estate 15.5%	Commodities 32.1%	Technology 47.2%	Energy 31.5%	Energy 31.4%	Telecom 36.8%	Energy 34.4%
2	Small-Cap Stocks 18.8%	Healthcare 13.7%	Financials 54.4%	Real Estate 35.7%	Healthcare 43.7%	Telecom 52.4%	Commodities 40.9%	Commodities 49.7%	Long-Term Bonds 12.5%	Intermediate-Term Bonds 11.4%	Small-Cap Stocks 38.8%	Real Estate 30.4%	Commodities 25.6%	Real Estate 34.4%	Commodities 32.7%
3	Industrials 18.6%	Consumer Staples 9.8%	Telecom 42.3%	Financials 32.1%	Telecom 41.2%	Healthcare 43.9%	Materials 25.3%	Healthcare 37.1%	Short-Term Bonds 10.3%	Long-Term Bonds 11.4%	Real Estate 38.5%	Utilities 24.3%	Utilities 16.8%	Energy 24.2%	Materials 22.5%
4	Real Estate 18.5%	Materials 5.8%	Consumer Staples 39.6%	Commodities 33.9%	Consumer Discretionary 34.4%	Consumer Discretionary 41.1%	Consumer Discretionary 25.2%	Real Estate 25.9%	Intermediate-Term Bonds 10.1%	Short-Term Bonds 9.8%	Materials 38.2%	Small-Cap Stocks 22.6%	Mid-Cap Stocks 12.6%	Utilities 21.0%	Utilities 19.4%
5	Energy 15.9%	Commodities 5.3%	Technology 39.4%	Consumer Staples 25.9%	Consumer Staples 32.9%	Mid-Cap Stocks 19.1%	Industrials 21.5%	Financials 25.7%	Small-Cap Stocks 6.5%	Real Estate 5.2%	Consumer Discretionary 37.4%	Telecom 19.9%	Real Estate 8.3%	Financials 19.2%	Technology 16.3%
6	Telecom 15.1%	Energy 3.7%	Industrials 39.1%	Energy 25.9%	Mid-Cap Stocks 32.3%	Consumer Staples 15.8%	Telecom 19.1%	Mid-Cap Stocks 17.5%	Materials 3.5%	Consumer Staples -4.3%	Mid-Cap Stocks 35.6%	Industrials 18.0%	Small-Cap Stocks 7.7%	Consumer Discretionary 18.6%	Consumer Staples 14.2%
7	Consumer Discretionary 14.6%	Real Estate 0.8%	Utilities 32.7%	Industrials 25.1%	Technology 28.5%	Utilities 14.6%	Energy 18.7%	Consumer Staples 16.8%	Consumer Discretionary 2.8%	Materials -5.5%	Industrials 32.2%	Commodities 17.3%	Financials 6.5%	Materials 18.6%	Industrials 12.0%
8	Mid-Cap Stocks 14.0%	Short-Term Bonds -0.8%	Energy 31.0%	Small-Cap Stocks 21.3%	Industrials 27.0%	Financials 11.9%	Mid-Cap Stocks 14.7%	Energy 15.7%	Mid-Cap Stocks -0.6%	Energy -11.1%	Financials 31.0%	Mid-Cap Stocks 16.5%	Healthcare 6.5%	Small-Cap Stocks 15.1%	Telecom 11.9%
9	Long-Term Bonds 13.9%	Industrials -2.4%	Mid-Cap Stocks 30.9%	Healthcare 21.6%	Small-Cap Stocks 25.6%	Industrials 10.9%	Small-Cap Stocks 12.4%	Small-Cap Stocks 11.8%	Industrials -5.7%	Mid-Cap Stocks -14.5%	Utilities 26.3%	Consumer Discretionary 13.2%	Materials 4.4%	Consumer Staples 14.4%	Small-Cap Stocks 8.0%
10	Utilities 13.7%	Financials -3.5%	Small-Cap Stocks 30.0%	Mid-Cap Stocks 19.2%	Energy 25.3%	Long-Term Bonds 9.5%	Financials 4.1%	Intermediate-Term Bonds 10.7%	Consumer Staples -6.4%	Small-Cap Stocks -14.6%	Energy 25.6%	Materials 13.2%	Consumer Staples 3.6%	Industrials 13.3%	Healthcare 7.2%
11	Materials 13.5%	Intermediate-Term Bonds -3.6%	Long-Term Bonds 26.4%	Materials 15.8%	Utilities 24.7%	Short-Term Bonds 8.8%	Short-Term Bonds 1.4%	Short-Term Bonds 8.8%	Financials -9.5%	Financials -14.6%	Commodities 20.7%	Financials 10.9%	Long-Term Bonds 3.5%	Mid-Cap Stocks 10.3%	Short-Term Bonds 5.7%
12	Intermediate-Term Bonds 13.0%	Mid-Cap Stocks -3.6%	Intermediate-Term Bonds 21.9%	Consumer Discretionary 12.4%	Real Estate 18.9%	Intermediate-Term Bonds 8.3%	Intermediate-Term Bonds -2.2%	Long-Term Bonds 8.7%	Energy -10.4%	Healthcare -18.8%	Healthcare 15.1%	Long-Term Bonds 9.2%	Industrials 2.3%	Technology 8.4%	Intermediate-Term Bonds 4.4%
13	Financials 10.9%	Telecom -4.8%	Commodities 20.3%	Utilities 5.7%	Long-Term Bonds 13.5%	Energy 0.6%	Long-Term Bonds -8.8%	Industrials 5.9%	Healthcare -11.9%	Consumer Discretionary -23.8%	Consumer Staples 11.6%	Consumer Staples 8.2%	Intermediate-Term Bonds 1.8%	Healthcare 7.5%	Long-Term Bonds 3.4%
14	Short-Term Bonds 9.8%	Small-Cap Stocks -4.8%	Consumer Discretionary 20.3%	Intermediate-Term Bonds 4.7%	Intermediate-Term Bonds 9.4%	Small-Cap Stocks -1.3%	Real Estate -6.5%	Materials -15.7%	Telecom -12.2%	Industrials -26.3%	Long-Term Bonds 10.7%	Intermediate-Term Bonds 6.0%	Technology 1.0%	Short-Term Bonds 4.8%	Mid-Cap Stocks -0.3%
15	Consumer Staples -3.9%	Long-Term Bonds -4.9%	Materials 20.0%	Long-Term Bonds 2.3%	Materials 8.4%	Materials -6.2%	Utilities -9.2%	Consumer Discretionary -20.0%	Technology -25.9%	Utilities -30.0%	Intermediate-Term Bonds 9.1%	Short-Term Bonds 3.4%	Short-Term Bonds 0.9%	Intermediate-Term Bonds 4.4%	Consumer Discretionary -13.2%
16	Healthcare -8.2%	Consumer Discretionary -8.3%	Real Estate 18.3%	Short-Term Bonds 3.3%	Short-Term Bonds 8.0%	Real Estate -18.8%	Healthcare -10.7%	Telecom -38.8%	Utilities -30.4%	Telecom -34.1%	Short-Term Bonds 7.1%	Technology 2.6%	Telecom -5.6%	Long-Term Bonds 3.7%	Real Estate -17.8%
17	Commodities -12.3%	Utilities -11.8%	Short-Term Bonds 16.6%	Telecom 1.1%	Commodities -14.1%	Commodities -35.7%	Consumer Staples -15.1%	Technology -40.9%	Commodities -31.9%	Technology -37.4%	Telecom 6.9%	Healthcare 1.7%	Consumer Discretionary -6.4%	Commodities -15.1%	Financials -18.6%

Of course, if you have an investment advisor, she can do it for you — and should be doing so on a continual basis. If she isn't, it may be time to find another advisor (see Chapter 16).

Here's a specific example of how rebalancing works, based on the example presented in Figure 5-2: At the end of 2006, given the outperformance of real estate and the underperformance of commodities during that year, the rebalancing angel on your shoulder would've prompted you to sell some of your real estate and buy more commodities. This would've paid off handsomely in 2007, because those two asset classes essentially switched places in the rankings. Other examples like this abound if you study the periodic table.

Does this always work? No. Getting back to the example in Figure 5-2, if you sold some energy at the end of 2004, it would've been too early, because it outperformed in 2005 as well. But the number of examples where it works outweigh the number of examples where it doesn't (because of reversion to the mean). At worst, with rebalancing, you may trim your holdings in a winner a bit too early, but it's virtually inevitable that it'll become a relative loser before long, when it reverts to its long-term average behavior. Over the long term, letting rebalancing dictate when you load up or lighten up in an asset class is the winning strategy. Although it may not beat every other strategy each and every individual period, over a number of periods, it'll outperform the guesswork of the market timers, and it'll outperform doing nothing.

One way to view all the essentially random activity evident in the periodic table is to think of it as representing a lot of kinetic energy. The total returns for those assets are moving all the time. Here's the crucial point: Rebalancing puts this energy to work for you. And it does so without having to take sides — without having to make a bet on which asset class will be the new "flavor of the month" at any point in time.

Making volatility work for you: Volatility pumping

There's another way to view how rebalancing works. Figures 5-3 through 5-6 illustrate a phenomenon called *volatility pumping*. When assets in a finely tuned portfolio are volatile, and you rebalance among them diligently, those assets act like the pistons in a finely tuned engine and "pump" — or generate — higher returns. Although volatility pumping is a very real phenomenon, the particular example used in these figures is a bit contrived, but it does a great job of showing you the key points.

Let's assume we have an asset, Asset A, with the ten-year return history shown in Table 5-1.

Table 5-1	A Ten-Year Return for Asset A	
Year	Annual Return	Account Balance
0	N/A	$100
1	20%	$120
2	−10%	$108
3	30%	$140
4	−10%	$126
5	30%	$164
6	−10%	$148
7	30%	$192
8	−10%	$173
9	30%	$225
10	0%	$225

Source: Brinton Eaton Wealth Advisors.

Figure 5-3 illustrates what would've happened to $100 invested in this asset at the beginning of the ten-year period. Clearly, this return history is quite volatile. You probably would've suffered through many sleepless nights if Asset A were the only asset in your portfolio.

Now, let's assume that we have another asset, Asset B, with a return history over the same ten years shown in Table 5-2.

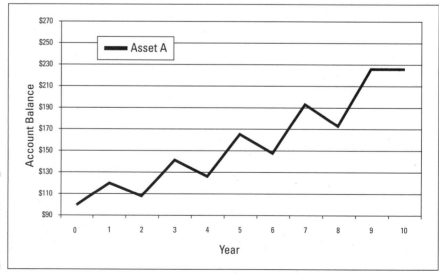

Figure 5-3:
How Asset A performed over ten years.

Source: Brinton Eaton Wealth Advisors.

Table 5-2	A Ten-Year Return for Asset B	
Year	**Annual Return**	**Account Balance**
0	N/A	$100
1	0%	$100
2	30%	$130
3	−10%	$117
4	30%	$152
5	−10%	$137
6	30%	$178
7	−10%	$160
8	30%	$208
9	−10%	$187
10	20%	$225

Source: Brinton Eaton Wealth Advisors.

The volatility of Asset B's return is identical to that of Asset A, but as you can see in Figure 5-4, it's exactly countercyclical to Asset A, meaning that it has perfect negative correlation with Asset A. (If you read up on correlation in Chapter 4, you'll know why it's obvious that this example is contrived — that level of correlation would be a once-in-a-lifetime phenomenon.)

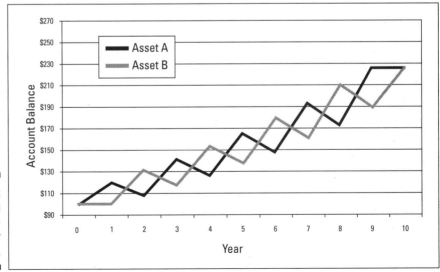

Figure 5-4:
How assets A and B performed over ten years.

Source: Brinton Eaton Wealth Advisors.

Here, and throughout this book, we reference correlation coefficients without showing you the calculations. If you want to verify that the returns for assets A and B do indeed have a perfect –1 correlation coefficient, enter their sequence of returns into an Excel spreadsheet and run the CORREL function on them. (If you're not familiar with Excel, check out the edition of *Excel For Dummies* [Wiley] that corresponds to your version of Excel.)

Is there a way to construct a portfolio so that you can reduce the return volatility associated with these two assets? Yes! You could build your portfolio with a 50/50 weighting of assets A and B. Let's assume you did that at the beginning of the ten-year period, and then you let the portfolio ride. In other words, you invested your $100 by putting $50 in Asset A and $50 in Asset B, and you did nothing else for ten years. Your result — the growth of your $100 initial investment — is shown in Table 5-3.

Table 5-3	A Ten-Year Return for Asset A and Asset B				
	Asset A		**Asset B**		
Year	**Annual Return**	**Account Balance**	**Annual Return**	**Account Balance**	**50/50 Mix**
0	N/A	$100	N/A	$100	$100
1	20%	$120	0%	$100	$110
2	–10%	$108	30%	$130	$119
3	30%	$140	–10%	$117	$129
4	–10%	$126	30%	$152	$139
5	30%	$164	–10%	$137	$151
6	–10%	$148	30%	$178	$163
7	30%	$192	–10%	$160	$176
8	–10%	$173	30%	$208	$191
9	30%	$225	–10%	$187	$206
10	0%	$225	20%	$225	$225

Source: Brinton Eaton Wealth Advisors

In Year 1, the $50 in Asset A would've grown 20 percent to $60, and the $50 in Asset B would've stayed at $50, for a total portfolio value at the end of Year 1 of $110. In Year 2, your $60 in Asset A would've shrunk 10 percent to $54, and the $50 in Asset B would've grown 30 percent to $65, for a total portfolio value at the end of Year 2 of $119. If you look at the graph of the growth of the 50/50 portfolio in Figure 5-5, you can see it traces a nice smooth curve — the jaggedness of the growth of Asset A and Asset B has disappeared. You've managed to remove much of the volatility of your returns. You would have been able to sleep much better over the ten years had you held this portfolio.

But even though your sleeping patterns would've improved, you still would've missed an opportunity. Because the 50/50 portfolio ended up at $225, just as Asset A and Asset B did on their own, the ten-year return on your portfolio is no better than the return of either asset by itself. It's as if you put Asset A in one pocket, put Asset B in another pocket, and never took advantage of the fact that the pockets were in the same pair of pants.

Now, what would've happened if, instead of letting your 50/50 portfolio simply ride, you rebalanced it back to 50/50 each and every year?

For example, in Year 1, the $50 invested in Asset A would've grown 20 percent to $60; the $50 in Asset B would've stayed at $50. At that point, your portfolio wouldn't be in 50/50 balance, so at the end of Year 1, you would've rebalanced by selling $5 of Asset A and buying $5 more of Asset B with the proceeds. You would, therefore, have begun Year 2 with $55 in each asset, and the 50/50 rebalance would be restored. If you rebalanced that way for each of the rest of the nine years, you would've ended up in a situation like the one shown in Table 5-4 and Figure 5-6. You would've ended up considerably wealthier, with $259 instead of $225. And the volatility of your returns would've been exactly zero, meaning that your return would've been a constant 10 percent each year. That's a win-win. It's the power of volatility pumping — that's what rebalancing can do for you.

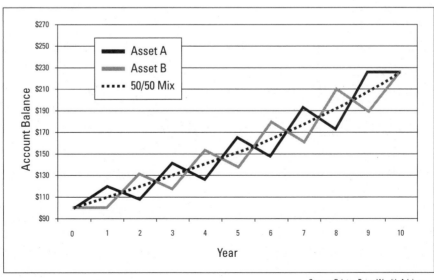

Figure 5-5:
How assets A and B performed individually over ten years compared to a 50/50 mix of assets A and B.

Source: Brinton Eaton Wealth Advisors.

Table 5-4	A Ten-Year Return for Asset A and Asset B (Rebalanced)					
	Asset A		Asset B			
Year	Annual Return	Account Balance	Annual Return	Account Balance	50/50 Mix	Rebalanced 50/50 Mix
0	N/A	$100	N/A	$100	$100	$100
1	20%	$120	0%	$100	$110	$110
2	−10%	$108	30%	$130	$119	$121
3	30%	$140	−10%	$117	$129	$133
4	−10%	$126	30%	$152	$139	$146
5	30%	$164	−10%	$137	$151	$161
6	−10%	$148	30%	$178	$163	$177
7	30%	$192	−10%	$160	$176	$195
8	−10%	$173	30%	$208	$191	$214
9	30%	$225	−10%	$187	$206	$236
10	0%	$225	20%	$225	$225	$259

Source: Brinton Eaton Wealth Advisors.

Figure 5-6:
How assets A and B performed individually over ten years compared to a 50/50 mix of assets A and B and a rebalanced 50/50 mix of assets A and B.

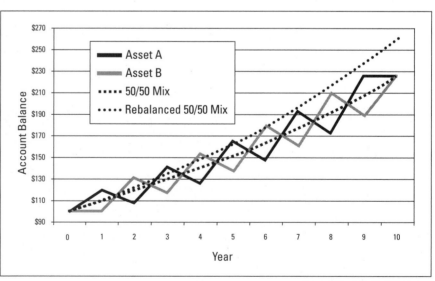

Source: Brinton Eaton Wealth Advisors.

Memorizing the mantra: How rebalancing forces you to buy low and sell high

At its simplest, rebalancing is a discipline you impose on yourself to dispassionately buy low and sell high, with ruthless regularity. Will you always manage to sell out of an asset at its absolute peak, and buy into an asset at its absolute bottom? No. But you'll be close enough. And you'll be forced to do it often enough to get a material benefit over the long term. (For more information on how often is often enough, skip ahead to "Following the Right Rebalancing Schedule," later in this chapter.)

Everybody knows that buying low and selling high is a good thing. The benefits don't really need to be explained. But buying low and selling high has benefits beyond the obvious. When you trim your holdings in a winner before it becomes a loser, that means you'll have less at stake in that asset and will suffer a smaller loss than you would've otherwise. Similarly, increasing your stake in a loser before it becomes a winner amplifies your eventual winnings. The hits just keep on comin'!

Rebalancing is really the antidote to the urge to engage in active investing or dabble in market timing. It doesn't require you to have a crystal ball. It doesn't require you to be able to correctly pick winners, losers, and turning points. It simply requires you to shove emotion to the side, where it belongs, and to have the fortitude to be a contrarian when it makes sense, no matter who knows it.

Rebalancing imposes a discipline that essentially forces you to buy low and sell high — the goal of any winning investment strategy.

Being a contrarian: Making sure you have the right mindset for rebalancing

Rebalancing can sound simple, but in reality it's very hard to do — not because it's technically difficult, but because it's counterintuitive. When you rebalance, you may be considered a contrarian because you'll be doing exactly the opposite of what your friends are doing and what the news media are telling you to do. You'll be selling out of your hottest investments. Worse, you'll be buying more of the investments that have been the coldest, and may have even been losing money for you. This isn't an easy thing for most investors to do. It's painful. But successful investors learn to leave their feelings out of the equation and let the science of probabilities work to their advantage.

As you rebalance, selling some of your winners and buying more of your losers, you'll get the undeniable feeling that you're making a big mistake. Plus, you'll be constantly bombarded with newspaper stories and television and radio commentary touting the glories of the investment you just sold a big chunk of, and pooh-poohing the investment you just loaded up on. And, to the extent you share your investing activities with your friends and family, they may also think you're making some questionable decisions, and they may not be shy about telling you so.

The pain is worth it. But how do you stand it? Remind yourself of these facts:

- **Rebalancing is a scientific, time-tested, reliably reproducible way to get extra return while at the same time controlling your risk.** It's based on sound economic fundamentals and rooted in well-established statistical theory.

- **Rebalancing doesn't rely on hot tips or fads, which aren't a good way to inform your investing strategy in the first place.** By the time investment advice makes its way to the general press, it's almost always already too late to act on it. If it's in the papers, it's already in the price. So, unless you can get wind of the headlines several weeks in advance, don't base your investment decisions on what you read in or hear from those sources. More generally, never let unsolicited advice from sources that really don't care if you do well or not sway you from your path.

- **The most successful and sophisticated professional money managers engage in rebalancing.** Reassure yourself with that knowledge. Your friends and family may think you're a bit wacky when you begin to rebalance, but in most cases they haven't done the research and analysis necessary to refute decades of the best research and analysis the finance community has to offer. The professionals are rebalancing, and there's no reason that you can't do it, too.

Rebalancing may make you seem like a contrarian to those around you, but it'll likely help make you richer in the long run than those who invest less scientifically.

Following the Right Rebalancing Schedule

All the other sections in this chapter should convince you that it's smart to rebalance, but how often should you do it? If you do it too often, you'll sell your rising assets too early, before they peak. You'll also invest in falling assets too early, before they bottom out. And you'll spend too much money on transaction costs. If you rebalance too seldom, you'll ride your winners too long, after they peak and become losers. You'll also let your portfolio drift away from its intended asset allocation, with the harmful effects we describe at the beginning of this chapter.

You need to schedule your rebalancing efforts wisely, and in this section we tell you how to do just that.

Rebalancing on fixed calendar dates

One approach is to rebalance on a fixed schedule — once a year, for example. Annual rebalancing is quite popular, because it's not overly burdensome, and it's easy to remember, particularly if you do it in concert with another annual event, like celebrating your birthday or filing your income-tax return.

For most portfolios, rebalancing once a year isn't often enough to take advantage of market changes. For the average investor looking to rebalance on specific calendar dates, it's reasonable to rebalance about three times a year, or every four months; a little less often if your portfolio is under about $500,000, and a little more often if your portfolio is an aggressive one, with lots of volatile investments in it.

But there's a better approach than rebalancing on a fixed schedule, as we describe in the next section.

Planning your rebalancing for the greatest opportunity

The best schedule for rebalancing your portfolio is one that you can't set in advance. It's the schedule that's triggered by your portfolio itself. Specifically, you rebalance when your portfolio drifts too far away from its intended allocation.

But how far is too far? There's no universally applicable, perfect answer, but you can't go too far wrong if you set your *tolerance* (the amount of drift you're willing to tolerate) at ±20 percent around your target allocation for each asset class. For example, if your target allocation to a particular asset class is 10 percent, then ±20 percent of that target is ±2 percent (0.10 × 0.20 = 0.02). In that case you'd rebalance if that asset class drifts above 12 percent or below 8 percent of your total portfolio. If another asset class has a target allocation of 5 percent, then ±20 percent of *that* target is ±1 percent (0.05 × 0.20 = 0.01), so you'd rebalance if that class drifted outside of a range of 4 percent to 6 percent of your total portfolio.

You'll need to monitor your portfolio frequently to determine if any of your asset classes have drifted outside their tolerance bands. But that doesn't mean you'll be rebalancing frequently. There may be some years during which you won't rebalance at all, if the markets are tame. If markets are tumultuous, though, you may find yourself rebalancing every other month or so. It all depends on the markets.

Volatile markets create more opportunities for productive rebalancing. You'll want to rebalance more often in those markets and less often in docile markets.

Monitor your portfolio frequently (at least monthly), and rebalance when — and only when — your portfolio drifts outside its intended asset allocation.

Part II
Getting Started

The 5th Wave
By Rich Tennant

"I've always used historical data analysis to rebalance my assets, but lately it's been pretty much hysterical data analysis that I've been working with."

In this part . . .

We lay the foundation on which you can build a solid portfolio by helping you set your unique investment parameters (for risk, return, constraints, and so on). In this part, you discover how to project your lifetime financial plan, as well as how to link your strategic investment decisions to that plan. In other words, you map out an investment strategy that's tailored to your own long-term goals. We also assist you in setting up your asset allocation, which flows naturally from your investment strategy. And we even give your process a kick-start by exploring some sample allocations.

Chapter 6

Laying the Foundation for Your Plan

*I*n this chapter, we help you nail down your investing plan. Here you can find guidelines that serve as an important step toward establishing your investment strategy and then setting up your asset allocation. You don't want to skip this step!

We start with your time horizon. Many investors don't realize how long their horizon truly is. Your time horizon directly influences your choice of investment strategy: The more time you have to invest, the more short-term risk you may be able to take.

We also help you to consider the returns you'll require from the assets in your portfolio. And we show you how to gauge your risk tolerance, because the risk you're willing, and able, to take along the way is a particularly important consideration.

You'll need to think about a few pragmatic constraints that you'll have to impose on your portfolio, and we show you how to deal with those in this chapter. For example, you may have holdings you won't relinquish, or investments — even whole asset classes — you won't even consider.

And don't forget taxes. They're one of the last things any of us wants to think about, but they're a priority in planning a portfolio. You want to be aware of your income-tax situation and its impact on your portfolio choices. For example, which is the better choice for you: a municipal bond or a Treasury bond of equivalent maturity? The answer depends on your tax bracket.

Finally, we explain how you can avoid overlooking any special considerations, such as protecting your assets from unnecessary estate taxes or from unexpected litigation.

Seeing Your Investment Horizon Clearly

Before deciding on your asset allocation, you'll need to determine your *investment horizon* — the length of time your assets will, on average, be invested. In general, the shorter your investment horizon, the more conservative your investment strategy should be, and the more weighted toward fixed-income investments your asset allocation should be. Conversely, the longer your investment horizon, the more aggressive your strategy should be, and the more weighted toward equities your allocation should be.

To help explain, we offer the following two extreme cases.

- ✔ **Case 1:** This case involves a college student, Dakota, whose invested assets are in a college fund. There's just enough left in the fund to cover the remaining two years of Dakota's tuition. The time horizon in this case is a very clearly defined two years. Dakota is in the homestretch — it's time to play it safe and cruise to victory! It would be foolish to risk the fund's principal on a highly aggressive investment strategy. The appropriate asset allocation should be one that emphasizes capital preservation, which means it should be quite conservative (more bonds than stocks, for example). The always-present risk that a conservative portfolio may fall behind inflation and see its purchasing power eroded is a very small risk here, because there are only two years left in the life of the fund. And bonds (of suitable maturity, of course) are much less likely than stocks to lose their value over that period of time.

- ✔ **Case 2:** This case features Ann, a widowed grandmother with considerable invested assets to her name. She has more than enough income from other sources (pensions, Social Security, a structured settlement on an old personal liability claim) to cover her modest living expenses, and enough insurance to cover any foreseeable catastrophic event. Ann's grown children are self-sufficient — they have good jobs and don't rely on her financially. She really sees her assets as ultimately being for the benefit of her grandchildren, ages 2 through 8, whose education costs through college have already been fully funded by their parents. Because Ann's investment horizon corresponds to her *grandchildren's* life expectancy, it's on the order of 70 years. This case argues for a fairly aggressive investment strategy and asset allocation. The grandchildren won't be accessing the assets for several decades, so short-term portfolio volatility is of very minor concern. The main concern is staying ahead of inflation. As you can see in Figure 6-1, over long enough holding periods the volatility of "riskier" assets, such as stocks, isn't much greater than that of "safer" investments, such as bonds. And stocks, with their higher expected long-term returns, are much better at beating inflation than bonds.

The length of your investment horizon should have a definite impact on the mix of assets in your portfolio. For example, the longer your horizon, the more comfortable you can be considering equities. Look at the impact of investment horizon (or holding period) on the three broad asset classes of Treasury bills, intermediate government bonds, and large-company stocks in Figure 6-1. We show the historical range of *compound average annual returns* (flip back to Chapter 2 if you need to read up on returns) for each of these assets.

The worst one-year return for T-bills was 1 percent, and the best was 15 percent, for a range of 14 percentage points; the worst one-year return for large-company stocks was –26 percent, and the best was 53 percent, for a range of 79 percentage points. Over longer holding periods, these ranges narrow considerably: Over a ten-year holding period, the worst compound average annual return for T-bills was 0 percent, and the best was 9 percent, for a range of 9 percentage points. For stocks, the range narrowed all the way down to 18 percentage points (worst was 1 percent; best was 19 percent).

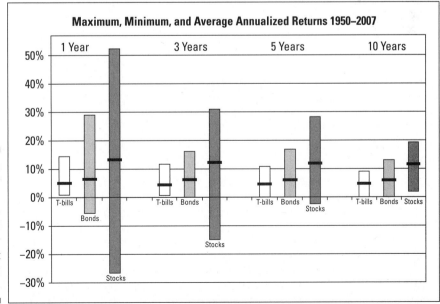

Figure 6-1: A range of compound average annual returns over different holding periods.

So as the investment horizon lengthens, the risk associated with stocks declines. (***Note:*** There hasn't been a single ten-year period since 1950 during which the worst returns for stocks wasn't above zero. That's not true for T-bills or bonds.) At the same time, the average return for stocks was always much better than that for T-bills and bonds. What happens is an investing phenomenon called *risk-spreading over time* — the good years and the bad years tend to offset each other.

The length of your investment horizon should have an impact on the mix of assets in your portfolio. The longer your horizon, the more comfortable you can be considering equities.

So, what's *your* investment horizon? It's probably longer than you think.

If, for example, you're 65 years old and planning to retire at 67, at which time your compensation, which is your only source of income (you have no pension), stops, it's natural to consider your horizon to be two years. After all, that's when you'll start to depend entirely on your accumulated savings to cover all your living expenses for the rest of your life. But that's far too short a period. According to current actuarial tables, if you're a reasonably healthy male, you could live another 25 years. And if you have a younger and similarly healthy wife, your joint life expectancy can be longer still. Your combined assets will need to support you both for that extra quarter-century! An investment strategy, and resulting asset allocation, that assumes a two-year investment horizon (a conservative, bond-heavy allocation, for example) may leave you seriously behind inflation in your later years, when it'll be too late to make an adjustment. This is an example of a strategy that appears quite conservative but is actually risky as can be.

Whatever your current age, over your remaining life expectancy, you'll probably have big-ticket expenses to cover (children's and grandchildren's educations, weddings, relocations, and so on) in the near term that'll have an impact on your overall investment horizon. You don't want to run dry in later years because you didn't take such expenses into consideration in your calculations. (We cover those details in Chapter 7, when you develop your investment strategy, and test several "What if?" scenarios.)

As you continue to age and your life expectancy naturally shortens, it's wise to consider dialing your asset allocation down to something more conservative, by shifting from equities to fixed-income investments. But this should be a slow, gradual process, and you shouldn't begin at too conservative a starting point.

This bears repeating: The first step in deciding on an asset allocation is to clearly determine the length of time your assets will need to be working for you. And remember, you have your whole lifetime to cover. Here's hoping that you have many, many years to plan for.

Setting Your Return Objectives

How hard do you need your assets to work for you? In other words, what kind of return do you need from your portfolio? These are important questions and, by forcing yourself to answer them, you can nail down how conservative or aggressive your investment strategy needs to be.

When we talk about return objectives, we're talking about what you need, not what you want. Clearly, all investors want their returns to be as high as possible. But as we discuss in Chapter 2, there's usually no free lunch; higher returns typically come only with higher risk. So when it comes to setting guidelines for your investment strategy, you want to make sure that you don't take on unnecessarily high risk by shooting for a higher return than you actually need.

The answer to the question, "What kind of return do you *need* from your portfolio?" may not be obvious or straightforward. It depends on your lifestyle, your other sources of income, your insurance and benefit plans, your age, your health, your dependents, and more.

When it comes time for you to figure out your return objectives, turn to Chapter 7. We devote much of that chapter to going through an exercise that helps you understand the nuts and bolts of setting a return objective, and we show you how you can do it yourself. This chapter doesn't deal with as much of the nitty-gritty detail, but it's critical that you grasp the importance of your return objective when you're making decisions about your asset allocation.

The connection to asset allocation is clear and direct. The higher your return objectives, the more aggressive your investment strategy needs to be and, hence, the more you should allocate to equities.

Making Decisions about Your Risk Tolerance

Your risk tolerance is one of the most important things (if not *the* most important thing) you'll need to determine to develop your specific asset allocation. To see why, take a look at the risk/return map in Figure 6-2.

As we explain in Chapter 2, all investment choices can be mapped on a risk/return map. On a risk/return map, an efficient frontier of choices emerges. The *efficient frontier* identifies those investments that you can't improve upon — for a given level of risk, there's no investment that gives you a higher return; for a given level of return, there's no investment that gives you a lower risk. Because all the investments along the frontier are equivalently efficient, the only way to increase your return is by increasing the degree of risk you take (by moving northeast along the frontier).

You want to maximize your return — assuming the associated level of risk was tolerable — so the only thing you need to do is determine how much risk is too much for you. That tells you how far east you dare go, and because you want to stay on the frontier, it also tells you how far north you can go. The efficient frontier uniquely determines the investment choice you should make, and you should tap into its usefulness when you're working on your asset allocation plan.

There are two aspects to risk tolerance. One is your financial *ability* to tolerate risk; the other is your *willingness*. Your ability to tolerate risk can be determined objectively, through the exercise we outline in the next chapter. Your willingness is subjective — it's your call. No one can stand in your shoes and determine for you what's going to keep you awake at night with worry about your portfolio. It is, though, very useful to know your ability to withstand risk before you decide your willingness. As subjective as the "risk willingness" decision is, it doesn't hurt to arm yourself with as much relevant objective information as you can before you make the call.

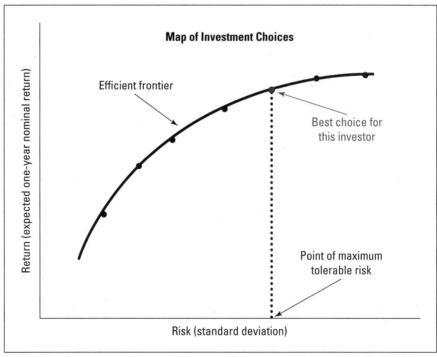

Figure 6-2:
Using your risk tolerance to make your investment choice.

Source: Brinton Eaton Wealth Advisors.

Flip ahead to Chapter 7 for a detailed explanation of how you can determine your risk-tolerance ability. To help you come to grips with your risk-tolerance willingness, read on!

Should you try to figure out on your own just how much risk you can tolerate, or should you seek help? Many investors consider risk tolerance an area that is a little too daunting to tackle alone, and they choose to consult with a professional. Good financial planners and investment advisors are well versed on and experienced in this topic and can be of great assistance to you. If you read through this section and still don't feel comfortable answering the question of your risk tolerance on your own, then by all means seek out a professional to guide you through the exercise. (See Chapter 16 for a discussion of the kind of help you can get and where you can get it.)

Evaluating your experience

Most everyone has an investing horror story to tell. Maybe Aunt Mabel put her life savings in a hedge fund that took a nose dive, or Uncle Fred made a killing in tech stocks in the 1990s until the tech bubble burst and he lost it all. Your feelings about investment risk are formed by the stories you've heard, and from your own personal experience. There are valuable lessons to be learned from virtually all these stories. But let the stories *inform* your judgment, not cloud it.

Learn the lessons from investment failures — both yours and those you hear and read about — but don't shy away from the level of risk that's appropriate for you. If you dwell on past failures, you won't make intelligent decisions about your risk tolerance and, therefore, about your investment strategy and asset allocation. Make sure that your primary goal isn't to avoid bad outcomes at all costs.

Think about your experiences, and those of others you've heard about, and then set your emotions aside as you ponder what you'd consider an intolerable outcome. Is it losing 15 percent of your portfolio's value in a given year? Is it not staying ahead of inflation over an extended period? Is it having your portfolio's value bounce around more than ±10 percent in a given quarter? (Flip back to Chapter 2 if you want to revisit the different ways to measure risk.) Pick the risk measure that best suits you, and then determine the critical number of that measure that you don't want to exceed. And be sure to remember that number when you get to Chapter 8, where you use it to help nail down your asset allocation percentages.

Considering risk questionnaires and other tools

Determining your risk tolerance can be a tricky undertaking. To help make the process a bit more straightforward, you can consider using a risk-tolerance questionnaire or a similar tool.

Most of these questionnaires are driven by psychology and are quite general — and the link to investment risk tolerance isn't direct. They don't offer a clear road map to translate the results into an investment choice, so you may not want to spend too much time with them for investment purposes.

Some of the other available questionnaires are investment specific, and ask you about some combination of your investment time horizon, past invest-ing experience, and emotional reaction to volatility. These questionnaires are usually found on brokerage and mutual-fund company Web sites, but the goal of the questionnaires is narrow: to direct you to which of the company's products and services it believes would be most suitable for you. The ques-tionnaires are basically sales tools; keep that in mind if you choose to fill them out.

We can't recommend either type of risk-tolerance questionnaire.

The advisors at Brinton Eaton Wealth Advisors try to fill this void by provid-ing a simple worksheet that boils down the determination of a client's risk tol-erance to five choices. (Other advisory firms may have similar tools.) You can see Brinton Eaton's worksheet in Figure 6-3. The features of each of the five risk-tolerance choices are expressed in various ways:

- ✔ The relative emphasis on income and growth
- ✔ The rough asset allocation (in particular, the percentage allocated to equities)
- ✔ Representative historical returns
- ✔ The range around those historical returns

Clients have found this a simple exercise to bring all the relevant consider-ations together in a very practical and understandable way. They've been able to have a focused and meaningful conversation with their spouses about risk, and make their choice with confidence. You may find it useful yourself.

Investment Strategy	Investment Philosophy	Investment Objective	Typical Asset Allocation		Risk/Return Profile	Historical Annual Benchmark Returns		
			Bonds/ Alternatives	Stocks		15-Year Low	15-Year Average*	15-Year High
A	Conservative	Income	67%	33%	Low	−2.1%	9.3%	24.5%
B	Conservative/ Moderate	Income with Growth	61%	39%	Low/Medium	−4.3%	9.9%	25.6%
C	Moderate	Growth and Income	49%	51%	Medium	−6.9%	10.5%	27.9%
D	Moderate/ Aggressive	Growth with Income	37%	63%	Medium/ High	−9.5%	11.0%	30.1%
E	Aggressive	Growth	27%	73%	High	−11.6%	11.3%	32.0%

measured by the compound annual growth rate

Notes:

"Typical Asset Allocation" is a simplified construction for broad illustration purposes. Actual asset classes employed within client portfolios may include, but are not limited to, cash and cash equivalents, money market instruments, individual fixed-income securities and fixed-income funds of varying maturities, real estate investment trusts, commodities, individual equities and equity funds of various company-size categories and within various industry sectors, **and so on.**

The "Risk/Return Profile" scale (along with the "Historical Annual Benchmark Returns" table) illustrates the fact that, in general, higher returns are associated with higher risk. Risk can be characterized in various ways, and individual investors will have different perceptions of what constitutes risk for them; risk is captured in the table above by the *range* of historical annual returns.

"Historical Annual Benchmark Returns" were derived from index data compiled by Ibbotson & Associates, a reliable industry source. The index used for bonds is the Lehman Aggregate Bond Index; for stocks, the S&P 500 Index; for commodites, the Goldman Sachs Commodity Index; and for real estate, the Dow Jones Wilshire Real Estate Securities TR Index. The index data consists of monthly total returns for each index, which assumes reinvestment of investment income into the index. The monthly returns for each index were annualized and weighted consistent with the "Typical Asset Allocation" in the table above (details available upon request), with annual rebalancing. In this compilation, alternative investments are evenly split between commodities and real estate. The 15-year period used is calendar years 1993 through 2007. "15-Year Low" and "15-Year High" returns represent the lowest and highest single year's return during the 15-year period. "15-Year Average" is the compound annual growth rate (or, equivalently, the geometric mean return) over the 15-year period.

Index return data have been provided for general illustration purposes only and generally do not reflect the deduction of transaction and/or custodial charges, the incurrence of which would have the effect of decreasing historical performance results. It should not be assumed that your portfolio holdings would correspond directly to any of the indexes. Past performance may not be indicative of future results.

Selection of an investment strategy should be done in consultation with your Brinton Eaton financial advisor, and should consider your return requirements, risk tolerance, time horizon, liquidity needs, applicable laws and regulations, taxes, and any unique circumstances and/or constraints.

Selected Investment Strategy (circle one): A   B   C   D   E

Investor/Trustee:_____   Date:_____

Investor/Trustee:_____

Advisor:_____

Figure 6-3:
Brinton Eaton's risk tolerance worksheet.

Source: Brinton Eaton Wealth Advisors.

Setting Your Portfolio Constraints

In addition to your investment horizon, your return requirements, and your risk tolerance, there may be certain overriding considerations that will constrain the way you build your portfolio. You need to deal with these, and in this section we let you know how to do just that.

Recognizing positions you won't get out of

You may have certain holdings in your portfolio that you just won't part with, because of emotional reasons. For example, you may have inherited some stock from a beloved departed family member and you never want to sell it, for sentimental reasons. You may have bought shares in a startup company founded by your college roommate and want to hold them as a gesture of your support for his dream. Or you may still own a modest position in the company where you worked for 30 years, and you can't bear losing that reminder of what got you where you are today. Coldly rational investors may quibble with these emotional choices, but you just can't relinquish those positions.

There are also a variety of unemotional, policy-related reasons for holding onto a position. For example, you may be prohibited from selling your company stock for a period of time.

How do you deal with the holdings in your portfolio that you just can't live without? Simply recognize those investments when you design your portfolio, and when you rebalance. Select the rest of your securities around your "sacred cows," and take them into consideration when it comes time to rebalance. If you care enough to hold onto them, you can find a way to work around them.

Identifying investments you won't consider

Another set of portfolio constraints can involve specific investments that you won't consider under any circumstances. These can often be ethical or moral decisions. For example, you may be firmly committed to never investing in the tobacco company that you believe played a role in the premature death of a loved one.

Some investments may also be off limits to you because of more formal restrictions. For example, you could be prohibited from investing in companies that the company you work for consults with or audits. Or, because of your position with your employer, you may be privy to certain inside information and have *blackout periods* imposed by regulatory authorities, during which you can't buy (or, for that matter, sell) your company's stock.

The simple strategy for working with off-limits assets is very similar to the one we explain in the preceding section. All you really need to do is keep the restricted investments in mind as you build your portfolio and when you rebalance it. Working around these types of constraints is generally quite easy, given the vast number of available asset opportunities. (Turn to Chapter 3 for our extensive discussion of asset classes.)

Limiting your exposure to certain asset classes

In the previous section, we describe a few situations in which you may completely refuse to invest in specific companies for one reason or another. There's another, somewhat similar set of portfolio constraints that can prevent you from being willing to consider entire asset classes, not just specific investments. For example, religious considerations may cause you to avoid healthcare stocks or shares in companies that promote gambling. Social concerns may prevent you from pursuing industrial companies that pollute the environment, or energy companies that burn fossil fuels without funding research for alternative energy solutions.

These types of constraints are harder to cope with than the ones we cover in the previous sections, because they can blackball entire asset classes. If you just have to dodge certain companies, then you really don't have to tinker with your overall asset allocation — just with your security selection and rebalancing. But if you're looking to avoid one or several asset classes, then you have to reevaluate the way you determine your asset allocation, which could compromise the performance of your portfolio. You may have to accept a portfolio that is not strictly on the efficient frontier (see Chapter 2). Have a look at Figure 6-4 to see what we mean.

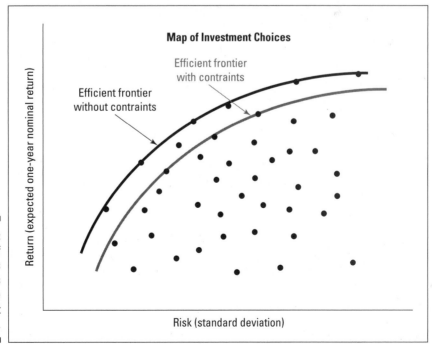

Figure 6-4:
The effect of asset-class constraints on the efficient frontier.

Source: Brinton Eaton Wealth Advisors.

In Figure 6-4, we plot some available investment choices on the risk/reward map (see Chapter 2). As you can see, the introduction of asset-class constraints eliminates some of these investment choices from consideration. Typically, those eliminated choices include some that lie on the efficient frontier. When all the eliminated choices are removed from the map, the efficient frontier formed by the remaining investment choices will almost always be inferior to (southeast of) the original frontier. (At best, it could overlap the original frontier at some points.) The more stringent your constraints, the farther the efficient frontier will move to the southeast on the risk/reward map.

Reviewing Your Tax Situation

Investing isn't an isolated activity in your financial life. It's intimately connected with your long-term financial plan (see Chapter 7), as well as with your income-tax and estate-tax situation. You have to take into account taxes and their effects when coming up with your investment plan. In this section, we help you figure out how you can factor in your income-tax considerations. (***Note:*** We touch on estate taxes later, in the "Taking Account of Special Circumstances" section.)

Being mindful of your current and future tax brackets

The tax bracket you're in — whether high or low — should influence your investment decisions in a number of ways. It's important that you keep in mind your tax bracket — and how it may change in the future — as you plan your investment strategy.

For example, buying municipal bonds (which are exempt from federal income tax — see Chapter 3) in your taxable accounts is generally more tax efficient. But if your tax bracket is low, you may get a better after-tax result by choosing Treasury bonds instead.

A quick calculation will point you in the right direction: Assume that the yield on the municipal bond you're interested in is 3 percent. If you're in the 15 percent tax bracket, and the Treasury bond of equivalent maturity is yielding 3.7 percent, you're better off after taxes buying the Treasury bond. Why? Because, $0.037 - (0.15 \times 0.037) = 0.03145$, which is greater than 0.03. In other words, the 3.7 percent you get from the Treasury bond, minus the tax you have to pay on it, is still greater than the 3 percent you get from the municipal bond.

As another example, suppose you're in a high tax bracket and your rebalancing trigger causes you to consider selling a stock that you've held for 11¹/₂ months in a taxable account. If you sell the stock, the gain will be taxed at your high-bracket ordinary income-tax rate; if you wait until after the 12-month anniversary, the gain will be taxed at the lower long-term capital-gains tax rate. In this case, it may pay to wait a couple weeks (as long as you're willing to accept the risk that the stock price doesn't drop in the meantime!).

You also need to consider whether you expect a material change in your tax bracket in the future. For example, if you retired this year and also exercised a large lot of employer stock options immediately after calling it quits, your bracket is high this year, but it will be considerably lower next year. In that case, you may want to delay short-term capital gains that you may otherwise take in December of this year, and take them in January of next year instead, when the tax bite will be lower.

Looking for opportunities in prior tax returns

You may be able to inform your investment plan by taking a look at past tax returns. The primary reason is that you may have what's called a *tax loss carryforward* (an IRS term that designates tax losses that accrued in earlier years and that, because of IRS limitations, couldn't be used at the time but can be used against gains in subsequent years). If, in prior years, you realized considerable tax losses on your security sales, you may still have a tax loss carryforward. You can use the tax loss carryforward to offset gains in the current and future years.

How can you tell if you have a tax loss carryforward? Simply have a look at your last tax return. If a tax loss carryforward is available to you, it'll be listed in Schedule D of your return.

If you enter a tax year with a tax loss carryforward, you have greater flexibility than you would otherwise in taking gains in that tax year. Your gains will be offset dollar for dollar by the amount of the carryforward. You'll owe no capital-gains tax until your gains exceed the carryforward. As a result, you may be more inclined to take gains in the current year — when, for example, your rebalancing trigger tells you to do so — instead of delaying them and running the risk that the rebalancing opportunity may pass you by.

Considering which of your assets are in tax-deferred accounts

If you're like most investors, you probably have your family's invested assets housed in a number of different accounts. If you're striving to be as savvy as possible when you're formulating your investment plan, you'll take the tax characteristics of each of those accounts into consideration.

First off, keep in mind that the most efficient route is to treat all your household accounts as one big pie to be allocated and rebalanced in the aggregate. We cover this in more detail in Chapter 10, but it's an important concept to remember when thinking about the ways that taxes can affect your various accounts.

By viewing your assets holistically across all your accounts, you can exploit the fact that the accounts receive very different tax treatment. Here's the gist of the tactic: Some assets are more *tax efficient* than others — meaning, they generate relatively less ordinary income and more long-term capital gains. (**Remember:** Ordinary income is taxed at higher rates than long-term capital gains for most taxpayers.)

For example, the income from real estate investment trusts (REITs — see Chapter 3) is taxed as ordinary income, while growth stocks generate very little income and their dividends typically qualify for tax rates equivalent to long-term capital-gains tax rates. So, in achieving your overall asset allocation, take advantage of the fact that your IRA and 401(k) are tax-deferred accounts, and put all the REIT allocation that you can in those accounts. Save the growth stocks for your taxable accounts.

Taking Account of Special Circumstances

When you're working out your asset allocation, you need to take into consideration a few other factors beyond those listed in the first sections of this chapter. These special circumstances may not apply to every investor in every situation, but you definitely need to be aware of them (some more than others) and be prepared to incorporate them into your plan.

Protecting your assets from lawsuits

Some investors are particularly subject to litigation. Doctors, accountants, architects, and engineers, notably, are more often targets of plaintiffs and their attorneys than are people in other professions. Whether or not you feel you're especially vulnerable to people trying to lay claim to your assets, you may be interested in taking steps to protect your assets from that potential threat.

If you feel your risk of litigation is high, you'd do well to speak with an asset protection professional (often an attorney) about how you can shield your portfolio from litigants and potential creditors. You need an expert qualified in this area who can advise you on the dangers and pitfalls of the various tactics; ask around (canvass your professional colleagues) to find and qualify these experts. Tactics include moving possession of the assets to another family member and/or setting up trusts, including offshore trusts.

Be careful when considering ways to protect your assets from the threat of litigation. There are legal and acceptable ways to accomplish that goal, but the courts are very unsympathetic to people whom they feel have structured such arrangements purely for the purpose of protection from creditors instead of for legitimate business/financial purposes.

If you want to protect some of your assets but don't feel the need to consult a professional, there are some perfectly acceptable and easy things you can do:

- ✔ An employer-sponsored 401(k) plan, or a *rollover IRA* — specifically designed to accept funds from your 401(k) — can offer better protection than your traditional IRA. (But see "Simplifying your holdings," later in this chapter, which describes the tradeoffs of keeping your money in a 401[k] or spread among too many IRAs.)

- ✔ Your primary residence has a higher degree of protection than your invested assets, generally speaking.

- ✔ If you've set up 529 plans for your child's education, these funds are protected from bankruptcy proceedings to the extent they were held in the plan for a sufficient number of years.

The degree to which you exploit any of these opportunities should depend on how likely you believe you are to be sued.

Protecting your estate from taxes

Estate taxes — unlike income, property, and sales taxes — have been referred to as "voluntary taxes," because there are many legitimate means to reduce or even eliminate the bite from federal and state estate taxes when you pass along your assets to your heirs. We don't go into much detail on estate-tax strategies in this book (see *Estate Planning For Dummies,* by N. Brian Caverly, Esq., and Jordan S. Simon [Wiley], if you want more information on the subject), but there are a few tactics you can easily incorporate into your portfolio construction plan.

One theme that should run through your planning is the equalization of assets as much as possible between you and your spouse. For example, if your IRA and 401(k) are much larger than your spouse's, you should consider putting more of your combined taxable assets in your spouse's name. (Although this is an easily foiled tactic when it comes to creditor protection, it's a perfectly valid and very common practice when it comes to estate planning.) This strategy allows both you and your spouse more flexibility, after the death of the first of you, to shelter assets from estate taxes through so-called disclaimer provisions. (The details of disclaimers are beyond the scope of this book — the point here is to allow yourself the flexibility to exploit them by spreading out the ownership of your assets.)

For similar reasons, you should review the assets you own jointly with your spouse — both invested assets and use assets (such as your house) — and determine if they are titled as Joint Tenants with Right of Survivorship (JTWROS) or Tenants in Common (TIC). TIC titling gives the surviving spouse more flexibility at the death of the other spouse to shelter the deceased spouse's share of the joint asset from estate tax.

Some states, such as California, deem all marital assets to be neither TIC nor JTWROS, but instead consider them to be Community Property (CP) assets. CP titling doesn't provide the flexibility you'd like, so if you live in a CP state you should consider establishing lifetime trusts, individually for you and your spouse, to effectively achieve the same result as if the titling were TIC.

Some investors have spouses who aren't U.S. citizens and aren't subject to U.S. taxation. The U.S. estate-tax laws, when it comes to the estate of the U.S.-citizen spouse, are particularly unmerciful in these situations. Here again, the use of trusts can allow you the flexibility to avoid estate taxes.

Each of the tactics mentioned in this section should be undertaken only with the assistance of a qualified financial planning and/or estate planning expert. (See Chapter 16 for a discussion of the relevant professionals you can turn to for help.)

Simplifying your holdings

It's common for investors to have too many investment accounts. When you're hammering out your asset allocation plan, remember that consolidating some of those accounts can be an excellent move. Aside from simplifying your paperwork, consolidating your assets makes it much easier for you to allocate your assets and periodically rebalance them. The fewer your accounts, the easier your job!

For example, you and your spouse may have several joint and individual accounts, perhaps one for each broker or custodian through which you originally set up the account. You may have a number of IRAs, some of which may have resulted from rolling over your 401(k)s from prior employers. You may even have left some of your old 401(k)s sitting in the prior employers' accounts. We've seen some investors of fairly modest means with as many as a dozen different accounts. That's too many.

First of all, there's usually no good reason for each taxpayer to have more than one IRA. Your IRAs, including those that are rollover IRAs, can be consolidated into one IRA with no tax impact — and they should be. There's even less reason (unless you're especially concerned about creditors, as we discuss a little earlier in this section) to leave an old 401(k) sitting in the account of a prior employer. Roll it into your existing IRA; you'll save on expenses (401[k] expenses are typically large and hidden) and you'll have a broader array of investments to choose from. (Most 401[k]s have limited investment menus.)

Beyond your tax-deferred accounts, there's little reason to have your taxable assets scattered across multiple broker accounts, if you're going to manage your portfolio yourself. Consolidate them into one account (or as few as possible, given the ownership issues discussed in the preceding section). Life is complicated enough — keep it simple where you can.

Chapter 7

Developing Your Investment Strategy

*H*ere's a big-time question for you: Do you know if you can afford your own retirement? If you're going to need $50,000 a year to maintain your lifestyle, but you have only $350,000 in assets at the moment, do you have any idea how you're going to get from where you are financially to where you need to be?

Maybe you're not even close to retirement. Maybe you're still changing diapers or trying to keep an eye on teenagers. But there are still big-time questions to be considered. Have you sat down and figured out if you can pay for their expected education expenses in five or ten years, or will you need to take out a loan (or several)?

Your investment strategy must match your life goals and circumstances — not the other way around. In thinking about future needs and wants, it's helpful to start by looking at your current lifestyle, but your investment plan must be broad enough to cover your future lifestyle, too.

In this chapter, we take you through a systematic, step-by-step process that will help you to build the investment portfolio that best suits your needs. We guarantee that you'll be glad you put in the work, because, in the end, you'll see the clear link between your ideal investment strategy and your long-term financial plan.

This chapter centers on a tool that can crystallize the future financial effects of your life choices. We call this tool the *Lifetime Cash-flow Projection* (LCP). We go through a careful, comprehensive exercise to nail down all the nuts and bolts of your LCP. Then, we show you how to use this projection to answer numerous questions — in particular, how to determine the asset allocation strategy that best helps you meet your lifetime financial needs.

Understanding the Lifetime Cash-Flow Projection

So what is a Lifetime Cash-flow Projection? An LCP is a very powerful tool that captures all the important information about your assets, liabilities, income, and expenses, and projects them into the future, so that you can make informed decisions today about things that will have an impact on you many years down the road. This section is designed to fill you in on a few LCP basics.

As you'll soon see, your LCP is really a living document that you can change as your life changes — it's not a one-time exercise.

Getting a feel for the basics

A well-crafted LCP allows you to see your present financial situation in a snapshot, which can be a real eye-opener. The LCP starts out looking a lot like a personal *balance sheet* (a list of your current assets and liabilities) and *income statement* (a list of your current income and expenses), and those two features combined can tell you quite a bit about where you stand financially. But the LCP doesn't stop there: It also helps you project what your situation might look like in the future. No LCP can perfectly predict what's going to happen in the future, but it can alert you to potential problems and areas of financial vulnerability. The LCP ties together all aspects of your financial plan. And, as you'll see, your asset allocation is a big part of that.

For an even fuller discussion on putting together your financial plan, we recommend *Personal Finance For Dummies,* 5th Edition, by Eric Tyson, MBA (Wiley).

You'll need to work to produce a good LCP. You'll have to gather a lot of information, some of which you probably haven't thought about in years. You may feel a little tempted to skip some of the work and take a few shortcuts. Our advice: Don't! The work will be worth it because detailed information will allow you to conduct a more accurate analysis, which will make pinpointing your optimal asset allocation strategy much, much easier. Your results just won't be as good if you're using incomplete or inaccurate info.

You can prepare an LCP in several ways:

- ✔ **By simply putting pencil to paper:** But don't reach for the old no. 2 pencil just yet. You may want to work out your LCP electronically — the arithmetic quickly becomes tedious if you take the manual route.

- ✔ **By using an off-the-shelf computer program, such as Quicken:** These programs help you keep track of a lot of the information we discuss in this chapter, and they even prepare a projection for you.

- ✔ **By doing it yourself using a spreadsheet program such as Excel:** Spreadsheets are quite easy to use, and you can customize them to fit your own unique situation.

- ✔ **By hiring a qualified expert to do it for you:** A professional will know what to do with all the information, but you're still going to need to provide her with the raw data — your assets, liabilities, income, and expenses. (See Chapter 16 for a discussion on hiring experts to help you.)

Recognizing the link between your asset allocation and your Lifetime Cash-flow Projection

As we explain in Chapter 6, your time horizon, return objectives, and risk tolerance are three of the most important factors that determine your asset allocation. You'll be able to better gauge all three as you develop your LCP. Why? There are three main reasons:

- ✔ **Your LCP will help you pinpoint your true time horizon.** If you haven't read Chapter 6, you may still think of your investment time horizon as lasting only until the beginning of your retirement, which may lead you to invest more conservatively than you should. The LCP will broaden your perspective to see just how long your investments need to last and how important investment growth is over the long term.

  You may also realize that an event that seems very far away is coming up relatively soon. For example, if you have a child in middle school, envisioning her old enough to attend college may be very difficult. Paying for her college expenses may not seem like a pressing need. But when your LCP tells you that you only have five years until you need to start paying for your princess's college expenses, that need will feel a lot more pressing. This may lead you to start investing part of your funds differently with this shorter time horizon in mind.

✔ **The LCP will help you more accurately figure out your required rate of return.** Just how much do you need to earn to support your lifestyle and reach your goals? Although you may not like the volatility inherent in more aggressive investments, the LCP may convince you that, if you don't want to scale back your lifestyle, you need to reach for higher returns. On the other hand, your LCP may indicate that you can afford to invest much more conservatively than you are, and there's no cause to take on risk you don't need to.

✔ **The LCP will help you define your risk tolerance.** The LCP makes it clear that risk isn't always the same thing as volatility (as we discuss in Chapter 2) and that risk doesn't exist in a vacuum. For example, many investors define risk as the chance that they might lose money. However, when you create your LCP and see your expenses increasing with inflation every year, it becomes apparent that "not losing money" isn't the same thing as "not losing purchasing power." To maintain your lifestyle, you may have to reach for higher returns and accept the higher volatility that comes with them. Paradoxically, this may be the only way you can reduce your risk of failure (your failure to maintain your style of living).

When you complete the exercise we describe in this chapter, you see the impact of different asset allocations on your lifetime cash flow directly, using your LCP. This is how your LCP helps you derive your optimal asset allocation strategy.

Coming Up with an Outline for Your Long-Term Financial Plan

The LCP has four main parts: assets, liabilities, income, and expenses. Table 7-1 shows the framework of an LCP. Keep this framework in mind and refer back to it as we explain each of the parts of the LCP in the next few sections.

Table 7-1	**The Framework of a Lifetime Cash-Flow Projection**		
Assets	*Liabilities*	*Income*	*Expenses*
Savings account	Mortgage (current balance, interest, annual payment, number of years left)	Salary	Annual living expenses
Certificate of deposit (CD)	Home equity line of credit (current balance, additional available balance, interest, expected annual payment, expected number of years left)	Pension	Mortgage payments

Assets	Liabilities	Income	Expenses
Brokerage account		Social Security	Home equity line of credit payments
IRA		Withdrawals	Medical care
401(k)			Extra expenses
			Savings (taxable accounts and tax-deferred accounts)
			Tax due (salary, pension, Social Security, investment growth on taxable account, withdrawal from tax-advantaged account)

Source: Brinton Eaton Wealth Advisors.

Try to keep in mind that, if you're still employed, your *net cash flow* (income minus your expenses) will generally be positive, but it will probably turn negative when you retire and start to draw down from your assets to cover expenses. Make sure that you have enough to meet your lifestyle needs when you start to make withdrawals by keeping track of your projected assets now. For most people, loan payments (such as mortgages and home equity lines of credit) are a large part of expenses in retirement, which is why keeping track of liabilities is another key part of the LCP.

You'll want to avoid a couple of common LCP mistakes:

- ✓ **Make sure that all income and expense amounts reflect the same period, such as a month or a year.** Be careful not to enter a monthly salary and quarterly insurance payments.

- ✓ **Don't skip any of the categories we list in this section just because they don't currently apply to you.** They may apply in the future.

Assets

For the purposes of creating an LCP, the term *asset* can mean money — bank accounts, brokerage accounts, IRAs and 401(k)s — as well as investment property (such as an apartment building on which you collect rent, or your business).

If you're like most people, you consider your house to be a significant asset, but it isn't included here because it's actually not a source of income. It's a source of expenses (property taxes, repairs, upkeep, and remodeling), which we get to in the next section.

Keep track separately of the equity you have in your home because you can use it to secure a home equity loan or line of credit if you need it, and it can be a source of funds if you downsize later.

When you list your assets, distinguish between three types of assets:

- **Taxable assets:** Your taxable assets are generally funds in non-retirement accounts. These are accounts for which there are no tax deductions when you make contributions and no taxation when you make withdrawals, but income and realized capital gains on these accounts are taxed in the years in which they're earned.

- **Tax-advantaged assets:** Your tax-advantaged assets are generally assets held in 401(k) plans, IRA accounts, 529 plans, education savings accounts (ESAs), and health savings accounts (HSAs). Income and capital gains in these accounts aren't taxed. Contributions to these accounts (other than Roth IRAs) are tax-deductible. Withdrawals from traditional IRAs and 401(k)s are taxed at your ordinary income-tax rates. Withdrawals from Roth IRAs, 529 plans, ESAs, and HSAs are not taxed, provided that the withdrawals are done in accordance with the rules applicable to each of those plans.

  Ask your financial or tax advisor for help with these rules if you're unfamiliar with them. (See Chapter 16 if you need to find an advisor.)

- **Non-invested assets:** These funds are your "rainy-day money," or money that you expect to use in the near future. Typically, you stick these assets in your savings or checking accounts.

For each of these, you need an *assumed earnings rate,* which is the rate (a percentage) at which each asset will generate income. We discuss how to estimate these assumed earnings rates in "Investment returns" and "Estimating returns," later in this chapter. Because your asset allocation should comprise both your taxable and tax-advantaged accounts in the aggregate, these should have the same assumed earnings rate. Because the non-invested funds (savings account, checking account) will be in very conservative instruments, they should have a different assumed earnings rate that is relatively low but fairly stable.

Experimenting with the assumed earnings rate (trying different rates and noting how they change your LCP) on your taxable and tax-advantaged accounts will allow you to see how asset allocation affects your cash-flow projections. That's one of the key links we develop in the "Determining How Your Asset Allocation May Affect Your Lifetime Cash-Flow Projection" section, later in this chapter.

In Table 7-2, we show you an example of what the asset portion of your LCP may look like. In this example, assets include taxable money held in a savings account, a certificate of deposit, and a brokerage account. Assets also include tax-advantaged accounts held in an IRA and a 401(k) plan.

Table 7-2	An Example of an Asset Summary	
Account	*Balance*	*Asset Type*
Savings account	$10,000	Non-invested
Certificate of deposit	$20,000	Non-invested
Brokerage	$190,000	Taxable
IRA	$200,000	Tax-advantaged
401(k)	$350,000	Tax-advantaged

Source: Brinton Eaton Wealth Advisors.

Liabilities

To develop the second part of your LCP, you need to keep track of *liabilities* (your outstanding financial obligations), which can include your mortgage, school loans, car loans, and unpaid credit card balances. Make sure you include all the necessary details. In Table 7-3, for example, details on your mortgage include balance, interest (fixed or variable), annual payment, and number of years left. You'll need this information on every loan you hold.

The annual payment, and how long you have to pay it, will be expense items that you'll enter on the expense portion of the LCP, which we cover in the "Expenses" section, later in this chapter, but it's good to simply note those items here as well, so that all your loan information is summarized in one place.

Your mortgage payment is probably one of your biggest expense items. Is the interest rate fixed or variable? If it's variable, what will the new payment be at different interest rates? (By the way, while you're compiling this information, it may be a good time to review the loan terms and conditions, if it's been a few years since you originally got the mortgage.)

What other loans do you have? What interest are you paying on them? Keep in mind that loans secured by the home, such as a home equity line of credit (HELOC), generally have lower interest rates than other loans.

In Table 7-3, we show you an example of what the liability portion of your LCP may look like. In this example, liabilities include a mortgage and a HELOC.

Table 7-3	An Example of a Liabilities Summary			
Type of Account	*Balance*	*Interest*	*Annual Payment*	*Number of Years Left*
Mortgage	$132,000	5% fixed	$26,021 (principal and interest)	6
Home equity line of credit	Current $10,000; available $60,000 additional	5% variable	$3,700 currently	3

Source: Brinton Eaton Wealth Advisors.

Income

To develop the third part of your LCP, look at *all* your sources of income. These may include compensation (while you're still working), pensions and deferred compensation (after you've stopped working), and also annuities, Social Security benefit payments, and income from your investments.

Table 7-4 shows a sample of what the income portion of a person's LCP may look like over the next ten years. (Don't worry just yet how we got data for years 2 through 10 — we get to that in the "Putting It All Together: Making Lifetime Cash-Flow Projections" section, a little later.) In this figure, we assume that the person is 60 years old and planning to work for five more years before retiring. The current salary is $120,000 per year, which is expected to grow at 3 percent every year. This person will qualify for a fixed pension in retirement. Social Security payments will start at normal retirement age and will also increase at 3 percent. Withdrawals, which are counted as income, are expected during retirement and are assumed to increase at 3 percent.

Table 7-4				The Income Portion of an Example LCP — The First Ten Years							
Income	**Growth Rate**	**Year 1 (Age 60)**	**Year 2 (Age 61)**	**Year 3 (Age 62)**	**Year 4 (Age 63)**	**Year 5 (Age 64)**	**Year 6 (Age 65)**	**Year 7 (Age 66)**	**Year 8 (Age 67)**	**Year 9 (Age 68)**	**Year 10 (Age 69)**
Salary	3%	$120,000	$123,600	$127,308	$131,127	$135,061					
Pension	0%						$50,000	$50,000	$50,000	$50,000	$50,000
Social Security	3%						$25,000	$25,750	$26,523	$27,318	$28,138
Withdrawals	3%						$52,000	$23,000	$25,000	$25,000	$24,000
Total Income		$120,000	$123,600	$127,308	$131,127	$135,061	$127,000	$98,750	$101,523	$102,318	$102,138

Source: Brinton Eaton Wealth Advisors.

In the following sections, we go into greater detail on the various sources of income you may have.

Compensation: Wages, salaries, and bonuses

If you're currently working, *direct compensation* — base wages or salary and any cash incentive pay — is probably your primary source of income. Business owners have self-employment income and profit. List your gross compensation, not what you actually take home. In the next section, you list each deduction from your paycheck — taxes, insurance payments, and 401(k) contributions — separately under expenses. Catalog each source of compensation income separately on your LCP.

If you're married and your spouse works, list your compensation and your spouse's compensation separately. This will help you address key questions such as: What happens if my spouse or I retires earlier or later? Can either one of us afford to work part-time or stop working altogether to take care of the children? If so, then at what point will we have to go back to work? (We get to those types of questions in the "Testing 'What If' Scenarios" section, later in this chapter.)

In order to project your compensation into the future (more on that later), start thinking about the following questions: At what rate will various parts of my compensation grow? How many more years do I intend to work?

You may also be entitled to deferred compensation benefits. Determine (with assistance from your company's human resources department, if necessary) what the amounts and timing will be of these benefits and include them as part of your future income.

Pensions and retirement account distributions

Are you entitled to a government or corporate pension? Companies have largely abandoned pensions in favor of 401(k)s and/or cash balance plans, but pensions are still a standard benefit for government employees and some teachers. Many companies also still have a pension program for their key executives.

If you aren't receiving a pension yet and you aren't sure of your benefit, contact your company's human resources department to help you estimate what the amount will be when you retire. If you're married, that amount may depend on how much you decide you want your spouse to receive if you die first. Be sure to ask what your options are and what the pension amounts are under each option. Also, ask when you'll first be eligible and, after you start receiving the benefit, whether it'll increase over time for inflation.

The pension you're currently entitled to may be significantly lower than the pension you'll likely be entitled to when you retire. In the LCP, enter the amount you expect to receive when you retire, as well as how much you expect it to grow each year.

Traditional 401(k) and IRA accounts will be subject to mandatory distributions at certain ages and count as income. Roth 401(k)s, Roth IRAs, and inherited accounts are subject to different rules. Ask your financial or tax advisor to estimate the amounts and timing of income from these accounts. (Find out how to pick an advisor in Chapter 16.)

Stock options

Are you entitled to stock options from your employer? Do you know if the options are qualified or non-qualified? When do they vest? When do they expire? When is the best time to exercise? What will they be worth when you exercise them? What taxes will you pay when you exercise the option or sell the stock?

You may be able to get answers to these questions from your human resources department, but a financial professional with expertise in stock options may be an even better choice. No matter how you locate the information, you'll need it as you complete your LCP.

Due to the volatility of a typical company's stock price, you may want to enter 0 for how much you'll receive unless your stock options vest soon and are already valuable, just to be on the safe side.

Annuities

Do you own any annuities? What is the annuity payment? Is it a fixed amount or does it increase with inflation or vary according to the performance of some market index? When do the payments start and when do they end? Note the answers to these questions, because they come into play in the "Putting It All Together: Making Lifetime Cash-Flow Projections" section, later in this chapter.

If you don't already own an annuity, should you purchase one? This is a question that the LCP will help you address. (It's an example of a "what if" question, other examples of which we cover in the "Testing 'What If' Scenarios" section, a little later in this chapter.)

Social Security

Once a year, the Social Security Administration mails all taxpayers a statement of their projected Social Security benefits at different retirement ages. (This information is also available online at www.ssa.gov.) Social Security payments increase annually with inflation.

With the concern over the viability of Social Security, one question today is whether you should even include these benefits in your LCP. If you're within ten years of retirement or you're already receiving benefits, it's a safe assumption to put in your expected or current level of benefits. If you have longer than that until retirement, then it's difficult to predict what benefit you'll actually receive. On the one hand, it's unlikely that the government will suddenly discontinue a program that provides the only source of funds for a large number of people. But on the other hand, a decrease in benefits is possible, because the current level of benefits isn't sustainable at current levels of funding.

You can test your vulnerability to changes in Social Security by using your LCP. Set the benefit to the amount shown on your Social Security statement, as well as to a lower amount, and don't escalate future payments for inflation. If, for example, you set your benefit to zero and you're still in the black (your income exceeds your expenses) every year, then the viability of Social Security isn't something you need to worry about — at least not for yourself.

Withdrawals

During some years, your expenses (which we catalog in the next section) may exceed your income. In those years, you'll need to make withdrawals from one or more of your asset accounts to make up the shortfall. Because those withdrawals represent cash inflows to you, they should be counted in the income category.

As we mention earlier, some minimum distributions (from your traditional 401(k)s and/or IRAs, for example) are required beginning at age $70^{1}/_{2}$. These should also be included in withdrawals and, thus, counted as income during those years.

Expenses

The final part of your LCP covers your expenses. The degree of detail is up to you — you can simply get an annual estimate using the "total withdrawals" value on your monthly bank statements, or you can do a full accounting of exactly where your money is going.

If you do a full accounting of your expenses when working on your LCP, double-check your total numbers with the bank statements. Don't overlook other places where you're paying out money, such as paycheck deductions.

Table 7-5 shows a sample of what the expense portion of your LCP may look like. Note that the income tax on investment growth for the taxable account is based on the assumed amount of taxable assets, which we calculate in the "Assets" section earlier in this chapter. Remember to estimate a lump sum figure for annual living expenses, even though you may have used a detailed worksheet to get there, and inflate it each year at 3 percent. Mortgage and medical care are listed separately, and are inflated at different rates (0 percent and 6 percent, respectively).

Table 7-5		The Expense Portion of an Example LCP — The First Ten Years								
Expenses	**Growth Rate**	**Year 1 (Age 60)**	**Year 2 (Age 61)**	**Year 3 (Age 62)**	**Year 4 (Age 63)**	**Year 5 (Age 64)**	**Year 6 (Age 65)**	**Year 7 (Age 66)**	**Year 8 (Age 67)**	**Year 9 (Age 68)**	**Year 10 (Age 69)**
Annual living expenses	3%	$50,000	$51,500	$53,045	$54,636	$56,275	$57,964	$59,703	$61,494	$63,339	$65,239
Mortgage	0%	$26,021	$26,021	$26,021	$26,021	$26,021	$26,021				
Home equity line of credit	0%	$3,700	$3,700	$3,700							
Medical care	6%	$7,500	$7,950	$8,427	$8,933	$9,469	$10,037	$10,639	$11,277	$11,954	$12,671
Extra expenses							$10,000	$10,000	$10,000	$7,500	$5,000
Savings											
Taxable accounts			$1,000		$2,000	$2,000					
Tax-deferred accounts				$1,500	$3,500	$3,500					
Tax Due	Tax Rate										
Salary	25%	$30,000	$30,900	$31,827	$32,782	$33,765					
Pension	20%						$10,000	$10,000	$10,000	$10,000	$10,000

(continued)

Table 7-5 (continued)

Expenses	Growth Rate	Year 1 (Age 60)	Year 2 (Age 61)	Year 3 (Age 62)	Year 4 (Age 63)	Year 5 (Age 64)	Year 6 (Age 65)	Year 7 (Age 66)	Year 8 (Age 67)	Year 9 (Age 68)	Year 10 (Age 69)
Social Security	20%						$5,000	$5,150	$5,305	$5,464	$5,628
Investment growth on taxable account	17%	$2,363	$2,525	$2,700	$2,883	$3,105	$3,343	$3,215	$3,160	$3,078	$2,993
Withdrawal from tax-advantaged account	20%						$4,400				
Total expenses		$119,584	$123,596	$127,220	$130,755	$134,135	$126,764	$98,706	$101,235	$101,334	$101,530

Source: Brinton Eaton Wealth Advisors.

In the following sections, we go into detail on the various expenses you may have.

Annual living expenses

The first item in the expense portion of your LCP is your annual living expense estimate. This is likely to be your largest expense item, and is probably the single most important item in your entire LCP. Annual living expenses are expenses that you expect to have every year, and that you expect will grow with the general rate of inflation.

Annual living expenses include such items as housing, clothing, personal care, food, insurance, transportation, gifts, charitable contributions, entertainment, and capital expenditures (things like new roofs and replacement cars that you don't necessarily expect to incur every year, but you want to anticipate and set aside an appropriate amount to cover — for example, if you expect to buy a new car every five years, set aside one-fifth of the expected cost in your annual living expense estimate).

You'll notice, in Table 7-5, that we don't list a cost for each and every annual living expense item in the LCP — we just have the lump sum. What you buy may change over time, but the amount you spend annually will likely stay relatively stable, inflation aside.

Other expenses — those that are either not expected to be ongoing, or will grow at a different rate of inflation — are treated separately. We cover those expenses in the next few sections.

Loan payments

Calculate loan payments when you prepare your liability statement (see the "Liabilities" section, earlier). For each loan, enter the payment amount and the time over which you'll be making the payments.

List your mortgage separately. If you're paying a fixed interest rate, then your loan payments shouldn't increase with inflation. Payments for home insurance, property taxes, and private mortgage insurance (PMI) are often bundled with the actual loan payments. Include only the actual principal and interest payments here. At some point, mortgage payments will stop. If you're paying PMI, then those payments will stop well before the mortgage payments. (***Note:*** Include home insurance and property taxes in the annual living expense category, as we describe in the preceding section.)

Medical care

If you're in good health and have a generous health insurance policy through your employer, then this may be an easy expense to overlook. Why include an expense that currently may be minimal? Because, as you age, medical care may become a significant part of your budget. Over time, you're likely to have more health problems, which will require more doctor's visits, exams, and prescriptions. Unless of course you manage to find that pesky fountain of youth, and if you do, please give us a call.

If you don't have retiree health benefits through your employer, then you'll rely on Medicare and supplemental insurance products, which will probably not be as comprehensive as the corporate policy you enjoyed while working. Medical costs have been increasing at the rate of about 6 percent per year — or twice the general rate of inflation — and are projected to continue to do so.

Education costs

List higher-education costs separately, because they're a significant expense over a limited period of time and have been increasing as quickly as medical costs. In estimating what the costs may be, include not just tuition but also room and board, books, travel, and incidentals. In developing your LCP, think about what you'll be able to pay and how much in loans you'll need to cover everything.

Pay particular attention to two sets of costs in developing your LCP. Education costs, along with medical costs, have been increasing at a rate of 6 percent annually — twice the general rate of inflation — and are expected to continue to do so.

Weddings, vacations, and other special events

Weddings, bar mitzvahs and bat mitzvahs, big vacations — these are all wonderful events, but they usually come with big price tags. Because these costs are not recurring and you have some control over the amount and/or timing, you may want to put them in a separate category, which we call "extra expenses." Any other large expenses, such as home remodeling (and maybe that Faberge egg collection you've been thinking about for years), should go here as well.

Taxes

How much are you paying in income taxes now? To project how much you might pay in income taxes in the future, calculate an *average tax rate* (your taxes divided by your gross income) instead of the dollar amount of taxes you currently pay. Doing so will allow you to automatically adjust your tax estimate in future years as your income changes.

Your average tax rate isn't the same thing as your *marginal tax rate;* your marginal rate indicates how much you pay on your last dollar of income in a given year (it reflects your highest tax bracket), and doesn't take any deductions or credits into account. For these reasons, your marginal tax rate will generally overstate your average tax rate.

When calculating your average income tax rate, be sure to include

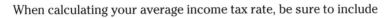

- ✔ Federal taxes
- ✔ State and local taxes
- ✔ Social Security and Medicare taxes

Consider the tax rate on each current source of income you list in the income statement.

What portion of your current income do you earn through your job? Your business? Your taxable investments? If you're self-employed, you pay up to an additional 7.65 percent in self-employment tax. You don't pay any Social Security or Medicare taxes on realized long-term capital gains and qualified dividends, which are also currently taxed at lower rates than ordinary income. And you don't get taxed on withdrawals from taxable accounts.

If you're not currently retired, what might your average income tax rate be in retirement? Depending on your income from other sources, up to 85 percent of your Social Security payments may be taxable. Your pension is taxable. Annuities are partially taxable. Any withdrawals you make from a traditional IRA or 401(k) are taxable, too. Clearly these are important considerations. The LCP will help you estimate what income you will have in retirement and the source of this income, which will help you determine your average tax rate.

Withdrawals from certain other tax-advantaged accounts aren't taxable, provided that the necessary conditions are met. Examples are Roth IRAs, 529 plans, ESAs, and HSAs.

Your accountant, or a financial program such as Quicken, can help calculate your future average income tax rate.

Taxes other than income taxes, such as property taxes, should be included in the annual living expenses portion of your LCP.

Savings

How much do you need to save to achieve your goals? How much can you afford to save at different times in your life? And in which account should the money be saved? The LCP will help you answer all these questions. When you estimate your savings amounts each year, enter them into your LCP.

Just as withdrawals from your asset accounts represent cash inflows to you and are counted as income (per the earlier section), savings you deposit into those accounts represent cash outflows to you, so they're categorized with expenses. In that sense, savings are a "good" kind of expense. (A "bad" expense might be the 30-foot ice sculpture of yourself that you commissioned, or that pair of $500 glow-in-the-dark sunglasses you picked up on vacation.)

Putting It All Together: Making Lifetime Cash-Flow Projections

If you work through all the steps in the previous section, you have all the pieces you need to put together your LCP. Table 7-6 is an example of what a finished LCP looks like. As you can see, after the initial amounts are entered for Year 1 it's possible to make some calculations to project what your LCP might look like in the future. In this section, we guide you through some of the key calculations you need in order to make these revealing projections.

Table 7-6 A Complete Sample LCP — First Ten Years

Income	Growth Rate	Year 1 (Age 60)	Year 2 (Age 61)	Year 3 (Age 62)	Year 4 (Age 63)	Year 5 (Age 64)	Year 6 (Age 65)	Year 7 (Age 66)	Year 8 (Age 67)	Year 9 (Age 68)	Year 10 (Age 69)
Salary	3%	$120,000	$123,600	$127,308	$131,127	$135,061					
Pension	0%						$50,000	$50,000	$50,000	$50,000	$50,000
Social Security	3%						$25,000	$25,750	$26,523	$27,318	$28,138
Withdrawals							$52,000	$23,000	$25,000	$25,000	$24,000
Total Income		**$120,000**	**$123,600**	**$127,308**	**$131,127**	**$135,061**	**$127,000**	**$98,750**	**$101,523**	**$102,318**	**$102,138**

Expenses	Growth Rate	Year 1 (Age 60)	Year 2 (Age 61)	Year 3 (Age 62)	Year 4 (Age 63)	Year 5 (Age 64)	Year 6 (Age 65)	Year 7 (Age 66)	Year 8 (Age 67)	Year 9 (Age 68)	Year 10 (Age 69)
Annual living expenses	3%	$50,000	$51,500	$53,045	$54,636	$56,275	$57,964	$59,703	$61,494	$63,339	$65,239
Mortgage	0%	$26,021	$26,021	$26,021	$26,021	$26,021	$26,021				
Home equity line of credit	0%	$3,700	$3,700	$3,700							
Medical care	6%	$7,500	$7,950	$8,427	$8,933	$9,469	$10,037	$10,639	$11,277	$11,954	$12,671
Extra expenses							$10,000	$10,000	$10,000	$7,500	$5,000
Savings											
Taxable accounts			$1,000		$2,000	$2,000					
Tax-deferred accounts				$1,500	$3,500	$3,500					
Tax Due	Tax Rate										

(continued)

Table 7-6 (continued)

Expenses	Growth Rate	Year 1 (Age 60)	Year 2 (Age 61)	Year 3 (Age 62)	Year 4 (Age 63)	Year 5 (Age 64)	Year 6 (Age 65)	Year 7 (Age 66)	Year 8 (Age 67)	Year 9 (Age 68)	Year 10 (Age 69)
Salary	25%	$30,000	$30,900	$31,827	$32,782	$33,765					
Pension	20%						$10,000	$10,000	$10,000	$10,000	$10,000
Social Security	20%						$5,000	$5,150	$5,305	$5,464	$5,628
Investment growth on taxable account	17%	$2,363	$2,525	$2,700	$2,883	$3,105	$3,343	$3,215	$3,160	$3,078	$2,993
Withdrawal from tax-advantaged account	20%						$4,400				
Total expenses		**$119,584**	**$123,596**	**$127,220**	**$130,755**	**$134,135**	**$126,764**	**$98,706**	**$101,235**	**$101,334**	**$101,530**
Net cash flow		**$416**	**$4**	**$88**	**$372**	**$926**	**$236**	**$444**	**$287**	**$984**	**$608**

Assets		Year 1 (Age 60)	Year 2 (Age 61)	Year 3 (Age 62)	Year 4 (Age 63)	Year 5 (Age 64)	Year 6 (Age 65)	Year 7 (Age 66)	Year 8 (Age 67)	Year 9 (Age 68)	Year 10 (Age 69)
Assumed growth rate		7%	7%	7%	7%	7%	7%	7%	7%	7%	7%
Taxable Assets											
Balance at beginning of year		$190,000	$203,300	$217,531	$232,758	$251,051	$270,625	$261,569	$278,978	$296,680	$314,666
Growth		$13,300	$14,231	$15,227	$16,293	$17,574	$18,944	$18,310	$19,528	$20,768	$22,027

Assets	Year 1 (Age 60)	Year 2 (Age 61)	Year 3 (Age 62)	Year 4 (Age 63)	Year 5 (Age 64)	Year 6 (Age 65)	Year 7 (Age 66)	Year 8 (Age 67)	Year 9 (Age 68)	Year 10 (Age 69)
Contribution				$2,000	$2,000					
Withdrawal						$30,000	$23,000	$25,000	$25,000	$24,000
Tax-deferred assets										
Balance at beginning of year	$550,000	$588,500	$629,695	$675,274	$726,043	$780,366	$812,991	$869,901	$930,794	$995,949
Growth	$38,500	$41,195	$44,079	$47,269	$50,823	$54,626	$56,909	$60,893	$65,156	$69,716
Contribution			$1,500	$3,500	$3,500					
Withdrawal						$22,000				
Non-invested assets										
Assumed growth rate	2%	2%	2%	2%	2%	2%	2%	2%	2%	2%
Balance at beginning of year	$30,000	$31,016	$32,641	$33,382	$34,422	$36,036	$36,993	$37,776	$38,819	$40,580
Growth	$600	$620	$653	$668	$688	$721	$740	$756	$776	$812
Contribution		$1,000								
Withdrawal										
Total assets at end of year plus net cash flow	$822,816	$662,336	$708,655	$760,464	$816,402	$893,984	$907,677	$969,613	$1,036,529	$1,107,665

Source: Brinton Eaton Wealth Advisors.

Before we get into the calculations that give you your future LCP projections, though, we want to call your attention to two key items in the LCP:

✔ Your net cash flow, which is your income less expenses

✔ Your assets at the end of the year plus your net cash flow

While you're working, it's good to have your net cash flow be positive. This may not happen every year, particularly when there's a large expense such as college or a wedding. When you stop working, you want to make sure the sum of your assets and net cash flow remains positive throughout your lifetime. When that number hits zero or below, that means you've run out of money — you've outlived your assets — which is not a good thing. Ways to avoid such a bad outcome, before it's too late, include working more, adjusting your lifestyle, and considering a different investment strategy. (These and other approaches are discussed in the "Testing 'What If' Scenarios" and "Determining How Your Asset Allocation May Affect Your Lifetime Cash-Flow Projection" sections, later in this chapter.)

The example LCP in Table 7-6 shows what a current LCP can look like, and it projects the next ten years. How can you make the same projections on your LCP? Read on to find out.

Salary and other income

To project your salary and other income into the future, first increase all your income items throughout the years by the growth rate you assumed. In the sample LCP presented in Table 7-6, we assume an annual salary of $120,000 with 3 percent growth per year. In Year 2, here's the projected salary:

Salary in Year 1 × (1 + growth rate) = salary in Year 2

$120,000 x 1.03 = $123,600

Keep multiplying each year's salary by the growth rate to get the following year's salary.

You project your other income in the same way.

Expenses

To project your future expenses on your LCP, you need to start by increasing your Year 1 expenses by a percentage, and then continue to increase them by that percentage each year. For the expense in the LCP example in Table 7-6, we assume $50,000 for annual living expenses growing at 3 percent per year, not including mortgage and medical expenses. In Year 2, that means that the estimated expenses will be $50,000 \times 1.03 = $51,500. Because we assume a fixed mortgage, its growth rate is zero. Medical expenses start out at $7,500, but increase at 6 percent per year, which would make them $7,500 \times 1.06 = $7,950 in Year 2. Keep multiplying the expense in each year by the growth rate to get the projected expense in the following year.

Investment returns

For your investments, enter some constant rate of growth for now. This will keep the numbers simple and make it easier for you to check that the LCP is calculating everything correctly. Use the assumed growth rates to calculate your asset growth each year. For example, in the sample LCP presented in Table 7-6, we assume a beginning taxable asset balance of $190,000 with 7 percent growth per year. In Year 1, the growth amount on those assets would be as follows:

Beginning Balance of Assets in Year 1 × Growth Rate = Growth in Year 1

$190,000 \times 0.07 = $13,300

Beginning Balance of Assets in Year 2 × Growth Rate = Growth in Year 2

$203,300 \times 0.07 = $14,231

And so forth for subsequent years. (We look at how to make these growth rates more realistic in the "Determining How Your Asset Allocation May Affect Your Lifetime Cash-Flow Projection" section, later in this chapter.)

Taxes

Figuring out the tax projections on your LCP is relatively easy. For each year, calculate the estimated tax on each item of income, using the average tax rate you calculate in the "Expenses" portion of the "Coming Up with an Outline for Your Long-Term Financial Plan" section, earlier in this chapter.

Don't forget to include the tax on realized investment growth and dividends, as well as any withdrawals from tax-advantaged accounts.

Savings or withdrawals

You may want to enter the amount of savings or withdrawals last. If the LCP shows that your income exceeds your expenses, consider setting a goal to save what you estimate the difference to be. For example, the sample LCP in

Table 7-6 shows that in Year 4 there should be a surplus of almost $6,000. In that case, we suggest setting a goal for that year to save $2,000 in the taxable account and $3,500 in the tax-advantaged account.

You may be asking yourself, "What accounts should I save to or withdraw from?" When it comes to saving, priority should be given to tax-advantaged accounts to the extent you can (as long as you don't need the money prematurely or for purposes that would violate the tax-advantage rules of that account). When withdrawing funds, priority should be given to taxable accounts. You want the money to be in the tax-advantaged accounts for as long as possible to prolong the amount of time that you get the tax-deferred growth.

Don't forget to adjust the amount of projected assets by any contributions or withdrawals made.

When taking out required minimum distributions from your tax-advantaged accounts, do so toward the end of the year, so you can receive more months of tax-deferred growth out of those funds.

Time horizon revisited

In Chapter 6, and in the "Understanding the Lifetime Cash-Flow Projection" section, earlier in this chapter, we discuss the issue of investment horizon. It's an important issue, and you need to factor it into your LCP. Put simply: For how many years should the LCP continue? Ideally, it should continue throughout your investment horizon.

But let's be frank. The whole discussion about your expected time horizon is really a polite way of exploring the very uncomfortable question of how long you should assume you'll live. Unless you're already in poor health, a reasonable assumption is that you will live a long time. With advances in medicine, you may live well into your 90s.

A deceptively simple way to get a more precise number is to use your life expectancy, which you can get from online actuarial tables.

However, this is a misleadingly short amount of time. Life expectancy measures how long about half of the people your age will survive. In other words, roughly half the people are expected to outlive their "life expectancy". A financial plan that manages to get you safely to your life expectancy, and no further, has a 50 percent chance of failing! So, unless your health or your family's longevity argue for something much shorter, it would be prudent to project your LCP out to age 100.

However, as with any projection that tries to model something as uncertain as your financial life, going more than, at most, 40 years out from today introduces too much room for error. Cap your LCP projection period at 40 years. You'll want to update your LCP about every year anyway, so if you need to project over a longer span, you'll have plenty of time to get more years in there down the road.

Assets

You project the amount of assets in each type of account as follows:

> Balance at the Beginning of the Year + Investment Growth (Based on Assumed Earnings Rate) + Contributions (From the Savings in the Expense Section) − Withdrawals (From the Income Section) = Balance at the Beginning of Next Year

Any money left in "Net Cash Flow" in any year is added to your non-invested asset balance at the beginning of the next year.

Liabilities

There's no need to project liability balances directly on the LCP. You use the information you compiled on your liabilities to generate the related expense items (annual mortgage payments, for example) each year. That's all you really need the initial liability information for.

Testing "What If" Scenarios

Now comes the really interesting part — using your LCP to see how different life events and choices may affect you financially. In this section, we explore some of the common life events that have profound effects on people's financial situations. Seeing how we analyze these situations should help you address additional questions you may have about your own financial scenarios.

As you read through these examples, you'll notice that your LCP is really a living document, not a one-time exercise. After you've done the work to set it up, it should be easy to update it annually and to use it to answer all sorts of financial questions you'll be asking yourself throughout your life.

What if you retire early?

Although some people can't imagine life without their current career, other people have a whole to-do list of the things they can't wait to do when they retire. If you fall in the latter group, you may want to know if you can afford to get a head start on that list by retiring early.

To test if this is possible, make these adjustments to your LCP:

1. **Pick an age at which you plan to retire.**

2. **Stop all sources of income that you expect to end when you retire at your new retirement age.**

   When stopping your income, consider each item you listed separately. For example, your wages may end but your investment income will continue.

3. **Start any source of income you may be eligible for when you retire early.**

   If you're considering starting a new career in retirement, enter a conservative estimate of what you think your new salary may be in each year. Consider the earliest age at which you may be eligible to receive the new source of income, the amount if you start claiming it prior to full retirement age, and any penalties you may have to pay.

   For example, Social Security payments can be claimed starting at age 62, but will permanently be 20 percent to 30 percent less than what you'd receive at full retirement age (the Social Security Administration defines your full retirement age based on your year of birth). On retirement accounts, you can start drawing distributions without penalty starting at age 59$\frac{1}{2}$.

   You can start drawing distributions on retirement accounts before you turn 59$\frac{1}{2}$ years old without penalty, by making substantially equal periodic payments (SEPP), also called 72(t) payments (after the IRS rule that defines them), over your lifetime.

   In a 401(k) plan, funds can be withdrawn as early as age 55 without penalty. This option is no longer available if you roll over the 401(k) into an IRA. If you're considering retiring prior to age 59$\frac{1}{2}$, this may be a reason to leave the money in the 401(k). Contact your human resources department or your accountant or financial advisor to help you determine the consequences of starting withdrawals from different accounts at different ages.

4. **Adjust your expenses, if you think they'll be substantially higher or lower.**

   When you retire, do you see yourself doing a lot more traveling or maybe going back to school? Do you see these expenses as being permanent increases in your lifestyle or one-time events? Are there any large expenses that you'll no longer have when you stop working? Make sure to include the net difference in your expense estimates.

If your LCP shows that you can afford to retire early, then go ahead and enjoy yourself! But what if the results show that you'll run out of money? There are many adjustments to the LCP you can try. For example:

✔ Consider working part-time during retirement.

✔ Increase the age at which you claim Social Security or start taking withdrawals from your retirement accounts.

✔ Decrease current expenses and increase savings.

✔ Decrease future expenses.

✔ Delay your early retirement age.

Some combination of these changes may be enough to allow you to retire earlier (except for the last one, of course). If you have to make drastic and uncomfortable changes to your current or future lifestyle, that may indicate that early retirement is not a good option for you.

What if you start a family or have more children?

Few things have a more profound lifelong effect on your finances than having children. There are the additional expenses and possibly lower income levels. Plus, having kids puts a crunch on saving during your pre-retirement years, which makes it all the more urgent to diligently plan for retirement. Also, if one parent decides to stop working or work part-time while the young ones are growing, then planning is essential to ensure the family's long-term financial well-being.

One of the first questions that prospective parents must address is: Who will watch the kids? In the early years, one of the largest expenses will be the cost of the children's care. This may include the cost of babysitting if both parents work, or the loss of income from the parent who quits work or reduces his or her hours to stay home. Here's one question you may want to explore: If one parent stops working full time, for how long can your family afford that arrangement?

Housing is another child-related expense you may have to consider. If you have a larger family, you may need a bigger house. (Where else are you going to put all those toys?) This can mean a bigger mortgage, higher property taxes, additional maintenance costs, more furniture — the list goes on and on. Then there are all the day-to-day expenses of having children like buying diapers, extra food, various baby paraphernalia, activities, and much more.

After the kids get through high school, you may need to pay for college. This is a complex area of planning in itself. You can use the LCP to help you determine how much you can realistically save for college. If your children will be attending college soon, then you can also use the LCP to help you determine the amount of loans you can afford to take on.

Although our advice may go against parental instincts, planning for your own retirement should take precedence over planning for your children's college. There are many options for financing the cost of college, but you can't get a scholarship or even a loan for retirement! And the best gift you can give your kids is not being a financial burden to them in your old age.

As a parent of young children, you must also be concerned about what may happen to them if something happens to you. You may want to consider increasing your emergency fund, because there are a lot more emergencies that can come up and higher expenses to maintain. You may want to purchase or increase your life insurance and disability insurance.

And then there's the wedding to pay for. . . .

What if you want to change your career?

Today people often switch careers, sometimes several times over the course of their working lives. Maybe you're disillusioned with your profession and want to do something you'd find more fulfilling. Maybe you want to start your own business. If the change will entail significant expenses or a period of time when your earnings will be lower, then you may want to do some long-range planning with your LCP.

If changing your career will require you to go back to school, make sure to consider the cost of tuition and other fees, and include them in expenses on your LCP. If the training is to enhance your current career and you're paying for it yourself, then consider what the extra salary potential might be to determine if it's really worth it. The LCP will help you compare apples to apples by comparing the cost of the school to the *after-tax* increase in your salary.

Will the career switch require either a temporary or permanent reduction in earnings? Will you be able to support your lifestyle using current savings, or will you need to cut your expenses? If the LCP indicates that expenses would have to be significantly reduced to live on a lower projected salary, try to live now within what your *future* means will be to see if it's feasible for you. Giving it a try is a great way to figure out whether you'll be able to deal with it over an extended period of time.

How will the career switch affect your retirement? With your projected income and expenses, what will you be able to save? How might your benefits change? If, for example, you're considering becoming a teacher, you'll likely be eligible to receive a pension and you may get retiree health benefits. For government jobs, a lot of this information is available online. If you're leaving your current place of employment, are you giving up a pension or will it be significantly reduced? If so, make the appropriate adjustments to your income on your LCP.

Another way a new profession can impact your retirement is your chances of continuing employment after you're past normal retirement age. Certain professions (like teaching) offer many part-time opportunities; others force you to retire at a certain age (commercial airline pilots, for example, can't fly after age 65).

If the LCP shows that it would be very difficult to switch careers, then you may want to consider making adjustments to your initial assumptions. Maybe instead of quitting your current job, you can continue employment there while starting the new business on the side or going to school on nights and weekends. You might consider delaying the start of the new venture until you can save more money to fund the business or to help meet expenses. The LCP will help you make these important decisions.

Determining How Your Asset Allocation May Affect Your Lifetime Cash-Flow Projection

One of the most important ways you can use your LCP to help you achieve your financial goals is to test how various asset allocations will perform for you. This section shows you how to do just that.

The idea is to try different asset allocations, run them through your LCP, and see which of them gets you the best result. By *best result,* we mean the "what if" scenario that has your assets outliving you with the highest probability.

How do you get to this best-case scenario? Start with getting a handle on the risk and return characteristics of various asset allocations. To keep the number of possible asset allocations manageable, we confine our review to those on the efficient frontier (see Chapters 2 and 6). In fact, for purposes of this discussion, we confine the candidate asset allocations (portfolios) to three, representing investment strategies we'll call conservative, moderate, and aggressive.

Now we need to determine the risk and return characteristics of each of these three candidate portfolios, and work those characteristics into the LCP. We start with return.

Estimating returns

You're surely familiar with the mantra "Past performance is no guarantee of future results," but the truth is that historical returns are often the starting point for projecting future returns.

For each asset that you're considering investing in, obtain the historical returns over as long a period of time as you can get your hands on. You want to make sure that the returns span a long enough time so that you can see how the asset behaved in both bull and bear markets. To get a head start, flip to Chapter 17 and look at the annual returns for ten common asset classes for the years 1988 through 2007.

You can calculate how a specific asset allocation would've performed in each year by taking the weighted average of the component assets' annual returns. For example, say you're interested in a very simple moderate portfolio that is invested 50 percent in corporate bonds and 50 percent in large-cap stocks. (See Chapters 3 and 9 for descriptions of corporate bonds and large-cap stocks.) In 2007, their respective returns were 4.6 percent and 5.5 percent. Your portfolio would've had the following return that year:

$$(0.5 \times 0.046) + (0.5 \times 0.055) = 0.023 + 0.0275 = 0.0505, \text{ or } 5.05 \text{ percent}$$

By doing the preceding calculation for each period of available data, you can find out how each candidate asset allocation would've performed in the past. You can do this for as many different periods as you want and compare the relative historic returns of your three candidate portfolios. From this history, you can then select a return that fairly represents the expected future return for each of the three portfolios.

Reckoning risk

Next, you need to derive a measure of risk for each of the three portfolios. One way to do that is to calculate the range of returns for each candidate portfolio for each of the previous years you can get your hands on. (You can again use Chapter 17 as your source for this information.) Another way is to calculate the standard deviation for each portfolio over the same period. (We cover how to calculate range and standard deviation in Chapter 2.)

Working risk and return into your Lifetime Cash-flow Projection

After you figure out your measures of risk and return for each of your three candidate portfolios (conservative, moderate, and aggressive), you need to work them into your LCP.

Working in your return is straightforward — for each portfolio, you can simply use the portfolio return you just derived to calculate the investment growth we talk about earlier in the "Investment returns" section (also see Table 7-6).

It's a good idea to add an element of conservatism whenever you make long-term projections, so you may want to use a return a percentage point or so less than the one you calculated. If you're going to be surprised, it's better for it to be a pleasant surprise than the alternative.

Reflecting the risk of each portfolio is a little more complicated. A very simple way to reflect risk is to use the high and low ends of the range of returns you derived earlier for each portfolio and run them through your LCP. This will give you a range of potential LCPs, but because this approach is so simple, the results can be unrealistic. However, if the worst of these LCPs shows your assets outliving you, then you can be quite confident that you'll be okay no matter what happens. For most investors, though, this worst-case scenario won't work out well for you — it'll likely show you outliving your assets. In that case, you might try different "what if" scenarios, using a different return for each year of your LCP, drawing from within the historical range of returns. This will give you some indication of the safety of your financial future, but it doesn't quantify it in any systematic way.

What you really need is a way to calculate something more useful and meaningful, namely the *probability* that your assets will outlive you. How do you do that? You can either try to go it alone (see the next paragraph) or hire a professional. (You can read all about how to hire a terrific financial advisor in Chapter 16.)

Professional investors use the risk (standard deviation, for example) and return measures for each portfolio to create probability distributions of returns for each asset class. They then simulate thousands of different possible LCPs based on those probability distributions. In other words, for each portfolio, they generate thousands of scenarios of what the portfolio's returns might be like in the future. This process is called Monte Carlo simulation. Its advantage is that instead of looking only at what has already happened, it also helps you project what might happen in the future. There are financial programs available that will allow you to do Monte Carlo simulations, based on expected returns and standard deviations that you input.

Whether you do it yourself or hire the work out, the result you're looking for after all this analysis is this: Which of the candidate portfolios (that is, which of the three — conservative, moderate, or aggressive, in our example) gives you the greatest probability of your assets outliving you in your LCP? That's the portfolio for you.

For some investors, that ideal portfolio may be the most conservative one. For others, it might be the most aggressive. Or it could be something in the middle. It all depends on your lifetime cash-flow needs. You just don't know for sure without going through the exercise.

For many investors, it makes sense, no matter where you start, to move to progressively more conservative investment strategies as you age. (We also address this issue in Chapter 8.) Using your LCP, you can plan how to make that transition — that is, what transition plan results in the highest probability of your assets outliving you? In doing this exercise, you make the leap from deciding on an asset allocation, to deciding on a long-term asset allocation *strategy*.

Are there any shortcuts to all this work, especially if you're willing to accept a portfolio that may not be ideal but that's good enough? Sure there are, and we cover some of them in Chapter 8.

Documenting Your Strategy: Drafting Your Investment Policy Statement

After you determine your investment strategy (conservative, aggressive, or something in between), document your decision in an *Investment Policy Statement* (IPS), which helps you (and your financial advisor, if you have one) stay focused and not veer off the path you want to take. Even if you don't hire a financial advisor, we recommend that you create your own IPS. It's simple to do so — just write down your selections for the following eight items:

- Your investment time horizon
- Your return objectives
- Your risk tolerance
- Your tax situation
- Your portfolio constraints

✔ Your special circumstances

✔ Your resulting investment strategy (for example, conservative, moderate, aggressive)

✔ Your asset allocation percentages

Each of these elements is introduced in Chapter 6 and revisited in Chapter 8. Your LCP will help you pinpoint what these should be for you.

Most financial advisors that you may hire to handle your investments would, in fact, require that you execute an IPS with them. The benefit of an IPS is that it clearly spells out all the key elements of your investment-strategy decision.

Chapter 8

Creating Your Allocation Plan

. . . .

. . . .

*I*n this chapter, we show you how to create your own asset allocation plan. This is where the magic happens!

We kick off the chapter with a quick review of the detailed discussion of asset classes and subclasses found in Chapter 3, so that you can be familiar with the types of assets you'll want to include in your allocation plan. Then we move on to establishing your own specific mix of these assets. In doing so, you'll want to keep your eye on the long term. Figuring out the right allocation percentages is a real science, and we show you how the pros do it. Then we talk about how you can do it on your own.

This chapter also contains some sample asset allocations, sharing some examples and guidelines across a range of investment strategies, from conservative to aggressive. And we walk you through a detailed portfolio, complete with asset classes and subclasses, that we develop for a fictional couple, John and Jane Doe.

Finally, even though your asset allocation decisions should be made for the long term, we discuss when you should do periodic reviews.

Before you dive into the important task of setting up your allocation plan, we suggest that you take a spin through Chapter 3 if you need to bone up on the various types of asset classes and subclasses that you can incorporate in your plan. It also wouldn't hurt to look at Chapter 4, especially if you don't feel quite up to speed on the concept of mixing assets together in the right proportions. Finally, check out Chapters 6 and 7 if you need to know more about developing your investment strategy.

Selecting Your Asset Classes

To create a balanced, effective portfolio, you need to take care to select the right asset classes. It's like preparing a gourmet meal: If you don't pick your ingredients wisely, your effort will be doomed from the get-go.

In Chapter 3, we discuss and describe the various asset classes and sub-classes. You can flip forward to Chapter 17 to see the historical performance of several of those assets.

Which of these asset classes are right for you? Well, it all depends on your specific situation. You can read all of those details in Chapter 3, but here's a quick rundown with some bits of universal advice:

- ✔ **Cash** is the least volatile asset class and can provide lots of stability to a portfolio. But it's also the asset class most likely to fall behind inflation over the long term. You should keep just enough cash in your portfolio to meet your short-term (less than 12-month) spending needs, and no more. Keep too much cash, and you run the very real risk of seeing your portfolio consistently lose purchasing power over time. Cash is for liquidity, not for investing.

- ✔ **Fixed-income investments** (bonds and bond funds) add stability to your portfolio. That's their role. Don't expect high returns from bonds. You can expect good solid bonds and bond funds to deliver returns several percentage points above inflation over the long term. But don't reach for higher returns by buying bonds of lower credit quality; it's not worth the gamble. High returns are the province of other asset classes.

- ✔ **Equities** (stocks and stock funds) belong in virtually every portfolio, regardless of how conservative they are. Don't be afraid to stock up on stocks! Over real-life investment horizons (several decades, for example), they're among the best inflation beaters you can find. Why? Over the long haul, the average annual total return for equities in general has exceeded 10 percent. And the short-term volatility in those returns becomes less and less material the longer you're invested.

- ✔ **Alternatives** such as real estate and commodities belong in most portfolios. Although they tend to be volatile, these asset classes paradoxically bring stability to the overall portfolio. Why? Because they tend to zig when the rest of your portfolio zags — meaning that when the rest of the portfolio underperforms, alternative investments will tend to outperform (see Chapter 13). And, over long investment horizons, alternatives also boast total returns that have averaged more than 10 percent per year.

- ✔ **Hedge funds, private equity, derivatives, and other exotic investments** aren't for you, unless you're a very seasoned, sophisticated investor. Think of them as you would exotic pets. It may be okay for a snake expert to keep a slithering python in the backyard, but for the average pet owner, it's a big mistake. Stay away from pythons — and from exotic investments.

When selecting your asset classes, stick to fixed income, equities, real estate, and commodities.

You may be thinking, how do you actually invest in each asset class? We discuss specific investments to buy in Chapter 9, but before you can do that, you first have to determine something pretty fundamental: how much of each asset class to buy. This is the next logical step in the systematic, scientific, top-down approach to investing.

As you work your way through this chapter (and this book), keep in mind that what you're allocating is your overall portfolio of invested assets. This portfolio may comprise several accounts (your IRA, your spouse's IRA, a joint investment account you share with your spouse, and so on). You want to allocate at the overall, aggregate portfolio level.

Don't be concerned just yet about how to allocate within each of your component accounts — we cover that in Chapter 10 (on asset location).

Establishing Your Asset Class Mix

Picking the asset classes you want in your portfolio is one thing. After you've made those decisions, though, you'll have to figure out exactly how much of each class you want to include. That's the focus of this section.

Establishing your asset mix means deciding on the specific allocation percentages to assign to every asset class and subclass in your portfolio. It's difficult to overestimate the importance of this decision — it's the essence of asset allocation. This decision will explain over 90 percent of your investment results. Although Chapter 4 discusses the concepts underlying the asset allocation process, this chapter delves more into the details of exactly how to put asset allocation into practice.

Go long! Finding percentages for the long haul

A key thing to keep in mind as you decide on your asset allocation is that you want these percentages to stand the test of time. This is a long-term, strategic decision you're making. These allocations are intended to last for several years.

Set your allocation percentages with the intent of keeping them intact for at least five years. Plan for less than five years only if your investment horizon (which we discuss in Chapter 6) is shorter.

If, instead, you intend to change your allocations more frequently — quarterly, or monthly, or in response to market news — stop! You're not striving to be an asset allocator — you're aiming to become a speculator. If that's the case, here's our advice: Don't do it! You need to make the decision to invest as most successful investors do — for the long term.

Now, it's not as though your asset allocation is untouchable for the rest of your life. In fact, later in this chapter, we discuss reasons to periodically review it. But, when you set it up, it should be done with the conviction that it'll remain intact for a good long time.

Picking the right percentages

How do you go about making the critical decision of determining your asset allocation percentages? Professional investors spend a lot of time, effort, and analytical firepower to get this right. As background for your own decision-making, let's look at how they go about it.

How the pros do it

Here's how professional investors figure out asset allocation percentages.

1. **They analyze the intrinsic characteristics of each of the asset classes and subclasses they're considering.**

   These characteristics include three important statistics:

   - The expected total return (see Chapter 2)

   - The volatility of those returns (see Chapter 2)

   - The correlations of the returns with those of the other assets under consideration (see Chapter 4)

   They also review the recent trends in these three statistics. Based on that intensive data review, they select values for each of these statistics that they believe will prevail over the foreseeable future.

2. **They plug the values into probability models.**

   These models project how the various asset classes will behave over the anticipated investment horizon. (We explain how you determine your investment horizon in Chapter 6.) There is no one universal model that everyone uses, and some are more sophisticated than others.

3. **Armed with the mathematical model, they estimate the risk/return behavior of entire portfolios.**

   They use this capability to test the behavior of thousands and thousands of different possible portfolios, each of which represents a different set of asset allocation percentages applied to the asset classes and subclasses they're considering. This procedure allows the experts to determine the efficient frontier of portfolios that outshine all the rest. (Turn to Chapter 2 for more on the efficient frontier, a key concept.) These portfolios are better than all the rest because you can't find other portfolios that have lower risk for the same level of return, or higher return for the same level of risk.

4. **From the efficient frontier, the pros choose a small set of portfolios that conform to different levels of a person's return objectives and risk tolerance.**

   We define these two parameters and their role in portfolio construction in Chapter 6. In particular, we specifically discuss how to use your risk tolerance to select the portfolio that's right for you, at the very end of Chapter 2 and again in Chapter 6.

The guiding principle of asset allocation (see Chapter 4) says that the characteristics and behavior of any single asset in isolation are inconsequential. The thing that really matters is the asset's effect on your portfolio in its entirety. The operative question should be: "Is my portfolio better, or worse, with this asset in it?"

How you can do it

The preceding section tells you how the pros pick the right percentages — they focus on the overall portfolio, and how each asset choice fits into the big picture. Now the question is, how can you?

We're not saying that you should do everything the pros do. We're just trying to be candid with you about the level of effort the pros put in to achieve optimal results. But can you get by with less-than-optimal results, and still do much better than most investors? Sure!

One way to do it yourself is to decide on a rough asset allocation, perhaps based on the samples we provide in the next section, and then to stick to it. How do you decide which is right for you? You could use the risk-tolerance worksheet we provide in Chapter 6. You could do the full exercise we outline in Chapter 7. Even if the allocation you decide on isn't perfectly right, just the act of sticking to it — rebalancing ruthlessly, as described in Chapters 5 and 11 — will put you ahead of most other investors. It may not be optimal, but it's a lot better than investing with no plan at all.

Another way to set your asset-allocation percentages is to temporarily hire yourself your own pro (an expert asset allocator like a Certified Financial Analyst) for the job. Some financial advisors would be happy — for a fee, of course — to review your situation and suggest an asset allocation that suits your needs. Use the information in Chapter 16 to identify and qualify the appropriate professionals whose help you may seek. After you've selected an advisor, share your relevant background information with her so she can help you establish your allocation. After that, you may (or may not) keep for yourself the job of sticking to it.

Regardless of whether you seek outside assistance, you may consider the sample asset allocations we discuss in the next section as a starting point, or at least a starting point for discussion.

Whichever approach you end up taking, make sure you consider your tax situation, honor any portfolio constraints you may have established, and reflect any special considerations you may have noted — all of which we discuss in Chapter 6.

Looking at Some Sample Allocation Percentages

As we stress throughout this book, the right asset allocation for you is specific to your unique situation. So why would we offer sample asset allocation percentages in this section, if they're not going to be tailored to your specific needs?

Because finding the optimal set of allocation percentages takes significant time, effort, data, expertise, analysis, and expense that you may not have available (see the "How the pros do it" section for a description of all the effort the pros put in to get it right). If you don't have loads of time and you aren't comfortable running those complicated analyses on your own, then starting with a reasonable (albeit less than optimal and not perfectly customized) set of percentages is significantly better than shooting from the hip with your investments.

We offer the sample allocation percentages below in that spirit — they're not a complete substitute for the thorough process the pros go through, but they're a reasonably good place to start. If you decide to use one of these sample allocations, we strongly recommend that you confirm the asset allocation you decide upon with a qualified professional (see Chapter 16).

We present several sample sets of percentages in the following sections, reflecting a range of investment strategies, from aggressive to conservative. In each of these sets, you'll notice that the asset classes stay the same — only the mix varies.

Aggressive: Higher equity percentage

Let's assume that you're an aggressive investor. You may

- ✔ Be young
- ✔ Have a promising career with solid earning potential

✔ Be in excellent health, and longevity runs in your family

✔ Be living well within your means

✔ Have a high personal tolerance for risk

If many of those traits describe you, then you have a long investment horizon, and your portfolio should have a healthy allocation of equities to reflect your ability and willingness to invest aggressively. And you recognize that, by investing aggressively over a long period, you have the potential to achieve much higher than average returns. This strategy may afford you the option of retiring early if you so desire down the road. A reasonable asset allocation for you would be one within the ranges outlined in Table 8-1.

Table 8-1   A Sample Asset Allocation for Aggressive Investors

Major Asset Class	*Sample Asset Allocation*
Fixed income	0%–15%
Equities	60%–80%
Alternatives	15%–35%

Source: Brinton Eaton Wealth Advisors.

As you can see in this table, the majority of your portfolio — anywhere from 60 percent to 80 percent — goes to equities. Alternatives are next, with 15 percent to 35 percent of the total. And the balance (a small percentage — as much as 15 percent, but as little as 0) is allocated to fixed-income assets.

Conservative: Higher fixed-income percentage

What if you're a classic conservative investor? If so, you may

✔ Be well into your retirement years

✔ Have no pension or other sources of income beyond Social Security

✔ Be in failing health

✔ Need to rely on income from your investment portfolio to pay your ongoing living expenses

✔ Have no stomach for risk

If some of those characteristics describe you, then you have a relatively short investment horizon. Your emphasis is on capital preservation, and you're comfortable sacrificing some return potential in order to lessen your risk of loss of principal. To conform to your desired conservatism, your portfolio should be lighter in equities and heavier in fixed-income investments than the aggressive investor's. Table 8-2 shows pertinent sample allocation ranges for you in this case.

Table 8-2	A Sample Asset Allocation for Conservative Investors
Major Asset Class	*Sample Asset Allocation*
Fixed income	35%–55%
Equities	20%–40%
Alternatives	15%–35%

Source: Brinton Eaton Wealth Advisors.

In this sample, fixed income gets the largest allocation: 35 percent to 55 percent of your portfolio. Next come equities, with 20 percent to 40 percent of the total. And the balance goes to alternatives. Note that the 15 percent to 35 percent allocated to alternatives is the same allocation range in the aggressive portfolio (see the preceding section). The real change when you move from aggressive to conservative is the shift from equities to fixed income.

Note that, even in conservative portfolios, equities deserve a substantial allocation. This is consistent with the point we make earlier, in the "Selecting Your Asset Classes" section: Equities belong in virtually every portfolio, regardless how conservative. That can't be said of fixed-income investments. Why? Because, over the long term, it's hard to beat equities in protecting your portfolio against inflation.

Moderate: Right in the middle

Perhaps you aren't quite an aggressive investor, but you're also not exactly conservative. You're somewhere in between. You'd like a decent return, but you don't want to take any above-average risks. You consider yourself a moderate investor, and the allocation ranges shown in Table 8-3 would be appropriate for you.

Table 8-3	A Sample Asset Allocation for Moderate Investors
Major Asset Class	*Sample Asset Allocation*
Fixed income	15%–35%
Equities	40%–60%
Alternatives	15%–35%

Source: Brinton Eaton Wealth Advisors.

Controversial asset classes

In the three sample allocations we feature in the last few pages, the range of percentages attributed to the alternative asset class (comprising real estate and commodities) doesn't vary. Even though these investments may be considered controversial by some and are, by definition, nontraditional, they aren't simply for the more aggressive investors. Their role is to stabilize the portfolio (see Chapters 3 and 13). Given that role, they belong in virtually every portfolio. (The modeling that the wealth advisory firm Brinton Eaton did at the time of this writing indicated that the allocation percentages for the alternative asset class should be roughly the same across all investment strategies. Other firms may have different opinions.)

Having said that, we should add that alternatives may not be for everyone. You may not be ready for them. As we point out in Chapter 13, you're ready to add alternatives when:

✔ You determine you have the stomach to tolerate their unusual behavior.

✔ You know you'll have the time to ride herd on them and pay attention.

If you are indeed ready for alternatives, though, they can be a real boon for your portfolio.

Here we allocate 40 percent to 60 percent of your portfolio to equities, and anywhere from 15 percent to 35 percent to both fixed income and alternatives.

What about Subclasses?

The sample allocations we present earlier in this chapter are at the asset class level. But you can't stop there. You'll also want to establish your asset allocation percentages at the subclass level.

Figuring out your fixed-income subclass allocation

Within the fixed-income class, consider laddering your investments. (Read more about laddering in Chapter 3.) Specifically, split your fixed-income allocation roughly equally among short-, intermediate-, and long-term bonds and/or bond funds. The only time you shouldn't ladder in this fashion is if the yield curve (also covered in Chapter 3) is flat or inverted at the time you set up your portfolio. In this case, you'd be better off tilting your allocation toward the short maturities, at least until the yield curve reverts to its more normal, upward-sloping shape.

Establishing your equity subclass allocation

Within the equity class, you'll also want to pay attention to several subclasses. With respect to size, make sure you allocate some of your equity exposure to small- and mid-cap equities. The amount to allocate should be anywhere from about 10 percent (for conservative portfolios) to about 20 percent (for aggressive portfolios) of your overall allocation to equities. For example, let's say you're a moderate investor and, consistent with Table 8-3, you allocate 50 percent of your portfolio to equities. Allocate 5 percent (0.50 × 0.10 = 0.05, or 5 percent) to 10 percent (0.50 × 0.20 = 0.10, or 10 percent) of your overall portfolio to small- and mid-cap equities, and the balance of the 50 percent to large-cap.

With respect to the industry sector within the large-cap equity subclass, you don't need to be in all ten of the subclasses we identify in Chapter 3. In fact, in our opinion, at the time of this writing you should concentrate on only these five:

- ✔ Healthcare
- ✔ Consumer staples
- ✔ Financials
- ✔ Energy
- ✔ Industrials (to a lesser extent than the other four)

Others may arrive at different conclusions about which sectors to leave in, or leave out, at different times.

Why leave out the other sectors? Different reasons. For example, the technology sector exhibits too much volatility for the return that that sector delivers, and, unlike the volatility you get with commodities, the volatility of the technology sector isn't the good kind of volatility, because its trends will tend to stay in step with the majority of your portfolio. Technology makes your portfolio riskier with no real added return over the long term. For another example, you can omit the materials sector, because you get a purer play with your direct investment in commodities, as part of the alternative asset class. Utilities and communications can be omitted, because they don't have impressive long-term returns. The consumer discretionary sector is cyclical, and may be attractive depending on where we are in the business cycle.

As far as equity style goes, to the extent you pay attention to this at all (we believe style is less important than size and sector, because there's nothing fundamental about a stock that makes it "growth" or "value" — these are merely terms that describe how a stock is priced on any given day), you should have a mix of value and growth stocks (and/or stock funds), with a bigger allocation to value, if you must take sides. Or, you can simply ignore style and focus on stock funds whose style is identified as "blend" or "core."

To wrap up the equity class, you should make sure you have a healthy dose of international exposure — particularly emerging markets — in your equity allocation. Shoot for anywhere from 15 percent or so (for conservative portfolios) to 33 percent to 50 percent (for aggressive portfolios) of your overall allocation to equities. We discuss this in more detail in the next section.

Arming your portfolio with the appropriate alternative subclasses

Within the alternative class, you should sub-allocate to real estate and commodities. (Both of these subclasses are discussed at length in Chapter 13.) All but the most conservative investors should consider placing 25 percent to 33 percent of their alternative allocation in real estate, with the rest going to commodities; for conservative portfolios, put a little less toward real estate.

As with equities, it would be prudent to have some international exposure in your real-estate allocation (although you may want to hold off on investing in that condo development in Antarctica). Consider putting anywhere from 33 percent to 50 percent (less if you're very conservative) of your real-estate allocation to international real estate.

When allocating to commodities, stick with the broad-basket index funds; don't dabble in individual commodities.

How you fill these subclasses with actual securities depends on the size of your overall portfolio. (We explain these choices in Chapter 9.) For example, if your portfolio is small, the process can be very simple: Fill your portfolio entirely with index funds (mutual funds and/or exchange-traded funds, as discussed in Chapters 3 and 9). In fact, if your portfolio is small enough (less than $250,000, say) you may be better off not allocating down to the subclass level at all, at least for some subclasses, such as the equity sector subclass. For smaller portfolios, the extra time, attention, and cost involved in monitoring tiny subclass allocations and rebalancing when necessary (in tinier amounts still) may offset the potential added benefit.

An Asset Allocation Case Study

To give you a concrete idea of how you can put all these asset allocation tips to good use, we present the following look at how John and Jane Doe construct their portfolio.

John and Jane have impeccable taste in top-notch books, so they pull *Asset Allocation For Dummies* from their shelves, read through Chapters 6 and 7, and determine their investment horizon, return objectives, risk tolerances, portfolio constraints, and special considerations. As a result, they decide that they're moderate/aggressive investors. (They're somewhere between moderate and aggressive.)

John and Jane put 15 percent of their portfolio in fixed-income investments, 60 percent in equities, and 25 percent in alternatives. Then they follow the guidelines in the previous section and allocate to subclasses, as shown in Table 8-4.

Table 8-4	**John and Jane Doe's Asset Allocation**	
Asset Class	*Subclass*	*Allocation*
Fixed income	Short term	5%
	Intermediate term	5%
	Long term	5%
	Fixed-income subtotal	**15%**
Equities	Small cap*	4%
	Mid cap*	6%
	Large cap*	50%
	Industrials	*5%*
	Consumer staples	*10%*
	Energy	*8%*
	Financials	*12%*
	Healthcare	*15%*
	Equities subtotal	**60%**
Alternatives	Real estate*	8%
	Commodities	17%
	Alternatives subtotal	25%

* Including international.

As you can see, the Does decide to fully ladder their fixed-income investments by spreading the 15 percent allocation in equal 5 percent allotments to short-, intermediate-, and long-term maturities. At the time they put their portfolio together, the yield curve slopes upward (normal), meaning that longer-term bonds have higher yields than shorter-term bonds.

Based on our guidelines, John and Jane decide to allocate 17 percent of their 60 percent allocation to equities (10 percent of their portfolio) into small- and mid-cap equities. Specifically, they put 4 percent in small-cap and 6 percent in mid-cap. The balance of the equity allocation goes to large-cap, spread over five industry sectors: The largest portion, 15 percent of the portfolio, goes to the healthcare sector; the smallest, 5 percent, to industrials. They decide on specific industry sectors after talking with their financial advisor, who provides a detailed analysis of the general economy. Smart move, Does!

With respect to their 25 percent allocation to alternatives, the Does put about a third of that, or 8 percent, to real estate, and the remaining 17 percent to commodities.

When the Does make their allocation to equities and real estate, they make sure that they earmark roughly 25 percent of that subtotal (or 17 percent of their total portfolio) to international investments in those areas.

Keep in mind that the Does' decisions are unique to them, not to you! Their choices may not be right for you, so don't simply jump in with the asset allocation they chose. Jumping into somebody else's allocation without doing your own homework is just plain irresponsible.

Setting Up a Schedule to Revisit Your Plan

Earlier in this chapter, we say that you want your asset allocation percentages to stand the test of time, that you should pick them with the conviction that they'll remain intact for the long haul. But how long is the long haul?

Certainly not for your lifetime. As you age, your investment horizon naturally shortens with your life expectancy. If you're typical, you also move from the asset-accumulation phase to the asset-distribution phase of your lifecycle, meaning that instead of adding to your invested assets from other income sources, such as wages, you may be drawing down your investment accounts to pay for your living expenses that your retirement income doesn't cover.

For these reasons, and others, many investors shift to a more conservative investment strategy over time, regardless of where they may start. This kind of change is very gradual.

So you do need to revisit your asset allocation, but when? Different occasions may trigger an accelerated review of your allocation (see Chapter 15). These include certain life events like a marriage or divorce, the loss of a loved one, a sudden change in health, or an unexpected child or grandchild. These are times that should cause you to step back and take a fresh look at the parameters you set when you established your current asset allocation. In Chapter 6, we identify those parameters: your investment horizon, return objectives, risk tolerance, portfolio constraints, tax situation, and special considerations. A change in any one of them, for whatever reason, is cause for a review of your asset allocation.

There are other triggering events that are less personal but can still warrant revisiting your allocation. For example, we mention earlier in this chapter that if the yield curve is flat or inverted when you set up your portfolio then it isn't a good idea to ladder your fixed-income investments so much; instead, tilt toward the short-term end of the maturity spectrum. Well, when the yield curve reverts to its normal shape, you should consider trading in some of your short-term bonds and bond funds for their intermediate- and long-term equivalents. (The reverse isn't true, by the way. If you started out with a well-laddered fixed-income portfolio, set up in a normal yield curve environment, you shouldn't unwind it and go short term if the yield curve later flattens or inverts. You're already where you want to be.)

Now, some of the triggering events we describe in this section may escape your notice. We're not going to shame you if you don't track the shape of the yield curve on a regular basis, for example. And some other events, such as the unanticipated arrival of a grandchild, may be so emotionally overwhelming and distracting that your asset allocation is far from the top of your priority list. Who can focus on bonds when there's babysitting to do? Because of these reasons, it's prudent to set a regular schedule to review your situation.

An annual review cycle is probably too often for most investors, but there's nothing wrong with setting the same time each year to do a review, especially knowing that in most years you'll do fine to leave well enough alone.

Make it easy to remember the date you set for an annual revisit of your asset allocation by tying it to something that'll be an automatic reminder, like your birthday.

For many investors, a quadrennial review (every four years) is plenty frequent. Again, tie the date to something you'll notice, like the presidential election, or the start of the Summer Olympic Games.

Whatever your schedule, remember that a review of your asset allocation is just that — a review. You shouldn't feel compelled to change your allocation — which is, after all, intended to be long-term and strategic — every time you review it.

Part III
Building and Maintaining Your Portfolio

The 5th Wave   By Rich Tennant

"We've got several hollow tree options to consider. How many nuts were you looking to invest at this time?"

In this part . . .

You need to know how to fill your asset allocation baskets with various types of investments, and this part shows you how. We also let you know how to exploit the tax characteristics of the different baskets by matching the right investments with the right baskets. Then we get into the details of portfolio rebalancing that'll give you extra return — if you do it faithfully. Finally, so that you know how well you're doing, we explain how to measure results by comparing your portfolio's performance with appropriate external benchmarks.

Chapter 9

Buying Securities

● ●

In This Chapter

▶ Deciding what securities to buy

▶ Knowing how to buy securities

▶ Understanding fees and expenses

● ●

*T*his chapter focuses on helping you roll up your sleeves and start build-ing your portfolio. The information we present here will get you ready to take the next step in asset allocation's systematic, top-down approach to investing.

As we mention throughout this book, asset allocation is mostly about determining the right baskets of investments to have in your portfolio. In this chapter, we show you how to fill those baskets with specific individual investments. You want nitty gritty? Look no further.

We start by guiding you through the different investments on offer — the standard stocks, bonds, and mutual funds, along with real estate investment trusts (REITs) and exchange-traded funds (ETFs). We also cover annuities, options, structured notes, and exchange-traded notes (ETNs).

After describing what's out there, we take a look at the best ways for you to buy the various investments. Should you buy directly (on your own) or through a broker? Is leveraging a good choice for you? How about shorting? You can find the answers to these questions and more in this chapter's second section.

Finally, we examine the fees and expenses involved in buying securities. Some of the fees are clear, but some can be tough to dig out if you don't know where to look.

How do you tell the good investment choices from the bad, or determine how much they really cost? If you have a small portfolio, should you even bother with individual securities? In this chapter, we give you the hands-on informa-tion you need to address these and other questions, so that you can build a solid portfolio.

Deciding What to Buy

There are different ways to own investments. You can own specific individual securities, which include the traditional choices of stocks and bonds, and the alternative choice of invested real estate, which is available through REITs.

You can also own shares in a diversified fund, which, in turn, invests in the types of securities that interest you. Fund choices are quite varied, and in this section we cover all the prominent options in enough detail so that you'll be able to make wise decisions about which funds are right for you and your portfolio.

Beyond individual securities and funds, there's still a range of investment choices you may want to consider, depending on your risk tolerance and investing experience. For example, annuities are for risk-averse investors who might prefer the guarantee of a steady return and don't mind the greater costs involved. More-exotic choices (options, structured notes) are for seasoned investors who are comfortable with more sophisticated products. We cover all those possibilities (and more!) later in this section.

Individual securities

Any discussion of individual securities starts with stocks and bonds. Stocks represent ownership in a company and come in two types: common and preferred. Bonds represent a loan you make to a company, municipality, or government agency. In addition to stocks and bonds, we also discuss real estate (through REITs) in this section.

Stocks

Stocks, or equities, which we introduce in Chapter 3, are the foundation of most portfolios because, over long periods of time, they tend to outperform most other types of investments. Broad stock-market indexes have, on average over many years, posted an annual total return of around 10 percent to 12 percent (depending on which years you average over).

Few investors understand equities as well as they should. For example, when the dot-com bubble was growing larger and larger in the late 1990s, many investors came to believe that stocks could pave the way to instant wealth, with little risk. Unfortunately, they found out otherwise when the bubble burst and took many portfolios with it. It just goes to show that potentially higher returns come with potentially higher risk. Stocks can be risky, but their potential for appealing returns justifies that risk.

You hear about stocks everyday, but what exactly is a stock? Plain and simple, a *stock* is ownership in a company. When a public company needs to raise capital to finance operations, it sells stock or *shares* (also known as *equity*) in the company to investors, who then become stockholders (or shareholders). As part owner of the company, you are entitled to a proportionate share of assets and earnings (no matter how small your share is).

Before buying, make sure you understand the differences between *common* and *preferred* stock, which are the two main types available:

- ✔ **Common stock:** When you buy common stock, your shares entitle you to a claim on assets and earnings. Earnings are paid out as dividends and can increase, which is a good thing. But you can also lose everything you invested — ouch! Ownership entitles you to vote at annual shareholder meetings, but that doesn't mean you have a say in how the company is run on a day-to-day basis. If the company goes bankrupt, you wait in line (figuratively speaking), after banks, bondholders, preferred stockholders, and all other creditors, are paid. You'd think all that standing in line would hurt your feet, but in this case it hurts your wallet. Double ouch.

- ✔ **Preferred stock:** When you buy preferred stock, you earn a fixed dividend and are paid ahead of common shareholders if the company goes out of business. And you usually don't have voting rights. For these reasons, preferred stocks behave more like bonds and less like common stocks, and they have lower expected returns than common stocks as a consequence.

With both common and preferred stock, your exposure to loss is confined to your investment in the stock; your other personal assets aren't at stake.

When you hear about stocks, including in this book, you're most likely hearing about common stocks.

So how do you pick a good stock? The answer to that question can fill several large books. We recommend *Investing For Dummies,* 5th Edition, by Eric Tyson, MBA (Wiley). But here's some quick advice: If you're considering buying shares of a company's stock, study the company's financial statements. You want to look for the following:

- ✔ A healthy income statement, with steadily increasing revenue and earnings

- ✔ A clean balance sheet with the ratio of the company's debt to its equity at or below the average for that company's industry

- ✔ A *price-to-earnings* (P/E) *ratio* (the share price divided by the company's latest, or projected, annual earnings) that is low relative to other firms in the same industry

If you don't have information like industry average debt-to-equity ratios or P/E ratios handy, ask your broker or financial advisor for them. (If you don't have a broker or advisor, see Chapter 16 for info on how to find a good one.)

You can check on a company's financial health by looking at the 10-K report, which is available from the Securities and Exchange Commission (SEC) Web site at `www.sec.gov/edgar.shtml`. This address takes you to EDGAR (the Electronic Data Gathering Analysis and Retrieval System), which offers more information, including balance sheets and income statements.

Holding individual stocks exposes you to considerable risk. Companies can, and do, go out of business; if they do, you lose your entire investment in them. So, it's not a good idea to have more than 5 percent of your portfolio in any one stock. For most small investors (those with portfolios of $250,000 or less), getting equity exposure through stock funds (discussed later in this chapter) is better.

Bonds

A *bond* is a loan to an issuer, which can be a government, municipality, or corporation. In return for lending the issuer your money, you periodically receive a fixed interest payment, with the promise that you'll get all your principal paid back by a certain date, known as a *maturity date.* Governments, municipalities, and corporations issue bonds when they need to raise capital.

Bonds are less volatile than stocks (meaning, they tend to hold their value more reliably), but their returns are lower over the long term. Bonds should be part of most portfolios for stability, as we explain in Chapter 3.

When you buy a *callable bond,* the issuer can ask for the bond back and pay you back early. You may lose interest and get stuck with a lower interest rate on a replacement bond.

Bonds can sound rock solid, but don't be fooled: Bonds aren't guaranteed. Some issuers will *default* (fail to pay you back all the interest — or even the principal that you lent them). Also, bond returns are generally lower than other asset classes.

Here's an overview of the risk involved in various types of bonds, from lowest to highest risk:

✔ **U.S. government bonds,** also called *Treasuries,* are the safest of bonds, because, by law, they must be paid ahead of the federal government's other obligations. Their income is free of state and local income taxes (but not federal income tax). Maturities range from T-bills (under 1 year) to notes (2 to 10 years), and bonds (10 to 30 years).

✔ **Municipal (or *muni*) bonds** are issued by states, cities, and towns, and when you buy them, your money goes to work for public projects, like the building of a road or a school. Munis are triple tax protected — free of local, state, and federal taxes — which makes them ideal for investors in high tax brackets. As a result, they generally have yields less than those on taxable bonds of similar risk. Default risk is lowest for *general obligation* (GO) bonds (backed by the state or municipality) and greater for *revenue bonds* (backed by the agency, commission, or authority created by law that builds a public project).

✔ **Corporate bonds** are generally the most lucrative of bonds — but also the riskiest. You've got only the issuer's (in this case, a company's) promise that they'll pay you back. Terms range from 1 year to 15 or more years. Corporate bonds usually offer higher yields than municipal bonds, but interest payments are taxable at all levels. Some corporate bonds feature a *convertible feature* (meaning that the bond can be converted into shares of common stock) or a *call provision* (the issuer can pay you back before the bond reaches maturity).

Use *zero-coupon bonds* if you're saving to achieve a long-term goal, such as college tuition, and you don't need a regular payout. These bonds, which are issued at a fraction of *par value* (face value), don't pay regular interest, but they increase regularly in value as the bond approaches maturity.

As with individual stocks, individual bonds expose you to risk that you can diversify away with bond funds (which we cover later in this chapter). Bond funds are also a better alternative than individual bonds for investors with less than $500,000 to invest, because you don't want to hold individual bonds of small amounts — they'll be harder to sell if you want to.

For more information on government bonds, go to www.treasurydirect. gov. For munis, consult www.municipalbonds.com. For agency bonds, check out www.freddiemac.com, www.fanniemae.com, and www.fhl banks.com. You can also check out www.bondbuyer.com, www.bondtalk. com, and *Bond Investing For Dummies,* by Russell Wild, MBA (Wiley).

Real estate investment trusts

REITs are companies that buy, own, and manage real estate properties on behalf of their investors. Most REITs invest in commercial properties such as apartment complexes, office buildings, warehouses, storage facilities, and retail malls. The other type of REITs are mortgage REITs, which offer debt financing for commercial as well as residential properties through investments in mortgages and *mortgage-backed securities* (MBSs). MBSs invest in an underlying pool of mortgages that are packaged and paid out as income to investors. If you decide to invest in real estate, we urge you to invest in a REIT that is tied to property — mortgage-backed securities are just too risky to consider (see Chapter 3).

Many investors find REITs very attractive. First, REITs distribute at least 90 percent of their taxable income annually to shareholders in the form of dividends. Second, over the long term, REITs have delivered equity-like (appealing) returns of over 10 percent per year.

On the downside, year-to-year returns for REITs can be quite volatile. If you'd like to see more information on returns for REITs, flip to Chapter 17 to see the return history of an all-REIT index, the FTSE NAREIT All REIT Index. Adding REITs to a well-diversified portfolio can increase return and reduce risk, because these assets have little correlation with the S&P 500. (Read all about correlation, a critical concept, in Chapters 3 and 4.)

For more information on investing in REITs, check out the Web site of the industry's trade association at `www.nareit.com`. Then search for a company's 10-K report in the EDGAR database on the SEC's Web site, as we explain in the "Stocks" section, earlier in this chapter.

Funds

Funds are privately or publicly owned investment companies that pool together money from many investors to buy financial securities. There are three basic types of funds:

- ✔ **Closed-end funds:** A closed-end fund sells a fixed number of shares at one time through an *initial public offering* (IPO), which occurs when a private company puts up its stock for purchase by the public for the first time.

- ✔ **Open-end funds:** An open-end fund sells shares on a continuous basis. Mutual funds are the most conventional type of open-end fund.

- ✔ **Unit investment trusts (UITs):** UITs create a specific, fixed number of securities, known as *units,* in a one-time public offering, which are redeemable at a set date in the future. UITs are unmanaged in that, after the securities are selected, they're held until the UIT ends.

Among these types, we focus here on open-end mutual funds because they're by far the most popular type.

A relatively new alternative to the mutual fund that has become very popular is the ETF. In this section, we describe ETFs and mutual funds. We also discuss passively managed index funds and actively managed funds (and a third type, the target or life-cycle fund, that doesn't fit neatly into either category). These choices are best understood as falling in two dimensions, as we show in Figure 9-1.

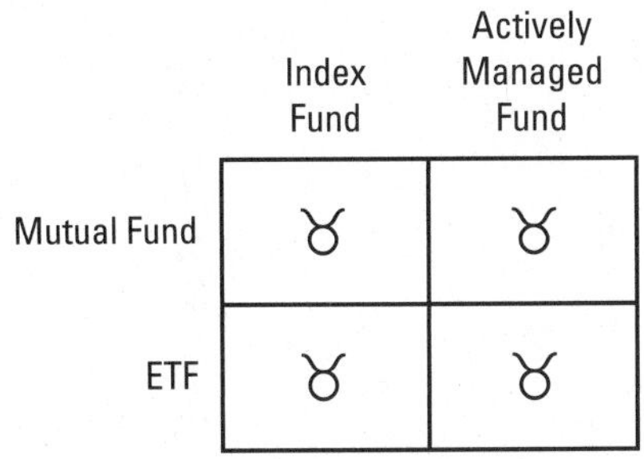

Figure 9-1:
Fund
choices.

Source: Brinton Eaton Wealth Advisors.

As the figure illustrates, a mutual fund can be either a passively managed index fund or an actively managed fund. Likewise for ETFs, although the actively managed variety is newer. To help you understand all this, we explain the details of mutual funds and ETFs, and then fill you in on the difference between an index fund and an actively managed fund.

Mutual funds versus exchange-traded funds

Mutual funds and ETFs have a few things in common, but there are also a number of key differences you need to be aware of.

Note: Mutual funds can be either passively managed index funds or actively managed funds — and so can ETFs.

Mutual funds

Mutual funds are the most common type of pooled investment. Funds "slice and dice" many types of investments — stocks, bonds, money-market instruments, and other securities — to offer diversified portfolios that would be difficult for investors to create with a small amount of capital on their own.

Here are some advantages of owning mutual funds:

- ✔ **Scalability:** Mutual funds allow investors to buy fractional shares. That means that you can invest all your money, even if the amount is small. For example, say a share is worth $30 and you're making a monthly investment of $115. With some other types of investments, you'd only be able to buy three shares for $90, and $25 would remain uninvested. With a mutual fund, the full $115 would be invested every month.

- ✔ **Affordability:** With some funds, you may only need as little as $50 or $100 to make an initial purchase.

- ✔ **Diversification:** By having the securities within the fund spread across a wide range of companies and industry sectors, you can lower your risk.

✔ **Liquidity:** You can redeem your shares at their current *net asset value* (NAV; the total market value of all the underlying securities in the fund divided by the number of fund shares outstanding), less any fees and charges, on any given day.

✔ **Professional management:** Professional managers do all the work, from researching individual companies to monitoring the performance of the securities the funds purchase.

✔ **Free income and dividend reinvestment:** When a stock pays a dividend or a bond pays income, you can either take it in cash or reinvest it. A mutual fund gives you the option to have all your dividends and income automatically reinvested at no extra charge. This is a significant benefit because, over the long term, these reinvested dividends and income payments make up a large portion of your total return.

And here are some disadvantages of owning mutual funds:

✔ **Expenses:** You'll pay sales charges, annual fees, and other expenses, even if your investment does poorly. (We cover expenses in the "Understanding Fees and Expenses" section, later in this chapter.)

✔ **Taxes:** Mutual funds typically generate capital-gains distributions that are taxable to you. You have no control over the amount or timing of these distributions.

✔ **Pricing:** You can't check a fund's price (its NAV) throughout the trading day as you can with a security. Mutual funds calculate their NAV once every business day, after the exchanges close.

There are various categories of mutual funds, corresponding to the various asset classes we describe in Chapter 3. For example, there are money-market mutual funds (representing cash equivalents), bond funds (representing fixed income), stock funds (representing equity), and real estate and commodity funds (representing the alternative asset class). (See Chapters 3 and 8 for more information on the risk and return characteristics of the various asset classes.) Because mutual funds correspond to those asset classes, the risk and return characteristics are the same as for the asset classes they represent. There are also mutual funds that invest in several asset classes at once. They can range from a conservative allocation (for example 80 percent bonds, 20 percent stocks) to an aggressive allocation (such as 20 percent bonds, 80 percent stocks).

When deciding among mutual funds, don't simply rely on each fund's historical performance. Focus more on such items as expenses and tracking error, which we discuss later in this chapter. As all investment prospectuses state, "Past performance is no guarantee of future results." However, past performance can help you get a handle on a fund's relative volatility over time. A fund with a lot of volatility may, for example, make it a bad choice for you if you really need your money to meet a short-term goal.

Mutual funds carry a number of costs that can lower your investment returns. We detail fees and expenses in the "Understanding Fees and Expenses" section, later in this chapter.

Exchange-traded funds

Exchange-traded funds are funds (typically modified UITs, which we describe earlier in this section) registered with the SEC. Each ETF represents a basket of underlying securities, like a mutual fund. But unlike a mutual fund, ETF shares can be bought or sold on a stock exchange throughout the trading day. This hybrid investment has become very popular with investors since it was introduced in the United States in 1993. The total ETF market is still smaller than the mutual-fund market, but at their pace of growth, ETFs may eventually overtake mutual funds in market share.

Their numbers continue to grow as originators (such as Barclays Bank and State Street Bank) create ETFs (with brand names such as iShares and SPDRs, respectively) that mimic the behavior of a wider and wider range of equity and bond indexes, including industry-sector indexes. In general, ETFs are *passively managed index funds* or *passively managed sector funds;* that is, they're usually designed to replicate the holdings, and the performance and yield, of specific underlying indexes, such as the S&P 500 Stock Index, the Russell 2000 Index (an index of small-cap stocks), the Barclays U.S. Aggregate Bond Index, and so on. Recently, actively managed, non-index-based ETFs have become available. (Read on for more information on the differences between index funds and actively managed funds.)

What benefits do ETFs offer that mutual funds don't? Consider the following:

- ✔ **Intraday marketability:** ETF shares, because they're actively traded on stock exchanges throughout the day, are quite marketable. Conventional mutual-fund shares are bought and sold only at end-of-day prices based on a share's NAV. ETF shares are bought and sold at intraday market prices, which means that they can trade at greater or less than their NAV at any point during the trading day, but these discrepancies are very small for the more popular ETFs.

- ✔ **Tax efficiency:** Conventional mutual funds must distribute the capital gains from their underlying portfolio of securities directly to fund share-holders, who are tax liable in the year of distribution. The legal design of ETFs allows certain capital gains on the underlying securities to not be distributed to investors at all, but instead serve to increase the share price of the ETF itself. Investors realize such capital gains only when they sell their ETF shares and, thus, can beneficially time the tax impact or defer it indefinitely.

- ✔ **Trading flexibility:** ETF shares can be bought on margin and sold short. These features, which we discuss in the "Buying on margin or shorting a stock: Not for the faint of heart" sidebar, in this chapter, are attractive to professional investors and sophisticated traders. We don't recommend that inexperienced investors toy with these features, but they do contribute to making ETFs so popular.

✓ **Low costs:** The fees and expenses embedded in ETFs are generally lower than in corresponding mutual funds. You can read all about these types of costs later in this chapter.

We're big fans of ETFs, and we believe that their popularity is well deserved. Their variety is broad enough that, if you wanted, you could construct a well-diversified portfolio across a wide range of asset classes using nothing but ETFs.

Although ETFs have evolved to cover more and more specific areas of the market, there are still some markets that are very expensive to invest in directly and match a specific index. A relatively new investment vehicle designed to address this difficulty is the exchange-traded note (ETN), a structured note where the issuer promises investors that they'll get the return on a specific index, less expenses. (ETNs and structured notes are both discussed in the "Other investments" section, later in this chapter.)

Buying on margin or shorting a stock: Not for the faint of heart

To enhance returns, some professionals use two investing techniques — leveraging and shorting. Both of these approaches are for seasoned investors, and they come with significant risk (as you'll pick up from our four uses of the word *warning* in bold). Here's the lowdown:

Some investors try to increase their returns by using *leverage*. Using leverage means buying securities using borrowed money from your broker. This is also called *buying on margin*.

If you buy a stock on margin, and it goes up in value, you can amplify your return. For example, if you buy a stock at $30 and it goes to $36, you get a return of 20 percent. But if, instead, you bought the stock on margin, putting up $10 and borrowing the remaining $20 from your broker, and the stock goes to $36, your return is much higher. Why? Let's say you sell the stock when

it hits $36, pay off the $20 loan, and pocket the $16 difference. That $16 represents a 60 percent return on your original $10 investment. You've "leveraged up" your return threefold.

Buying on margin works great in a bull market, when stock prices are rising — you can haul in a lot of money. But it can be devastating in a bear market, when stock prices are falling, because you stand to lose your shirt. If the stock goes down enough, the broker issues a *margin call,* meaning that you have to put up more money. In that case, you'll have to put up cash or sell some of the stock. If the stock price goes down far enough fast enough, this can end up in a very expensive spiral for you.

Warning: If you're going to use leverage, be sure that you fully understand your broker's margin rate and how the broker calculates its margin calls. You want to be very careful and fully understand margin before you try this technique. Make sure to consider what your maximum loss may be.

Using leverage in a bear market can force you to continuously sell stock into a declining market. There are examples of company executives who had a substantial portion of their personal wealth invested in company stock on margin. In an extended declining market, as stock prices fell precipitously, they were forced to sell most of their stock to cover the margin calls! Bottom line: Understand the risks of margin before proceeding.

Warning: Leveraging is for the seasoned investor, who has the credit to qualify for a margin account plus enough cash in his brokerage account to cover a potential loss.

Shorting is the practice of selling a stock you don't own. You might be thinking, "Huh?" Don't worry, you're not alone. Shorting can be a confusing concept.

The way it works is that you borrow the stock from your broker (for a small fee) and sell it to someone else. You do this if you expect the share price to go down. If and when it does, you then buy the stock on the open market for the lower price, and give the stock back to your broker. You've made a tidy profit, and you never technically owned the stock.

Here's an example: Suppose a stock is currently trading at $50. You borrow a share from your broker, and sell it to someone for $50. If the stock later trades at $40, you buy it at that price and give it to your broker, settling the loan. Your profit is $10.

Warning: This strategy allows investors to make money in a declining (bear) market. But you must really understand the risks of shorting. If instead of going down, the share price goes up, you can lose big — *very* big. If you buy a share of stock at $10 the old-fashioned way, you know that your maximum loss is $10 (if the stock goes to zero). However, if you short-sell a stock at $10 you have a potential unlimited loss! There's no limit as to how high a stock can go, so your potential loss can be much, much more than $10.

To qualify for shorting, you must be approved by your broker and meet minimum collateral requirements, usually $2,000 or 50 percent of the shorted stock's market value.

Warning: Like leveraging, shorting isn't for the squeamish or the uninitiated. If you're thinking about shorting, make sure you're extremely familiar with the ins and outs, and be certain you understand the consequences and implications.

Index funds versus actively managed funds

In this section, we tackle passively managed index funds versus actively managed funds.

Note: Index funds can be either mutual funds or ETFs — and so can actively managed funds.

Index funds

An *index fund* is a fund that follows a *passive* investing strategy, meaning that the fund managers attempt to match an identified benchmark index, not outperform it. (If benchmark indexes don't sound familiar, turn to Chapter 12 for more information.)

To get an index fund to work most effectively for you, you want to look for two things: a low expense ratio and a low tracking error.

- ✔ The **expense ratio** of a fund tells you how big a bite the fund's management fees and other ongoing expenses take out of your return. If the expense ratio is 1 percent, for example, and the annual return of its underlying holdings is 8 percent, you get to enjoy only a 7 percent return from the fund. Because an index fund tries only to passively match an index, not beat it, it doesn't need to hire an expensive portfolio manager to run the fund, so its expense ratio should be low.

  For funds that track broad indexes like the S&P 500 Stock Index, look for expense ratios of no more than 0.25 percent. For funds that track narrower indexes, such as the Dow Jones U.S. Health Care Index, seek out expense ratios of 0.5 percent or less.

- ✔ The **tracking error** of a fund measures how well the fund's return matches that of the index it claims to follow. A low tracking error means that the fund tracks its index relatively well. That's what you want from an index fund, after all — you want it to faithfully follow the index it's supposed to follow. You don't want it to stray off its path.

Where do you find information on a fund's expense ratio and tracking error? In the fund's prospectus and on its Web site. The expense ratio is usually shown explicitly, but the tracking error isn't always as easy to find. Some funds instead show the correlation of the fund with its index (see Chapter 4 for more on correlation). They may also show a comparison of the annualized returns of the fund as well as its index. Over time, you can expect the annualized return of the fund to gradually diverge from its index due to fees. If correlation is high (over 95 percent) and the annualized returns are close to each other, then the fund's tracking error is low.

Finding the right index fund for your portfolio is a two-step process:

1. **Decide what index you want to have represented in your portfolio.**

   For information on those decisions, which are the basis of your asset allocation plan, check out Chapters 4 and 8. For example, do you want an index that follows domestic large-cap stocks? Then you want the S&P 500 Stock Index.

2. **Find an investment that inexpensively and faithfully tracks the index you have in mind.**

   Here you need to do some scouting around. Lots of companies offer index funds, but you'll do well to start with Vanguard (`www.vanguard.com`), Fidelity (`www.fidelity.com`), and T. Rowe Price (`www.troweprice.com`) for mutual funds, and Barclays iShares (`www.ishares.com`), State Street's SPDRs (`www.statestreetspdrs.com`), and Vanguard (again) for ETFs. There are several others as well.

Actively managed funds

In most actively managed funds, the fund manager makes specific investments with the goal of outperforming a benchmark index. Managers do this by trying to identify investments that they believe will do better than the index. That's their objective anyway.

The truth is, most of them aren't very good at this on a sustained basis; actively managed funds rarely outperform their benchmark index over long periods of time. According to the Standard & Poor's Index Versus Active (SPIVA) quarterly scorecards, which rates index funds against actively managed funds, only a handful of actively managed mutual funds beat S&P's various index benchmarks. In fact, when all expenses are taken into account, they rather consistently underperform! A big reason is that actively managed funds are usually considerably more expensive than index funds; the expense ratio for an actively managed funds can be a full percentage point or more than its corresponding index fund. That's a tough difference to make up, even if the active manager was incredibly lucky, or good, over an extended period of time. The longer the period, the less likely this will happen, of course.

So why bother at all with actively managed funds? Well, for the most part, you shouldn't. But consider the type of fund we describe in the next section, which is something of a hybrid between an active and a passive fund.

Target and life-cycle funds

These funds fall into a third category of fund — they don't fit neatly into the active or passive categories. They're like a one-stop shop for investors. You choose one of these funds based on your retirement year or your current age. They determine your current asset allocation and then automatically adjust the allocation to be more conservative as you age. Often, these funds invest in other funds, which may be either passive or active.

Most fund companies offer target and life-cycle funds. They're particularly popular in 401(k) plans because they simplify your choices by automating your asset allocation according to when you want to retire — useful for investors who don't want to do their own asset allocation, rebalancing, and security selection. For those investors, these are the only types of actively managed funds that we recommend.

Other investments

In this section, we look at a few other investment choices, starting with annuities, which may be good choices for risk-averse investors who don't mind the extra expense for the peace of mind these investments buy. But if you're looking for a pure investment, think twice. Annuities are really an insurance product.

On the opposite end of the scale, we also look at options, which can work well as a risk-management tool for the expert investor.

Then there are structured notes. These deliver a guaranteed rate of return, like a bond, and match a predetermined index, but they're really for wealthy investors who have the money (several million dollars) to purchase them.

For the masses, there are ETNs, which are sliced and diced structured notes and, thus, much more affordable.

Annuities

Annuities are products, usually offered by insurance companies, that provide payments to you for a guaranteed period in return for a premium that you pay the annuity provider. The payments to you can be for a fixed amount (in the case of a *fixed annuity*) or for an amount that varies according to an underlying investment (in the case of a *variable annuity*). The guaranteed payment period can be for a specified number of years *(annuity certain)* or for the rest of your life *(life annuity)*. Those payments can begin immediately after you purchase the annuity *(immediate annuity),* or the first payment can be deferred for a specified period of time *(deferred annuity)*. And that's just the tip of the iceberg — there are many other varieties of annuities.

If you're considering an annuity as an investment, you need to be aware of a few things:

- ✔ **Terminal value:** In general, after you pay your premium, you don't get it back at the end of the term as you do with the par value of a bond, for example. Whether the term is fixed (as in an annuity certain) or for the rest of your life (as in a life annuity), when the term ends, so do the payments you (or your heirs) receive. There are variations on this (such as survivorship options), but one fundamental difference between annuities and regular investments is that annuities are designed to eventually exhaust your original investment; regular investments are not (or at least they're not designed to!).

- ✔ **Expenses:** The expenses embedded in an annuity are usually quite a bit higher than what you find in investments such as mutual funds and ETFs.

- ✔ **Taxes:** Income and capital gains aren't taxed to you as they occur. When you start receiving payments from your annuity, only part of the payment is considered taxable in the year you receive it. (The rest is considered return of your principal.) This is a nice tax-deferral feature that annuities provide and regular investments don't.

Some investors feel that the tax-deferral benefit offsets the higher expenses. This potential offsetting benefit disappears, though, if you buy an annuity inside your IRA or other tax-advantaged account, because you get the tax deferral anyway with those accounts.

Think twice about buying an annuity inside an IRA. You may be paying for a tax benefit that you can't use.

Make sure you truly understand all the costs involved in an annuity, how long you're locked in for, and what the guarantees (if any) really mean. Annuities' many bells and whistles generally make them more expensive than traditional investments.

On balance, our advice regarding annuities is this: If you're looking for an investment, buy an investment. An annuity is really an insurance product, and as investments go, it's an expensive choice.

That said, fixed annuities can be a good choice for investors who have a very low tolerance for risk and need a steady stream of guaranteed income. The exercise we go through in Chapter 7 can help you identify whether such an annuity would be a good choice for you.

Options

An option is a type of *derivative* — its value is derived from an underlying asset, such as a stock. The party that buys the option is called the *option holder;* the party that sells the option is called the *option writer.* An investor can be either a holder or a writer.

Options come in two types: *calls* and *puts.* A call option gives its holder the right, but not the obligation, to buy a certain security at an agreed-upon price (the *strike price*) for a specified period of time (the *term*). The strike price and the term are determined when the option is purchased. A put option gives its holder the right to sell a security at the strike price for a certain term. Just as with call options, the strike price and term for a put option are determined when the option is purchased.

A call option increases in value as the market price of the underlying security increases beyond the strike price of the option. So, if you own a call option on a stock with a strike price of $45 and the market price on that stock jumps to $90, that means you have the option to buy the stock for $45 when it is currently trading for $90 (sweet!). You're looking at a pretty substantial increase in value. The difference between the security's current market price and the option's strike price is called the *in-the-money value* (ITM value) of the option. For example, if the market price of stock XYZ is $50, and the strike price of the call option is $45, the ITM value of the option is $5 ($50 – $45). If the current market price is lower than the strike price, the ITM value of the call option is zero.

For a put option, the ITM value is positive if the security's current market price is below the strike price; it's zero otherwise. For example, if the strike price of the put was $45 and the stock price has plunged to $25, then you have the option of selling a stock for $45 that is currently worth $25. Your ITM value is $20 ($45 – $25).

Whether you're talking about a call option or a put option, there's no such thing as a negative ITM value. That's because an option is just that — an option, not an obligation, to buy or sell.

Sometimes options are used as risk-management tools. For example, if an investor is overly concentrated in a certain stock that she can't easily sell for some time (maybe it's her company's stock and she's prohibited from trading it for a time, given her position with the company), then she can buy a put to protect her downside risk.

How does that work? Let's say the company stock is currently worth $80 a share and our investor is concerned about her loss if the stock goes below $75 before she can sell it. She can buy a put option with a strike price of $75. If the stock price goes down, to $70, say, then her put option will still allow her to realize, in effect, $75 per share, which would be quite a relief. Why? In that case, the put option would be worth $5 (its ITM value), partially offsetting her $10 loss on the stock itself, and thereby limiting her net loss to $5. If, instead, it goes down to $60, then the put is worth $15, partially offsetting her $20 loss on the stock, limiting her net loss to, again, $5. No matter what happens to the price of the stock during the term of the option, her net loss is limited to $5 per share.

If you have a position in a security that you'd like to protect in this manner, and you're not familiar with trading options, then by all means hire a professional to help you. (See Chapter 16 for advice on finding a suitable professional.)

Other times, though, options are used as purely speculative investments. For example, an investor can buy or sell call or put options on securities she doesn't own. This practice is called *holding* or *writing naked options.* But the naked truth is that this practice is extremely dangerous. Leave options to the expert investors.

Structured notes

A *structured note,* in its most popular form, is essentially a bond that's structured so that it gives the *holder* (buyer) of the note a return that matches some predetermined index but may limit losses if the index declines. The index may be the S&P 500 Stock Index. In that case, the return on the bond follows a pattern that matches the return on the S&P 500 Stock Index, but it provides some minimum guaranteed return. In another variation, the note could provide the holder a return that's two or three times the return on the index. Or it could provide the "inverse" return — it goes up when the S&P 500 Stock Index goes down, and vice versa. Or, it could provide a return tied to the five best performing currencies out of a basket of ten world currencies. There's virtually no end to the possibilities — they're limited only by the imagination of the issuer and the holder.

Structured-note issuers will only be interested in buyers with the resources to purchase several million dollars' worth of notes, so they're out of reach for most investors. But there's a way for most any investor to participate — through exchange-traded notes, which we explain next.

Exchange-traded notes

An ETN is basically a structured note for the masses. Essentially, a master structured note is sliced, diced, and parceled out to smaller investors. As a smaller investor, what you lose in control over design of the note you gain in access to the product. In other words, you may not get a whole heck of a lot of say in how the note is set up, but at least you can get a piece of it for less than a million dollars.

Some popular structured notes are designed to track indexes such as broad baskets of commodities. You can think of ETNs as an alternative to ETFs. One advantage of an ETN over an ETF is that the ETN has no tracking error: The issuer promises that the ETN will exactly follow its target index (less the ETN's expense ratio). It's the issuer's responsibility to make that happen, and if it doesn't, it's the issuer's problem. A disadvantage of ETNs is that you're subject to the creditworthiness of the issuer to make good on the promise. Also, ETNs are generally more expensive (by 0.25 percent or so) than ETFs that track the same index.

Figuring Out How to Buy Securities

When you've got a firm grasp on the various securities available to you, you need to figure out the best way for you to go about buying those securities. Should you go through a broker or go it alone? We help you answer that key question in this section.

Buying through a broker

To buy most securities you need a broker, who acts as a middleman and handles the transaction for you. There are three different types of brokers:

- **Full-service brokers:** A full-service broker is a firm like Goldman Sachs or Smith Barney. They'll give you advice on what stocks to buy based on their own internal research. For this, you'll pay a higher commission. Firms like these will also help you with your financial planning, again all for a higher fee than the discount brokers charge. If you're looking for a one-on-one relationship and more specific advice on what to buy and sell, a full-service firm may be right for you.

✔ **Premium discount brokers:** A premium discount broker could be a firm like Fidelity or Charles Schwab. The commission rates are somewhere between the discount brokers and the full-service brokers. They have branch offices where you can go to get investment guidance, and they make investment research from third parties available to their customers.

✔ **Discount brokers:** A discount broker (E*TRADE is one example) allows you to make all your own investment decisions. These brokers have the lowest commission rates of the three broker types, but they may not offer you investment advice.

Currently, brokers aren't required to put your interests ahead of their own. It's perfectly legal for them to advise you to buy stocks for the sole purpose of making money for themselves. The stock can't be terribly inappropriate for you, but it may also not be the best choice. Before accepting investment or any other financial advice, make sure to ask if the advisor is legally obligated to adhere to a *fiduciary standard.* Being a fiduciary means they have to place your interests first, above their own and those of their company. If they're not a fiduciary, caveat emptor! (We talk more about this in Chapter 16.)

When choosing a broker type, in addition to considering the commission rates and level of control you'll maintain, you also need to think about how you want to do your business. Over the phone? In person? Online? Each firm has different rates and schedules for different services.

Buying on your own

Don't want to deal with brokers? No problem. You can buy securities directly from a company and skip the cost of a commission.

Some companies allow investors to buy stock directly from them through *direct purchase programs* (DPPs), also called *direct investment programs* (DIPs). You can buy shares all at once, or invest monthly, quarterly, or annually. This option is a good one for small investors. Minimum investments are low to start a DPP, and although more companies are charging service fees, these fees are lower than a typical brokerage commission.

If you're interested in a particular company, you can find more information on its Web site or through its investor relations department, or you can go to the Web site of the stock exchange that the company trades on. Services that specialize in helping small investors buy in small quantities are The Moneypaper (`www.directinvesting.com`) and ShareBuilder (`www.sharebuilder.com`); these services charge a fee.

After you become a shareholder, you then qualify for a *dividend reinvestment plan* (DRP), for companies that provide such a plan. DRPs allow you to automatically use your dividend to buy more shares of a company's stock, without paying a commission. If a company doesn't have a DPP, have a broker buy a share for you; after that, you qualify for the company's DRP.

A DRP can be a very appealing option. By *dollar cost averaging* — investing a small constant amount of money regularly — you buy less of an investment when it goes up in price and more when it comes down. It's also the only way, other than through a mutual fund, for you to have your dividends automatically reinvested at no additional cost. Because reinvested dividends make up a large portion of your total return over the long term, this is a significant benefit.

A disadvantage to doing it on your own is getting the best *execution* (the price at which you buy or sell your security). Let's say you're watching the stock of a particular company, you suddenly see a good price, and you want to buy it immediately to capitalize on the price. Well, it's unlikely that you'll be able to do that if you're buying through a DPP or DIP. By using a broker, you could log on to the Internet and buy the stock right away or call your broker and place the trade over the phone.

Another disadvantage to going it alone is that *reregistering* your stock (changing the title of ownership) is more difficult and complicated. Let's say you own stock in 20 different companies, each through a DPP or DIP. Upon your death, your beneficiary would have to go to each of the 20 different companies with a death certificate and all the other necessary paperwork to reregister the stock to his name. This is awfully time-consuming, and it's a paperwork nightmare! Holding all 20 of these stocks with one broker makes this process much easier.

Understanding Fees and Expenses

Fees, fees, fees. It seems like every time you turn around, another one catches you by surprise. Forewarned is forearmed, as the saying goes, so take the time in this section to become familiar with all the fees and expenses involved in owning an investment.

Mutual-fund fees

As with any sale, as a shareholder you may expect to pay for fees called *shareholder fees,* which are triggered whenever you buy or sell shares. But you may not be prepared for *operating expenses,* which a fund charges indirectly and passes along to you; these fees pay for all sorts of costs, and it's extremely helpful if you understand them. We take a closer look at both types of fees in this section.

It's important to know how much you pay in fees or commissions for an investment and services. They lower the total return your investment earns.

Shareholder fees

There are several fees you may pay, depending on the fund's policies:

- ✔ When you buy an investment, the fund may charge an initial **front-end load** (a sales charge), which typically goes to the brokers who sell you shares. The fee, which is based on the amount invested and deducted from each investment made into the fund, generally decreases as the amount of your investment increases.

- ✔ On the other end, when you go to redeem shares, you may pay a deferred or **back-end load** (also known as a *back-end sales charge*). Generally, the longer shares are held, the more this charge declines. This fee typically goes to the broker who sells you your shares. Some good news: This fee may decrease to zero if you hold your shares long enough.

- ✔ Some funds charge you a **purchase fee** to buy shares. This fee sounds like, but isn't, a front-end load that goes to the broker. Instead, a purchase fee goes to the fund.

- ✔ Okay, so if there's an additional fee on the front end, what can you expect to pay to some funds when you sell? A **redemption fee.** This fee goes to the fund, not the broker.

- ✔ Incredibly, some funds charge you an **exchange fee** (also known as a *transfer fee*), for moving your money from one fund into another after you're invested with them. If you don't want to be nickeled and dimed to death after the fact, before you invest, make sure you know if your fund will impose this charge.

- ✔ The fund may charge you an **account fee,** just to maintain your account, especially if your account's value falls below a certain dollar amount.

Front-end loads reduce the amount of your investment. If you invest $10,000 in a fund with a 5 percent front-end load, you pay $500 in a sales load and only $9,500 is invested in the fund. According to the organization that regulates the securities industry, the Financial Industry Regulatory Authority (FINRA), firms can't charge a front-end load of more than 8.5 percent.

Not all funds charge all these fees. Before buying a mutual fund, make sure you understand the fees involved. When it comes to fees, there are generally three types of funds you can purchase:

- ✔ **Load:** Load funds typically charge either an upfront fee (usually a percentage), a back-end fee (meaning when you sell it), or both.

- ✔ **No load:** No-load funds typically have no upfront fee, but both a short-term trading fee and a back-end fee may be charged when you sell. However, the short-term trading fee is eliminated after a matter of days (typically 30 to 90 days), while the back-end fee can take many years to phase out.

   Our advice: Stick with no-load funds that don't levy front-end *or* back-end charges.

- ✔ **Transaction fee:** Transaction-fee funds usually charge a flat dollar amount upfront to buy and also may have a short-term trading fee if you sell too soon.

All three types of funds have annual ongoing costs called *expense ratios,* which are intended to cover ongoing operating expenses of the fund (see the next section).

Annual operating expenses

Annual operating expenses are the fees a fund may charge you for the cost of doing business on your behalf. There are several categories of annual operating expenses:

- ✔ **Management fees:** Fund management taps these fees from a fund's assets to compensate them for their work and to cover any administrative fees that aren't absorbed in the "other expenses" category.

- ✔ **12b-1 fees:** These fees pay for the costs of marketing and distribution — the marketing and selling of fund shares — which includes compensating brokers and others who sell fund shares; the cost of advertising, which includes the printing and mailing of prospectuses to new investors and sales literature; and fees paid to those who respond to investor inquiries and provide investors with information about their investments.

- ✔ **Other expenses:** These expenses may include custodial expenses, legal and accounting expenses, transfer agent expenses, and other adminis-trative expenses.

- ✔ **Total annual fund operating expenses:** This fee is the percentage of operating expenses that it takes the fund to operate.

You'll find a fund's expense ratio on the fee table in the fund's prospectus. The expense ratio can help you make comparisons among funds.

Some funds call themselves *no load,* meaning that the fund doesn't charge a sales *load* (fee). But that gives investor the impression that there aren't any fees at all. In reality, a no-load fund may charge several fees — purchase fees, redemption fees, exchange fees, account fees, and operating expenses, for example. Carefully review the fee tables of any funds you're considering, including no-load funds; even small differences in fees can add up over time.

Brokerage fees

Whether you buy (and sell) funds or individual securities, the broker you use to execute your trades deserves a fee or commission for this service. In some cases, that fee is a percentage of the dollar amount transacted; in other cases, the fee might be a flat charge per trade; or it can be a combination, particularly for large trades.

Most fee-only advisors work for an independent firm under this model (meaning, they aren't associated with any of the brokerage firms on Wall Street). Typically, they'll have your assets kept at a brokerage firm acting as *custodian* (a firm that is legally responsible for holding and safekeeping your investments — Fidelity and Schwab are the largest players in this business). The commissions to buy and sell securities on your behalf are also kept by the custodian.

Some financial advisors who work for brokerage firms or banks are compensated by commissions only. Here, the commissions may get built into the total price of the product you're buying (meaning that you won't see what that commission really is). There could be commissions to buy and sell individual securities (again, this will vary depending on what type of broker you use and if you place trades over the phone or online). Also, you want to ask about whether there are any account maintenance fees, inactivity fees, or any other service fees associated with your account. If you're buying mutual funds or insurance products, typically fees are built into the price of the product. Last, be aware that there usually is a fee to close your account as well.

Under a *wrap-fee* approach, a brokerage house manages an investor's portfolio for an all-inclusive fee, charged on a quarterly or annual basis, that covers all administrative, commission, and management expenses. This means that you can trade an unlimited number of times for one set annual fee (usually some percentage of the value of the portfolio) that covers all costs and fees.

Think about what type of investor you are before committing to a wrap fee. Will you make enough trades to justify the annual percentage fee? If you're more of a buy-and-hold investor, this arrangement may not be the best for you. Usually, there is a minimum account size of at least $50,000 to qualify for this service.

The most important lesson in all this is for you as the investor or customer to fully understand how your advisor and broker are compensated. That way you know how they're paid and if they're a good fit for your needs. Define how you want the relationship to work and which services you require, and match that up with the right way to pay for those services. (Turn to Chapter 16 for more on financial advisors and their compensation structure.)

Chapter 10

Knowing Where to Put Your Assets: Asset Location

. . . .

In This Chapter

▶ Thinking about your accounts in a holistic way

▶ Understanding the tax characteristics of your investments

▶ Trying out an asset location exercise

. . . .

*W*ouldn't it be a shame if you did all the right things to get your assets properly allocated, and bought all the right securities, only to see your hard-earned gains go to the tax man? Wouldn't it be even worse if it happened unnecessarily? That's what can happen (and does happen to most investors) if you don't consider another step — asset location.

Asset allocation is all about decreasing risk and increasing return. Asset location is all about saving taxes.

Put simply, *asset location* is putting tax-inefficient (highly taxable) investments in tax-deferred accounts, and putting tax-efficient investments in taxable accounts. If asset allocation (Chapter 8) is picking the right (and right-size) baskets, and security selection (Chapter 9) is picking the right eggs to put in those baskets, then asset location is deciding on the right shelves on which to store those baskets.

That's what we cover in this chapter. First, we take a look at all the different types of accounts you may have, and what their tax characteristics are. Then we examine the tax efficiency of your different asset classes and investments. Finally, we give you hands-on information about how best to stock those shelves. We follow the progress of John and Jane Doe, a fictional couple whom we introduce in Chapter 8, as they tackle the issue.

Viewing Your Accounts Holistically

If you're like most investors, you have more than one investment account. If you're married, you may have six or more accounts within your family. Some investors have as many as a dozen accounts.

It may sound like an awful lot, but consider the following, which are just a few of the common types of investment accounts:

- ✔ A tax-deferred 401(k) account with your employer
- ✔ A tax-deferred individual retirement account (IRA)
- ✔ A tax-deferred health savings account (HSA)
- ✔ At least one taxable account, such as a brokerage account

If you're married, both you and your spouse could have each of those kinds of accounts. You may also have one or more joint accounts. It's really not that difficult for a family to end up with double-digit investment accounts.

But it doesn't end there. You could have even more investment accounts. You and your spouse may also own a Roth IRA (which you fund with post-tax dollars that then grow for you on a tax-free basis). And this doesn't even count any custodial or educational accounts you may have set up for your children and grandchildren (though you shouldn't include these accounts in your asset allocation, because they actually don't belong to you).

If you have several investment accounts in your family, you may be tempted to do the same asset allocation separately within each account. But it's better to apply your asset allocation holistically — in the aggregate across all your separate accounts. If you shoot for identical allocation within each account, then you can waste the tax advantages that some of your accounts provide you. And it's the overall allocation — across all your accounts taken together — that matters.

So, how should you allocate within each account? We answer that question throughout this chapter, but the following example offers a big clue: Say you have invested assets that total $500,000, spread across two accounts — an IRA and a taxable brokerage account — with $250,000 in each account. Assume that your chosen asset allocation calls for 10 percent of your portfolio to be allocated to real estate investment trusts (REITs). You could, of course, allocate 10 percent of each account to REITs, buying $25,000 of REITs in your IRA and another $25,000 in your taxable account. But is that the best way to do it? REITs are notoriously tax-inefficient, throwing off lots of ordinary income that gets taxed at your highest tax rate. (By the way, that doesn't make REITs a bad investment, just a highly taxable one.) So, why not buy all $50,000 of your REITs in your IRA? There, the income is tax deferred. Save your taxable account for assets that are more tax-friendly. After all, the thing that matters is that you have $50,000 (10 percent of $500,000) of REITs *somewhere* in your portfolio.

Sounds simple, right? In this case, it's pretty straightforward, but your decisions get a little more complicated when you have more than two accounts in your portfolio and you consider all the other asset classes you want to allocate to.

In this section, we take a closer look at your accounts to help you make the right asset location decisions, so you can be sure to place your assets where they'll do you (and your portfolio) the most good.

Considering taxable accounts

Most non-retirement investment accounts are taxable — the *investment income* (dividends and interest) and *realized capital gains* (profit that results from the sale of an investment) generated within such accounts are subject to income tax in the year in which they occur. Here are three types of non-retirement investment accounts:

✔ **Individual:** An individual account is registered to a single owner. Sometimes, this type of account can be a transfer on death (TOD) account, if the owner has designated a beneficiary in the event of her death.

✔ **Joint:** Joint accounts are typically owned by a husband and wife together. When it comes to investment accounts, the two most common types of joint ownership are

- **Joint tenants with right of survivorship (JTWROS):** In this type of account, accountholders have an equal right to the account's assets and survivorship rights. The survivor inherits the total value of the other member's share of account assets upon the death of that other member. A JTWROS account can have more than two owners.

- **Tenants in common (TIC):** In this type of account, accountholders have an equal right to assets on a pro rata basis. For example, if there are two accountholders, each share is worth 50 percent. They also have survivorship rights, meaning that they can retain their share of assets should the other accountholder die. But the survivor doesn't automatically acquire the rights (and assets) of the deceased accountholder unless that transfer is spelled out in a will.

Some states, such as California, consider all marital assets to be neither TIC nor JTWROS, but instead community property (CP) assets. CP titling doesn't give you the flexibility you'd like, so if you live in a CP state, you should consider establishing lifetime trusts, individually for you and your spouse.

✔ **Trusts:** Trusts may exist for any number of purposes. A *trust* is a property interest held by one person for the benefit of another. There are many types of trusts: Some are lifetime trusts that you set up while you're alive; others you receive as part of an estate. For example, a minor could have her assets held in a trust until she's old enough to receive income and/or principal. Investors living in CP states sometimes use lifetime trusts to effectively convert account ownership from CP to TIC (see Chapter 6).

There's an alphabet soup of trusts: CRUTs, CRATs, CLTs, GRATs, and QPRTs, to name just a few. Our purpose in this chapter isn't to define and describe each and every type of trust out there, but simply to point out that whatever trusts you may own, consider them part of your overall investment portfolio.

If you want more information on trusts, check out *Estate Planning For Dummies,* by N. Brian Caverly, Esq., and Jordan S. Simon (Wiley), and *Wills & Trusts Kit For Dummies,* by Aaron Larson (Wiley).

Taxable accounts — of all the types we describe in this section — are good locations for tax-efficient investments (see "Considering the tax efficiency [or inefficiency] of your investments," later in this chapter).

Getting the most out of joint ownership rules

Married couples should pay special attention to the rules that govern the ways in which assets are handled if one spouse passes away. It's certainly not the happiest topic for discussion but one that you should definitely bring up with your spouse so that you can be sure to get the most out of your assets if something awful were to happen.

For example, you and your spouse should equalize your assets as much as you can while you're still living. That way, if anything should happen to one of you, the surviving spouse will have more flexibility in sheltering assets from estate

taxes. This is particularly important if you have a spouse who isn't a U.S. citizen.

For similar reasons, you should also review the assets you own jointly with your spouse — both invested assets and use assets (such as your house) — to determine if they're titled as JTWROS or TIC. TIC titling gives the surviving spouse more flexibility upon the death of the other spouse to shelter the deceased spouse's share of the joint asset from estate tax.

Consult with a qualified financial planning and/or estate planning expert (see Chapter 16) before you consider an estate-planning strategy.

Understanding tax-deferred and tax-free accounts

With tax-deferred accounts, such as 401(k) plans, IRAs, and annuities, you don't pay tax until you begin withdrawals. With a tax-free account, such as a Roth IRA, you don't get a tax break on the front end, but you pay no tax when you begin withdrawals. With tax-free HSAs, you pay no tax at all, but with one stipulation: You have to use the money for the designated purposes of funding allowable health costs.

- **401(k)s:** A 401(k) plan is a qualified retirement plan offered by an employer that allows employees to defer a certain amount of their compensation from taxation. The income that goes into the 401(k) isn't taxed when it's received. The subsequent investment income and gains on the account are also tax deferred.

  But it's not all good news: When funds are removed from the 401(k), they're taxed at ordinary income-tax rates. There are IRS rules and regulations on the eligible amounts that can be contributed to the 401(k) each year, as well as on the timing and amount of withdrawals.

  When you no longer work for the employer, you can *roll over* the 401(k) balance into your IRA with no tax consequences. This rollover is often advantageous because investment choices within a 401(k) are limited to a menu provided by the employer, whereas, in an IRA, the choices are virtually limitless.

  There are also advantages to rolling over a 401(k) when it comes to fees. Fees within a 401(k) are often high and hard to identify, so an identical investment within your IRA may give you a higher net return.

- **Traditional IRAs:** Traditional IRAs are very similar to 401(k)s in terms of tax deferral, contribution limits, and withdrawal requirements. But you can set them up on your own — you don't go through an employer.

- **Roth IRAs:** Roth IRAs are similar to traditional IRAs, but instead of contributing pre-tax income, you contribute post-tax income to a Roth. Investment income and growth are tax deferred (just like in a traditional IRA), but withdrawals are totally tax-free (unlike in a traditional IRA) as long as the money doesn't come out too soon. The IRS makes the rules on the contribution limits and withdrawal timing. For more information, contact the IRS at 800-829-1040 or go to www.irs.gov.

- **HSAs:** HSAs allow you to put pre-tax income into an account that grows tax-deferred. If withdrawals are used to pay qualified healthcare expenses, those withdrawals are tax-free. HSAs need to be established in conjunction with a so-called high-deductible health plan (HDHP) and are typically available through your employer.

✔ **Annuities:** *Annuities* typically provide you with regular payments after you put up a premium to an issuer, usually an insurance company. Payments can be fixed, or they can vary (depending on the investment performance of the securities in the policy). In either case, payments can be for a specified number of years (in what's called an *annuity certain*) or for the rest of your life (in a *life annuity*).

There are enough annuity varieties to fill a book (check out *Annuities For Dummies,* by Kerry Pechter [Wiley], for more information), but here's one important annuity fact that you need to know: Annuities have an attractive tax-deferral feature that means income and capital gains aren't taxed as they occur. You pay tax only when you start receiving payments, and only on a portion of each payment. (The rest is considered return of your principal.)

Of all the types of accounts we describe in this section, tax-advantaged accounts (whether tax-deferred or tax-free) are good locations for tax-inefficient investments (see "Considering the tax efficiency [or inefficiency] of your investments," later in this chapter).

Understanding the Tax Characteristics of Your Investments

As we say throughout this book, it's not what you earn with your investments, but what you keep, that really matters. Taxes can have a major impact on the success of your investments, and you need to pay special attention to tax considerations when figuring out your asset location. Some investments are more tax-efficient, or tax friendly, than others. But how is that characteristic determined? It's simple: The tax efficiency of an investment is determined by the degree to which its income is taxed.

You can see the tax efficiency (or inefficiency) of several common types of investments in Table 10-1. Some, such as growth stocks and municipal bonds, are more tax-efficient than others, such as REITs and commodity funds. In this section, we provide you with plenty of details on the relative tax efficiency of each of these investments and more. Then we reveal how you should go about placing the investments in the most appropriate accounts to ensure excellent asset location. Read on to get a feel for how taxes can affect your investments, and how you should locate your assets based on those tax characteristics.

Table 10-1	**Tax Characteristics of Some Common Investments**	
	Tax Efficient	*Tax Inefficient*
Asset classes	Growth stocks, international stocks, municipal bonds	REITs, taxable bonds, commodity funds
Fund types	Exchange-traded funds (ETFs), exchange-traded notes (ETNs)	Mutual funds

Source: Brinton Eaton Wealth Advisors.

You might ask yourself, "Why would I want to include tax-inefficient investments in my portfolio at all?" Keep in mind that there are many other features of those investments — for example, high returns, attractive levels of volatility, and the potential for negative correlation with other assets in your portfolio — that can make them very valuable ingredients in your portfolio. Some investments may be quite taxable, but in most cases it's worth it to put up with the taxes to reap the rewards.

Considering the tax efficiency (or inefficiency) of your investments

As you decide which investments to buy in each of your accounts, it's important to recognize how tax-efficient each of those investments is. We discuss many details of these investments in Chapters 3 and 9, but here we focus on their tax characteristics:

- **Growth stocks:** Growth stocks are those that pay relatively small (if any) dividends. Instead, the upside of growth stocks lies in their potential for above-average share price growth. Because these stocks generate very little income, they're subject to little tax.

- **International stocks:** Stocks of non-U.S. companies, and funds that include these international stocks, are sometimes subject to foreign taxes. However, you can get a credit for the foreign taxes when it comes time to file your U.S. taxes, if these stocks are held in a taxable account.

- **Municipal bonds:** Interest income from bonds issued by states and municipalities is generally free from income tax at the federal level and in the state of issue. As far as tax efficiency goes, munis (as they're sometimes called) are tough to beat.

- **REITs:** REITs are required to pay a large portion of their income to investors each year. This income is categorized as ordinary income, which means it's subject to the highest tax rates. Taxes on REITs can get ugly.

✔ **Taxable bonds:** Interest income from corporate and Treasury bonds is fully taxable at the federal level. Corporate bond income is also taxable at the state level. The income is considered ordinary income, which means that it's taxable at your highest rate. Yikes! And the larger the *coupon rate* (the interest earned on the security), the more taxable income there is.

✔ **Commodity funds:** The commodity funds we discuss in this book have the potential to generate highly taxable income. This is because the securities that are held within those funds can throw off a lot of taxable gains, which are passed along to the fund's shareholders.

✔ **Mutual funds:** Mutual funds often have to sell some of their underlying securities, usually to raise cash to pay investors who sell their shares in the fund. The taxable gains resulting from those sales are distributed to the remaining shareholders of the fund, usually at the end of each year. You don't have a single ounce of control over those taxable gains, and you don't know their magnitude in advance, unfortunately. They just hit you with it.

This feature is much less common among ETFs and many ETNs, so you might consider those if you want to include funds in your portfolio (a good idea) but don't like the idea of losing out when other fund investors decide to sell their shares.

Knowing where to locate investments based on tax characteristics

If you read through the tax characteristics of the various investments we list in the preceding section, you know that different types of investments can have very different levels of tax efficiency. So how do you know where (in which accounts) you should locate those investments?

It's actually very simple: You use the relative tax efficiency of each investment that you're considering buying to decide which account to buy it in. So, to the extent you can, you want to buy your REITs, taxable bonds, commodity funds, and mutual funds (all tax-heavy investments) in tax-deferred accounts like your 401(k) and IRA. By the same token, it really pays off to use your taxable account(s) to buy your growth stocks, international stocks, municipal bonds, ETFs, and ETNs. You keep your highly taxed investments in the tax-deferred accounts and keep your tax-efficient investments in your taxable accounts.

That all sounds terrific — and it is — but, to be honest, you may not be able to accomplish it on the level you'd like. Why? There are several reasons. For example, your IRA may not be big enough to allow you to buy all the tax-inefficient investments that you want to buy. There are ways to deal with these challenges, though, and we tackle them in the next section.

Going through the Asset Location Exercise

The best way to grasp the importance of asset location for minimizing the negative effects of taxes and maximizing the quality of your portfolio is to take a good hard look at an example. That's exactly what we provide in this section — a useful example of how clever placement of investments in the right accounts can really cut down on the amount of taxes that are pulled out of your returns.

In Chapter 8, we discuss John and Jane Doe, and we explain the asset allocation they derived for themselves (okay, with a little help from us). The Does' asset allocation is shown in Table 10-2.

Table 10-2	Asset Allocation for John and Jane Doe		
Asset Class	*Subclass*	*Allocation*	
		Percentage	*Dollars*
Fixed income	Short term	5%	$25,000
	Intermediate term	5%	$25,000
	Long term	5%	$25,000
	Subtotal	**15%**	**$75,000**
Equities	Small cap (including international)	4%	$20,000
	Mid cap (including international)	6%	$30,000
	Large cap, industrials (including international)	5%	$25,000
	Large cap, consumer staples (including international)	10%	$50,000
	Large cap, energy (including international)	8%	$40,000
	Large cap, financials (including international)	12%	$60,000
	Large cap, healthcare (including international)	15%	$75,000
	Subtotal	**60%**	**$300,000**

(continued)

Table 10-2 *(continued)*

Asset Class	Subclass	Allocation	
		Percentage	Dollars
Alternatives	Real estate (including international)	8%	$40,000
	Commodities	17%	$85,000
	Subtotal	**25%**	**$125,000**
	Total	100%	$500,000

Source: Brinton Eaton Wealth Advisors.

As you can see in the table, the Does allocate 15 percent of their portfolio to fixed-income investments, 60 percent to equities, and the remaining 25 percent to alternatives. (We discuss asset classes in detail in Chapter 3.)

Now, suppose that the Does' investment portfolio is $500,000. In the right-hand column, we show their allocation in dollars. For example, $75,000 (which equals 15 percent of the total $500,000 portfolio) is in fixed income, $300,000 (60 percent) is in equities, and $125,000 (25 percent) is in alternatives.

John and Jane never seem to get too upset with us when we make assumptions about them, so we'll further assume that their portfolio consists of three accounts: an IRA for John, an IRA for Jane, and a TIC account for the two of them jointly. John's IRA is relatively small at $25,000, while Jane's is larger ($125,000). Their biggest account is their TIC account, consisting of $350,000. One more assumption: All their assets are in cash, waiting to be allocated.

So, how should the Does locate their assets in order to achieve their desired asset allocation in the most tax-efficient way? Have a look at Table 10-3 for one way they can do it.

Table 10-3   Asset Location for John and Jane Doe

Asset Class	Subclass	John's IRA	Jane's IRA	TIC Account	Total Portfolio
Fixed income	*Short term*			*$25,000*	*$25,000*
	Intermediate term		$25,000		$25,000
	Long term			$25,000	$25,000

(continued)

Asset Class	Subclass	John's IRA	Jane's IRA	TIC Account	Total Portfolio
	Subtotal	$0	$25,000	$50,000	$75,000
Equities	Small cap			$20,000	$20,000
	Mid cap			$30,000	$30,000
	Large cap, industrials			$25,000	$25,000
	Large cap, consumer staples			$50,000	$50,000
	Large cap, energy			$40,000	$40,000
	Large cap, financials			$60,000	$60,000
	Large cap, healthcare			$75,000	$75,000
	Subtotal	$0	$0	$300,000	$300,000
Alternatives	Real estate	$25,000	$15,000		$40,000
	Commodities		$85,000		$85,000
	Subtotal	$25,000	$100,000	$0	$125,000
	Total	$25,000	$125,000	$350,000	$500,000

Source: Brinton Eaton Wealth Advisors.

We'll walk you through the numbers in Table 10-3. The Does start with their tax-inefficient assets — a wise move. They know they want to buy $40,000 in real estate, and they decide to use up all of John's IRA to buy $25,000 worth of REITs. They then buy the remaining $15,000 of REITs (to complete their $40,000 allocation) in Jane's IRA. In her IRA, they also buy all $85,000 of their allocation to commodities via a commodities index mutual fund. It may seem like they should be worried about taxable distributions from the mutual fund, but that's not a concern because the fund will be housed in a tax-deferred account. That's one example of the savvy asset location that's at work here.

To continue with the asset location example in Table 10-3, the Does have $25,000 left over in Jane's IRA, which they use to buy an intermediate-term bond fund. Because the fund is in a tax-deferred account, they opt for a taxable bond fund, which has a higher yield than a tax-free municipal bond fund. Then all the rest of the purchases are made in the TIC account. To round out the fixed-income allocation — they still need to own $50,000 in fixed-income investments according to their asset allocation plan (refer to Table 10-2) — the Does buy $50,000 in municipal bond funds. (They buy $25,000 each in short-term and long-term bond funds.) They also buy all their equities in the TIC. That causes the Does no woes, because even the stocks and stock funds they bought that actually pay dividends will pay *qualified* dividends, which means that they're taxed at lower federal tax rates than what the Does would expect for ordinary income.

The Does have done a fine job of not only allocating their assets, but locating them as well. They've kept their highly taxed investments in their tax-deferred accounts, and their tax-efficient investments in their taxable accounts. You won't find these particular Does with a deer-in-the-headlights look when tax time comes around.

Suppose, though, that the Does' IRAs weren't large enough to accommodate their desired allocations to tax-inefficient assets. Jane's IRA could've been $25,000 instead of $125,000, and their TIC account $450,000 instead of $350,000. What would they do then? In that case, they'd buy $15,000 in REITs in Jane's IRA and only $10,000 in commodities, because that's all the room that was left in that account. The balance of the commodity purchase ($75,000) would have to be made in the TIC account, along with the $25,000 in intermediate-term bonds. Recognizing the taxable nature of the TIC account, the Does would make sure they bought an ETF or ETN instead of a mutual fund to cover their commodity exposure there, and a municipal bond fund instead of a taxable bond fund.

When it comes to asset location, it's usually a good idea to tackle your tax-inefficient investments first, and try to buy as much as you can of them in your tax-deferred accounts. When you complete that, you'll know whether you had enough room in your tax-deferred accounts to accommodate all of them. If you did, then you can fill up the rest of those accounts with tax-efficient assets (you really don't lose anything by doing so) and then buy the remainder of the tax-friendly assets in your taxable accounts. But if you don't have enough room in your tax-deferred accounts for all your tax-inefficient investments, then you have no choice but to buy the remaining portion of the tax-inefficient assets, as well as your tax-friendly assets, in your taxable accounts.

Do as good a job as you possibly can when it comes to asset location. You'll be glad you focused on the tax details and made the extra effort.

Chapter 11

Monitoring Your Portfolio: Rebalancing and Other Smart Strategies

. . . .

In This Chapter

▶ Understanding how to rebalance your portfolio

▶ Knowing how to keep tabs on the securities you own

▶ Taking advantage of smart and simple tax strategies

. . . .

*D*esigning and building your portfolio isn't the end of the asset allocation recipe we work at perfecting throughout this book. To keep delivering the appetizing portfolio results you desire, you need to do diligent maintenance to make sure your portfolio stays true to your recipe.

Your portfolio should be monitored for several reasons. You may need to replace individual securities that lose their luster. Taxes are always a part of the investing picture, so you can be sure that tax considerations may also dictate some remedial action. And, perhaps most important, your portfolio can drift away from its intended allocation due to the vagaries of the markets and occasionally need to be brought back to target by rebalancing on the right schedule.

In this chapter, we go through a helpful step-by-step rebalancing exercise with our fantastic fictional financial friends John and Jane Doe. We look at the details of how they rebalance their portfolio, so that you can understand how rebalancing can work for you and get you the benefits you deserve. We also show you a few other hands-on strategies, beginning with the importance of keeping tabs on the individual securities you own and always being aware of certain tax-driven opportunities, such as timing the sale of your securities and harvesting tax losses.

If you use the monitoring and opportunistic adjustment approach we recommend in this chapter, you'll end up ahead of most investors, because you'll decrease the risk of your portfolio and increase your returns over the long term.

Rebalancing Your Portfolio

In Chapter 5, we talk about the what and why of portfolio rebalancing. In this section, we take you through the how. Rebalancing is an incredibly important process, so flip back to Chapter 5 to bone up if you need to. If you already know the rebalancing basics, dive right in!

Dealing with portfolio drift

As we discuss in Chapter 5, not all your asset classes will grow at the same rate. In other words, you can count on the markets disrupting your asset allocation every day — it's the nature of the beast. Over time, your portfolio will drift away — sometimes far away — from its target allocation. When that happens, it's time to rebalance your portfolio.

Defining portfolio drift

When it comes to a drifting portfolio, how far is too far? In Chapter 5, we tell you about the importance of setting a tolerance band around your target allocations. A *tolerance band* is the range (usually plus or minus a certain percentage) within which you allow your asset allocations to fluctuate without taking action. If your actual allocation at any given time departs from its target by more than the tolerance you've set, then it's time to rebalance. That's how you know when to rebalance. It's as simple as that.

Tolerance bands can be of any size, but we suggest you go with ±20 percent around each of your allocation percentages.

For example, if your target allocation to the consumer staples asset class (check out Chapter 3 for more on asset classes) is 10 percent, then ±20 percent of that target is ±2 percent ($0.10 \times 0.20 = 0.02$). In that case, you rebalance if the size of your consumer staples investment drifts above 12 percent or below 8 percent of your portfolio. If another asset class has a target allocation of 5 percent, then ±20 percent of that target is ±1 percent ($0.05 \times 0.20 = 0.01$), so you'd rebalance if that class were to drift outside of a range of 4 percent to 6 percent.

Catching the (portfolio) drift

There's no better way for you to understand how to identify portfolio drift than by working through an example situation. The example we use is that of John and Jane Doe, whom you may remember (fondly, no doubt) from Chapter 8. The first step is to nail down the tolerance bands for the Does' portfolio, which is what we do for you in Table 11-1. (We use the same ±20 percent tolerance band guideline that we champion in the preceding section.)

Table 11-1	John and Jane Doe's Tolerance Bands		
Asset Class	**Subclass**	**Allocation**	**Tolerance Band**
Fixed income	Short term	5%	4%–6%
	Intermediate term	5%	4%–6%
	Long term	5%	4%–6%
	Subtotal	**15%**	
Equities	Small cap	4%	3%–5%
	Mid cap	6%	5%–7%
	Large cap, industrials	5%	4%–6%
	Large cap, consumer staples	10%	8%–12%
	Large cap, energy	8%	6%–10%
	Large cap, financials	12%	10%–14%
	Large cap, healthcare	15%	12%–18%
	Subtotal	**60%**	
Alternatives	Real estate	8%	6%–10%
	Commodities	17%	14%–20%
	Subtotal	**25%**	
	Total	100%	

Source: Brinton Eaton Wealth Advisors.

As you can see in the figure, the Does have a target allocation of 5 percent for each of the fixed-income asset subclasses. So using the ±20 percent tolerance-band guideline, the Does' fixed-income investments have a tolerance band of 4 percent to 6 percent (±20 percent of 5 percent). The 10 percent target allocation to the consumer staples sector within the large-cap equity subclass has a tolerance range of 8 percent to 12 percent.

Now that we've established the Does' target allocations and their tolerance bands, let's put some meat on the bones. Table 11-2 shows you what the Does' portfolio looks like in dollars.

Table 11-2	John and Jane Doe's Initial Portfolio		
Asset Class	*Subclass*	*Target Allocation*	
		Percentage	Dollars
Fixed income	Short term	5%	$25,000
	Intermediate term	5%	$25,000
	Long term	5%	$25,000
	Subtotal	**15%**	**$75,000**
Equities	Small cap	4%	$20,000
	Mid cap	6%	$30,000
	Large cap, industrials	5%	$25,000
	Large cap, consumer staples	10%	$50,000
	Large cap, energy	8%	$40,000
	Large cap, financials	12%	$60,000
	Large cap, healthcare	15%	$75,000
	Subtotal	**60%**	**$300,000**
Alternatives	Real estate	8%	$40,000
	Commodities	17%	$85,000
	Subtotal	**25%**	**$125,000**
	Total	100%	$500,000

Source: Brinton Eaton Wealth Advisors.

As you can see in Table 11-2, we assume that the Does have an initial investment portfolio of $500,000. Their allocation to short-term fixed income is $25,000 (which equals 5 percent of the total $500,000 portfolio); their allocation to small-cap equities is $20,000 (4 percent of $500,000); and on down the line.

Table 11-2 shows you where the Does started out in our example, and in Table 11-3 you can see how the Does were faring six months into our example. Six months later, the Does' portfolio is up to $530,000. As is typically the case, this growth didn't occur uniformly across all asset classes. Take a look.

Table 11-3		The Does' Portfolio after Six Months			
Asset Class	**Subclass**	**Target Allocation**	**Actual Portfolio after Six Months**	**Actual Allocation after Six Months**	**Tolerance Band**
Fixed income	Short term	$25,000	$27,000	5.1%	4%–6%
	Intermediate term	$25,000	$26,500	5.0%	4%–6%
	Long term	$25,000	$26,000	4.9%	4%–6%
	Subtotal	**$75,000**	**$79,500**		
Equities	Small cap	$20,000	$20,000	3.8%	3%–5%
	Mid cap	$30,000	$32,000	6.0%	5%–7%
	Large cap, industrials	$25,000	$34,500	6.5%	4%–6%
	Large cap, consumer staples	$50,000	$45,000	8.5%	8%–12%
	Large cap, energy	$40,000	$28,000	5.3%	6%–10%
	Large cap, financials	$60,000	$55,000	10.4%	10%–14%
	Large cap, healthcare	$75,000	$80,000	15.1%	12%–18%
	Subtotal	**$300,000**	**$294,500**		
Alternatives	Real estate	$40,000	$38,000	7.2%	6%–10%
	Commodities	$85,000	$118,000	22.3%	14%–20%
	Subtotal	**$125,000**	**$156,000**		
	Total	$500,000	$530,000		

Source: Brinton Eaton Wealth Advisors.

As the figure indicates, the Does' original $25,000 in short-term fixed income grew to $27,000 and their $50,000 in consumer staples shrank to $45,000. You can see some interesting movement in the other asset subclasses as well.

Just like what will inevitably happen to your portfolio, the Does' actual asset allocation saw some drift over their portfolio's first six months. But did the uneven growth or shrinkage in the Does' asset classes/subclasses take the Does' portfolio outside of its tolerance bands? For an answer, look at the Does' actual asset allocation percentages at the six-month mark. Their $27,000 in short-term fixed income, divided by their portfolio total of $530,000 is 5.1 percent; their $80,000 in healthcare, divided by $530,000, is 15.1 percent of the total portfolio; and so on through each asset class. You can see that the 6.5 percent in industrials now exceeds the 6 percent top end of the tolerance band for that sector. Also, 5.3 percent in energy is below the 6 percent low end of that sector's tolerance band. And the 22.3 percent in commodities exceeds the 20 percent high end of its tolerance band.

That's how you check for portfolio drift — and whether it's severe enough for you to stand up and take action. But how exactly do you take that action? Read on to find out.

Rebalancing back to target

When you have at least one asset subclass that has drifted too far away from its target allocation, that should trigger you to rebalance, as we discuss in Chapter 5. One way to rebalance is to buy and sell sufficient amounts by asset subclass to bring every subclass back to target. To continue with the John and Jane Doe example, Table 11-4 shows what trades the Does would have to make to bring their portfolio back to its target asset allocation. (Making adjustments to bring most but not all subclasses back to target is also an option, but we cover that in the next section.)

Table 11-4			The Does' Rebalancing Act		
Asset Class	Subclass	Target Allocation	Actual Portfolio after Six Months	Target Allocation	Necessary Trades
Fixed income	Short term	5%	$27,000	$26,500	–$500
	Intermediate term	5%	$26,500	$26,500	$0
	Long term	5%	$26,000	$26,500	$500
	Subtotal	**15%**	**$79,500**		
Equities	Small cap	4%	$20,000	$21,200	$1,200
	Mid cap	6%	$32,000	$31,800	–$200
	Large cap, industrials	5%	$34,500	$26,500	–$8,000
	Large cap, consumer staples	10%	$45,000	$53,000	$8,000
	Large cap, energy	8%	$28,000	$42,400	$14,400

Asset Class	Subclass	Target Allocation	Actual Portfolio after Six Months	Target Allocation	Necessary Trades
	Large cap, financials	12%	$55,000	$63,600	$8,600
	Large cap, healthcare	15%	$80,000	$79,500	–$500
	Subtotal	**60%**	**$294,500**		
Alternatives	Real estate	8%	$38,000	$42,400	$4,400
	Commodities	17%	$118,000	$90,100	–$27,900
	Subtotal	**25%**	**$156,000**		
	Total	100%	$530,000		$0

Source: Brinton Eaton Wealth Advisors.

Table 11-4 shows what the Does' target allocation is in dollars, now that their portfolio balance has grown to $530,000. (It's the updated version of Table 11-2, six months later.) For example, for short-term fixed income, 5 percent of $530,000 is $26,500; for small-cap equities, 4 percent of $530,000 is $21,200.

The necessary trades are simply the difference between the Does' actual dollar allocations to each asset subclass and their target dollar allocations. For example, for short-term fixed income, the target of $26,500 minus the actual $27,000 is –$500, which means that the Does need to sell $500 of their short-term fixed-income investments to get back to target. Likewise, for small-cap equities, the target of $21,200 minus the actual $20,000 is $1,200; the Does need to buy $1,200 more of small-cap equity investments.

If you add up every amount that needs to be bought and sold, the total is $0, meaning that the total buys and the total sells balance each other exactly, as they should! After the Does make these trades, they'll be back to their target allocations across the board.

Rebalancing close to target

In practice, the Does — that lovable couple from our running example who don't seem to mind us splashing their financial information all over a *For Dummies* book — may decide that some of their out-of-balance amounts aren't big enough to worry about. In that case, they may decide to forgo some of the trades shown in Table 11-4.

For example, they may decide that the $500 sale of short-term fixed-income investments and the $500 buy of long-term fixed-income investments are small enough to ignore. They can forgo those trades, and because their values are a wash, the remaining total buys would still equal the total sales.

They may also decide that the $200 sale of mid-cap equities is too small to concern themselves with. If they forgo that trade, they then must cut back on $200 of buys elsewhere. A logical place would be in small-cap equities — they might buy $1,000 instead of $1,200 there. We hate to see a good-timin', raucous, small-cap equity shopping spree cut short, but in this case it's the best choice.

Pragmatic decisions like this are perfectly acceptable. They'll save you time, effort, trading costs, and possible taxable gains — and they won't have a material effect on the performance of your portfolio. There are no hard and fast rules on where to draw the line on these too-small-to-worry-about trades, but you can use the Does' example as a guideline.

Using a working layer of exchange-traded funds

Throughout this book, we do a lousy job of hiding our love for exchange-traded funds (ETFs). We think ETFs belong in virtually every investor's portfolio, for a number of reasons. For example, they're typically low-cost and tax-efficient, and as we explain later in this chapter they present opportunities for tax-loss harvesting.

You should consider having ETFs in every asset class and subclass in your portfolio for yet another reason: ETFs can make rebalancing easier. Rebalancing trades are, by their nature, relatively small, fine-tuning trades. If you have ETFs in every asset class, you can easily use them to do the rebalancing trades you need to do without having to disrupt your holdings in bonds, stocks, REITs, and so on. For example, as we explain in Chapter 3, you don't want to sell a bond before it matures if you can help it. In contrast, ETFs are so liquid and marketable that trading any odd and/or small number of shares just isn't a problem. They're agile assets, and when it comes to investing, agility is a virtue.

Consider having a *working layer* (enough to cover about half the width of your tolerance band) of ETFs in every asset class and subclass in your portfolio. (You can apply the working layer concept to mutual funds as well — but, again, we just like ETFs better.)

Keeping Tabs on Your Securities

Security selection — picking the individual investments you want to own within each of your asset classes — isn't a one-time deal. After you pick 'em, you've gotta keep an eye on 'em. In this section, we let you know how to manage the securities in your portfolio. We also clue you in on when it's time to drop a dud, and we tell you how you can benefit by not being too greedy when a security has done well for you. Both moves may seem uncomfortably counterintuitive to you at first, but in this section, we explain how they can be a real boon to your investment efforts.

Knowing when to hold 'em and when to fold 'em

If you own a security that's done well, you may be tempted to hold onto it forever. But sometimes, an extended winning streak simply means that it's time for a hot security to turn cold. There are no hard and fast rules for when this may happen, but you don't want to just ride your winners blindly and indefinitely.

Similarly, if you own a security that's had a rough time and lost lots of market value, you may feel obligated to hang onto it until it recovers, and you recoup your loss. Sometimes that's a good strategy; other times, a loser is just a loser.

So how do you know when it's time to wave goodbye to a winner and to cut a loser loose? The secret is in the planning. (In the "Setting your security guidelines early" section, later in this chapter, we talk about some guidelines you'll want to put in place to protect yourself in both these situations.)

Taking some winnings off the table

In some instances, you may own a security that has done well — maybe even better than expected — but hasn't performed on a superstar level. In those cases, you should consider selling some of your investment (but not selling out altogether) and putting the proceeds to work in another security that has more potential for growth. When you do that, you are, in a sense, playing with house money in the new security, while still leaving enough behind in the hot (but not too hot) security to benefit you if it continues its upward ride. It's a conservative move, and one that can really help your overall portfolio health in the long run.

But how do you know when to sell off some of your shares of a good security in order to reinvest in another security? The guidelines we suggest in the next section will help you figure it out.

Setting your security guidelines early

So, how do you decide when to sell off (or at least reduce your ownership of) a security? Sometimes it can be really tough to make that call as events are unfolding. It's better to make the decision early on, so you won't feel as if you're under the gun when the time comes to decide.

When you buy a security, go ahead and make your decisions about when (at what price) you want to reevaluate your position. That way, if the security's price starts moving up or down erratically, you won't have to panic because you've already set guidelines for what to do when the price hits a certain level.

When you stop and think about it, planning your security guidelines makes sense, doesn't it? If you set your guidelines *before* you buy, you won't run around like a chicken with its head cut off when you feel that the market or your personal circumstances are forcing you to take action.

For example, say you buy a stock for $50 per share. To guide your future actions, you decide to establish a set of threshold prices around that purchase price. What are those? We'll say you decide on a *bottom alert price* of $40 (meaning, if the market price falls below that price, you'll investigate the causes). How do you do that investigation?

Well, if the fundamentals of the company are still sound and you believe that the market is underpricing the stock for no good reason, or that the stock's entire industry sector is under pressure, you may decide to stick with the stock. (For a primer on a stock's fundamentals, flip back to Chapter 9, where we tell you what you need to know about buying individual securities.) On the other hand, if the drop in price is triggered by a sudden change in management of the company, or the failure of an important new product launch — the new line of submarine screen doors doesn't tickle the market's fancy, for instance — then you may decide to cut and run. The bottom alert price doesn't trigger an automatic response from you; it simply warns you to take a close look.

In addition to the bottom alert price, you may want to set a pair of *upper alert prices,* perhaps one at $65 and another at $75. When you set an upper alert price, that means you decide to reevaluate a security when it reaches your set price. But why would you set two upper alert prices?

We'll start with the first upper alert price from our example. If the market price exceeds $65 for reasons other than the entire industry sector coming into favor, you should consider reducing your investment in a security by enough to take your profit. Here's how that works: Suppose your initial purchase (at $50 per share) was for 300 shares, costing you $15,000. When the market price hits $65, your 300 shares will be worth $19,500. Your profit is, therefore, the difference between $15,000 and $19,500, or $4,500. This $4,500 represents 69 shares at $65 a share (which you may want to round up to 70 shares so you're not dealing with "odd lots" of stock, simply because it makes buying and selling easier). You then sell 70 of your 300 shares to cash in your profits and put the proceeds to work in another security with more potential for growth, as we explain earlier.

But what about that second upper alert price? If the market price exceeds $75, you may consider exiting the position altogether and looking for another stock that has a lot more potential ahead of it. Here again, the alert prices don't set off automatic actions — they merely let you know when you should look more closely at the situation.

The close looks you take should include a survey of all the features you considered when you bought the security. Before you invest your hard-earned money in a stock, make sure you check out a company's 10-K report, which all public companies are required to file with the Securities and Exchange Commission (SEC) at `www.sec.gov/edgar.shtml`. (This address takes you to EDGAR, the Electronic Data Gathering Analysis and Retrieval System.) You want to see a healthy income statement (showing steadily increasing revenue and earnings), a clean balance sheet, and debt-to-equity and price-to-earnings ratios that are at, or below, their industry averages, as we explain in Chapter 9.

The time to decide how far you're willing to go with a stock is before — not after — you buy. When volatile changes occur, either in the market or in your own personal circumstances, you can be far too emotional and fail to think clearly at the time.

Making Smart Tax Choices

As we mention throughout the book, it's not what you earn that matters, it's what you keep — and we want you to keep every allowable penny of what you've earned! You don't need to pay more income taxes than you should — but you'll do exactly that if you overlook some perfectly legitimate ways of cutting down your tax bill. We cover tax strategies in more detail in Chapter 14, but we hit the highlights in this section. *Note:* Our discussion reviews only federal income taxes, which will be a permanent and important factor for you.

Paying attention to taxable gains and losses

As you're monitoring and maintaining your portfolio, be sure to keep an eye on the tax implications of what you're doing. Like any special language — and tax talk is certainly one of them — there are certain terms to master. But they're not that hard to grasp, when you take a few minutes to unscramble their code.

To begin, whenever you consider selling any security you hold, you should know what the *embedded taxable gain* or *loss* (also called the *unrealized gain or loss*) is in that holding. The embedded gain/loss is the difference between the current market value of your holding and its *cost basis* (what you paid for it). If the current market value is greater than the cost basis, you have an embedded gain; if it's less, you have an embedded loss. You realize the gain or loss when you sell the security. And you incur a tax liability (meaning, you get taxed) only on realized gains. The IRS can be harsh, but it won't tax you on a loss (or on a gain you haven't realized yet). So, if the security you're considering selling has an embedded tax loss, you can sell it without fear of a tax liability.

If you're selling a security and you're facing a realized tax loss, you can use that loss to offset taxable gains from your other transactions.

If, though, the security you're considering selling has an embedded tax gain, then you have more to think about. We get into those details in the next section.

Make sure you have a recordkeeping system to keep track of your securities' cost bases. That way you won't make mistakes or waste a lot of time later when you sell a security and need to know whether you had a gain or loss. Most brokers keep track of your cost basis and report it to you periodically. If you buy and sell securities on your own, you'll need to know — and keep track of — the cost basis for the securities you own. Personal finance software applications like Quicken or Microsoft Money can help you do that.

Deferring and offsetting taxable gains

You can do yourself a lot of good if you can remember a few key concepts about deferring and offsetting taxable gains.

When it comes to tax planning, a simple rule to follow is to take your taxable gains as late as you can, and to take your taxable losses as early as you can.

We talk about deferring your gains in this section and accelerating your losses in the next section.

There are several ways that you can defer or even offset your taxable gains, and all of them are allowable strategies that will help you to keep more of your hard-earned money. Here are some of the ways to defer or offset taxable gains:

- ✔ **Defer the gain into the next tax year.** If it's mid-December when you make your decision to sell a security and earn a taxable gain, you should consider waiting a couple of weeks and making the sale in January. That way, you'll have the rest of that year to try to generate tax losses to offset the gain. Even if you don't, you'll at least get to delay paying the tax man for a full year.

- ✔ **Wait until the gain is long term.** If you're selling a security that you held for almost a year at a gain, it may be a good idea to wait until after the one-year anniversary of your purchase. That way, the gain will qualify for a long-term capital gains treatment and get taxed at a lower rate.

- ✔ **Take advantage of realized losses.** You can offset taxable gains with *taxable losses* (what you get when you sell something for less than you paid for it) that you may have realized from other sales you made in the same tax year.

- ✔ **Capitalize on capital loss carryovers.** A *capital loss carryover* is a tax loss that you can't use to offset gains in the year of the loss (that is, your gains were not large enough to fully use up all your losses). You can offset gains in a given year with capital loss carryovers from prior tax years.

We offer some concrete examples in Chapter 14, where we talk about tax considerations in more detail.

If you're going to sell a security, make sure you know the tax implications of your decision and plan for its consequences in advance.

Harvesting tax loss opportunities with exchange-traded funds

The two previous sections show you why tax losses can be valuable. You should be alert to opportunities to generate them whenever you can, and one way to do that is through clever use of ETFs (see Chapter 9).

One of the notable things about ETFs is their popularity. For just about any of the asset class baskets where you may want to allocate your assets, you have a number of ETFs to choose from, and more are becoming available on a regular basis.

So how does this popularity allow you to harvest tax losses with ETFs? Here's an example: Say you decide to invest $20,000 in equities in the energy sector. You can choose from several energy ETFs. After considering the possibilities, you buy energy ETF A for $20,000 (that's your cost basis). Now let's assume that the market value of your holding in ETF A drops $2,000 to $18,000. That's probably not enough of a drop to cause you to rebalance your portfolio (because your tolerance bands are likely wider than that), but the drop does represent a sizeable embedded, or unrealized, tax loss. So what can you do to seize this tax loss opportunity without doing damage to your portfolio? You can sell your shares in ETF A, and realize a tax loss of $2,000. Then you can immediately buy $18,000 of energy ETF B with the proceeds from your sale. It's a smart move for several reasons, including the following:

- ✔ **You didn't change your portfolio's asset allocation one iota.** You had $18,000 in the energy sector before the swap, and you have $18,000 in the same sector after the swap.

- ✔ **You have a realized tax loss of $2,000.** You can use that loss to offset taxable gains elsewhere in your portfolio, in the current or in future years. (Check out the preceding section for more information.)

- ✔ **You're haven't run afoul of IRS rules.** More specifically, you did right by the IRS's rules against what they call *wash sales,* which disallow tax losses if the sale that generated the loss is followed by the purchase of an essentially identical security within 30 days. You can steer clear of wash sales as long as the ETFs you choose don't track identical indexes. For example, if ETF A tracks an S&P energy sector index and ETF B tracks a Dow Jones energy sector index, the ETFs are distinct for IRS purposes but basically the same when it comes to asset allocation.

If you've already worked your way through Chapter 9 or you're just familiar with how mutual funds work, you may be wondering if you can harvest tax losses with mutual funds the way you can with ETFs. Sure! We just generally prefer ETFs to mutual funds, for reasons we mention throughout this book (cost effectiveness and tax-efficiency, to name a couple).

For more details on tax loss harvesting, turn to Chapter 14.

Chapter 12

Measuring Your Results

. . . .

In This Chapter

▶ Calculating your investment return

▶ Using benchmarks for investment-return comparisons

▶ Using your Lifetime Cash-flow Projection to track your progress

. . . .

*T*o be the best investor you can be, you need to be able to gauge how well you're doing with your asset allocation recipe. That's what we focus on in this chapter — how to figure out how well your portfolio is doing with a high level of accuracy.

We begin the chapter by explaining how to express your investment results in a useful way — one that allows you to make meaningful comparisons — by calculating your investment return. You can calculate several different types of returns, and we explain which ones to use in various circumstances.

We then look at how to find and construct appropriate points of comparison (called *benchmarks*) against which you can gauge your return. And we wrap up the chapter by putting your investment performance in its most pertinent context: your long-term financial plan.

Throughout this chapter, we explain how the measurements we recommend touch upon the five key elements of understanding your investment results: principal, term, risk, opportunity cost, and suitability. We also make important connections to relevant concepts we introduce in other chapters, such as risk and return (see Chapter 2), the range of investment strategies and their associated sample asset allocations (see Chapter 8), and your Lifetime Cash-flow Projection (see Chapter 7). So get your page-flippin' fingers ready.

A wise man once said, "You can't manage what you can't measure." Knowing how to measure your results correctly is critical to being able to manage your financial future.

Figuring Your Investment Return

Say your neighbor tells you that that he made $10,000 on a recent investment. That's not chump change. But how good a result is that, really? The quality of that result depends on a whole host of factors, including the following:

- **How much he invested in the first place:** Was it $25,000? $250,000? More?

- **How long he was invested:** A month? A year? Longer?

- **The risk level of the investment:** Did he stand a realistic chance of losing his whole investment (or more)? Was he guaranteed a full return of his *principal* (the amount that he invested)? Did the value of his investment fluctuate wildly while he held it?

- **The health of the general investment environment at the time:** Was he investing in the middle of a *bear market* (a period when security prices are generally falling)? Or was he the beneficiary of a *bull market* (when security prices are rising)?

- **The suitability of the investment for him:** Did it help him achieve his financial objectives? Or did it put his financial future in unnecessary jeopardy?

These five considerations illustrate the five key elements of understanding your investment results and putting them in a meaningful context. Those five key elements are

- **Principal:** The amount you invested (your amount at risk)

- **Term:** The length of time over which you're measuring your results

- **Risk:** The degree of safety built into the investment

- **Opportunity cost:** The results you could've gotten for a typical alternative investment with similar risk over the same term

- **Suitability:** The degree to which this investment is in step with your financial plan

These are the most important considerations, but there are others, too, including the following:

- **Liquidity:** The ability of the investment to be converted to cash on short notice without affecting its market value

- **Marketability:** The attractiveness of the investment for buyers, at the price you want to sell it at

✔ **Cost:** The cost of the investment, including transaction expenses, management fees, and loads (see Chapters 9 and 16)

✔ **Taxes:** Perhaps the largest cost of all (see Chapters 6, 10, 11, and 14)

We touch on these other considerations in various chapters throughout this book. In this chapter, though, we focus on the five key elements in the first list. We cover two of those elements — principal and term — in this section. In the "Comparing Your Return to Relevant Benchmarks" section, later in this chapter, we address risk and opportunity cost. Then, in the chapter's final section, we take a look at suitability.

Calculating your return

Understanding how to calculate your return is of the utmost importance. We start with the basics, focusing on principal.

Paying attention to principal

You should express your results as a percentage of your principal. If you invest $250,000, and your investment earns $10,000, your return is 4 percent ($10,000 ÷ $250,000 = 0.04, or 4 percent). If you express your results this way, you normalize the results by essentially taking the size of your principal — the first of our five key elements — out of the equation. It also helps you compare your results with your neighbor's (or anyone else's) without either of you having to know how much the other invested. If your neighbor also made $10,000, but he only invested $25,000, his return was 40 percent, quite a bit better than yours, all else (term, risk, opportunity, suitability) being equal.

When you figure out your return as a percentage of your principal, make sure you include both income and growth. *Income* includes payments you received during the course of the investment, such as interest or dividends. *Growth* measures the change in market value of your investment, which can be positive or negative.

Income and growth are the two components of total return (see Chapter 2).

Coming to terms with term

The second key element for understanding your investment results is term.

Suppose you and your neighbor each had returns of 10 percent, but your investment was tied up for two years, while he made his in six months. Well, he did much better than you did, all else being equal. For a given return, the shorter the term, the better the actual result. After all, time is money.

Calculating your compound annual growth rate

Calculating a CAGR can be a tricky process. If you're interested and you're not scared of some math, follow these steps:

1. **Express your return in decimal form.**

    For example, a 10 percent return would be expressed as 0.10.

2. **Add 1 to your result from Step 1.**

3. **Express your term as a number of years.**

    For example, a 24-month term would be expressed as 2; a 6-month term would be expressed as 0.5.

4. **Take the inverse of your result from Step 3 (that is, divide it into 1).**

    For example, for the 24-month term, it's $1 \div 2 = 0.5$; for the 6-month term, it's $1 \div 0.5 = 2$.

5. **Raise your result in Step 2 to the power derived in Step 4.**

    For example, $1.10^{0.5} = 1.049$; $1.10^2 = 1.21$. (**Tip:** If you don't have a financial calculator, you can go to www.google.com, and enter **1.10^0.5** to get the results, and then do the same with **1.10^2**.)

6. **Subtract 1 from your result in Step 5.**

    That leaves you with 0.049 and 0.21.

7. **Express your result from Step 6 in percentage form.**

    For example, 0.049 is 4.9 percent; 0.210 is 21 percent. (**Remember:** To express something in percentage form, multiply by 100, or just move the decimal point to the right two places.)

So, how do you normalize your results for term, as we did in the preceding section for principal? You express your return on an annualized basis, because a year is the most popular period for comparison purposes. In Chapter 2, we explain two ways to do this: simple averaging and compound averaging. Compound averaging is more realistic and we much prefer it. (Turn to Chapter 2 if want to know why and to find out how to calculate it.)

Annualizing returns is so popular, there's a special name for the result: *compound annual growth rate* (CAGR). Coming up with a CAGR is a multistep process, and you can read about how to calculate CAGR in the "Calculating your compound annual growth rate" sidebar in this chapter. You don't have to know how to calculate it — there are plenty of programs that can do it for you — but just keep in mind that CAGRs are expressed as percentages, and the higher the CAGR, the better. In our earlier example, your two-year 10 percent return is equivalent to a CAGR of 4.9 percent. Your neighbor's six-month 10 percent return is equivalent to a CAGR of 21 percent. (We explain both calculations in the sidebar.) The higher CAGR belongs to your neighbor, so his investment did better than yours (all other factors being equal). But you knew that already. Using CAGR shows you precisely how much better than you he did, on a fair and objective, quantifiable, apples-to-apples basis.

Determining the return that's most meaningful to you

In Chapter 2, we fill you in on nominal versus real returns, and time-weighted versus dollar-weighted returns. In this chapter, and throughout this book, we use *nominal returns* (returns unadjusted for inflation) unless specifically noted otherwise, because nominal returns are, by far, the more conventional choice. (Real returns are most commonly used by professional analysts.) When it comes to choosing between figuring time-weighted returns or dollar-weighted returns, you need to make sure you're using the most appropriate measure.

The choice between time-weighting and dollar-weighting comes into play because, in real life, your investment situation is probably not as simple as the examples we present earlier in this chapter. Why not? Well, for starters, your principal may have been contributed in more than one installment. And your income may have been received periodically and reinvested along the way. The way to accommodate these and other real-life complications is to calculate time-weighted or dollar-weighted returns. Which weighting scheme you use depends on what you're really trying to do as you measure your return. (If these two weighting schemes are unfamiliar to you, then stop here and turn to Chapter 2 before you continue.) In other words, your choice should depend on the situation you're dealing with.

As we summarize in Chapter 2, time-weighted returns are the right choice if you want to compare your returns against other external returns, like your neighbor's, or broad index returns that you find in the newspaper. Time-weighting removes the distortions that can pop up when you make deposits into or withdrawals from your investments accounts, so that comparisons to other investments are more fair and meaningful. Therefore, when we talk about benchmark comparisons later in this chapter, we use time-weighted returns.

On the other hand, dollar-weighted returns are the better choice if you want a personally customized picture of how your wealth actually changed over the term of your investment. In this case, you want to reflect your actual deposits and withdrawals, because if you're just worrying about your own investment picture, then deposits and withdrawals aren't distortions that need to be removed. Therefore, when we discuss tracking your progress against your long-term plan at the end of this chapter, we use dollar-weighted returns.

Recognizing that making money isn't necessarily the same as doing well

So, your neighbor who told you he made $10,000 certainly made money (unless he's prone to telling fibs, which may explain why he swears he hasn't seen your power washer when his deck is looking sparkly clean). But do those $10,000 earnings really mean that he did well?

By considering what we cover earlier, you can express his result as a return (you adjust for his principal invested) and not just any return, but CAGR (you adjust for his term). That covers the first two of the five key elements we introduce at the beginning of this chapter and helps you put his performance in proper context.

But it doesn't go quite far enough. To fully answer the question of whether he truly did well, you still have to consider the other three elements — the risk, opportunity cost, and suitability of his investment, all of which we turn to in the next few pages.

Comparing Your Return to Relevant Benchmarks

What if you determine that, over the last five years, the compound annual growth rate (see "Coming to terms with term," earlier in this chapter) for one of your investments was 8 percent? It's always helpful to know your CAGR, but should you be satisfied with that performance? Disappointed? If you really want to get a feel for how your investment is doing, you need to have something relevant to compare your CAGR to.

That's where benchmark returns come in. A *benchmark* is a standard by which something is measured (for example, the Standard & Poor's 500 Stock Index is a common benchmark against which to measure the performance of stock investments). By comparing your CAGRs to the relevant benchmark returns, you can account for risk and opportunity cost, which are two more of the five key elements for understanding your investment results.

Knowing which indexes to use, and how to use them

So you understand that you have to compare the CAGR of your investments with benchmarks if you really want to get a handle on how well those investments are doing for you. That's easy enough. But which benchmarks do you use for comparison, and where do you find those benchmarks?

Selecting and using a benchmark for comparison

Two of the most common benchmarks, published in all the major news-papers, and widely available online, are

- ✔ **The S&P 500 Stock Index:** This index tracks the performance of 500 of the largest publicly traded companies — these companies are house-hold names (General Motors, Exxon, Procter & Gamble, Johnson & Johnson, and so on) and are sometimes referred to as *blue-chip stocks*.

- ✔ **The Barclays Capital U.S. Aggregate Bond Index:** Formerly known as the Lehman U.S. Aggregate Bond Index, this index tracks the perfor-mance of a mixture of corporate bonds, Treasury bonds, and so-called *agency bonds,* such as Government National Mortgage Association (GNMA) bonds.

These aren't the only two indexes for stocks and bonds — not by a long shot (see the next paragraph) — but they're the most widely referenced standards and they've been around for a long time. They're reliable indexes, and you can benchmark a wide range of portfolios using just these two indexes.

Hundreds of benchmark indexes exist, to gauge the performance of all kinds of investments. There are benchmark indexes that track all types of equities (small cap, mid cap, international, industry sector and subsector, and so on), all types of bonds (short term, long term, Treasuries, municipals, and so on), as well as real estate, commodities, and so forth. For example, if your portfolio is almost exclusively allocated to small-cap equities, you might use the S&P SmallCap 600 Index, or some other small-cap index, as the benchmark. But our advice is to keep it simple. In the vast majority of cases, just using the two major indexes (the Barclays Capital U.S. Aggregate Bond Index and the S&P 500 Stock Index) — and, as necessary, blending them together as we describe in the next section — is all you need to do to get a respectably representative benchmark for your portfolio.

When you look up the S&P 500 Stock Index or the Barclays Capital U.S. Aggregate Bond Index, make sure you're looking at their total returns. You don't want just the price return, because that ignores dividends and interest income.

If your portfolio is extremely conservative (if it's almost exclusively allocated to fixed-income investments), then you can use the Barclays Capital U.S. Aggregate Bond Index directly as your benchmark. Alternatively, if your port-folio is very aggressive (if it's allocated almost entirely to equity investments), then you can use the S&P 500 Stock Index directly as your benchmark.

So, if the portfolio you got the 8 percent on at the beginning of this section was very aggressive, and, over the same five years, the CAGR of the S&P 500 Stock Index was 9 percent, you didn't do so well, did you?

If, like most investors, your portfolio is somewhere between extremely conservative and very aggressive, check out "Blending benchmark indexes," later in this chapter.

Understanding why benchmark comparisons are useful: Risk and opportunity cost

You can accomplish a lot by comparing an investment's return to a benchmark. By using percentage returns, you adjust for principal amount (an important step, as we explain in the "Paying attention to principal" section, earlier in this chapter). By calculating CAGRs over the same five-year period, you've adjusted for term and removed that from the equation as well. (We cover term in the "Coming to terms with term" section, earlier in this chapter.)

But what else have you done? By comparing your return to a relevant benchmark, you've also adjusted for the third and fourth key elements — risk and opportunity cost — in one fell swoop.

Risk, as we point out in Chapter 2, is a subjective thing. What's risky for one person may not seem risky at all for another. But however you define risk, the risk characteristics of an all-equity portfolio are going to be equivalent to the risk characteristics of the S&P 500 Stock Index. So the comparison adjusts for risk, whether you define risk as volatility, loss of principal, loss of purchasing power, or something else. (In Chapter 2, we discuss ways to measure your personal definition of risk.)

Opportunity cost represents the result you could've gotten for a typical alternative investment with similar risk over the same term. Well, that's what you measured with your benchmark index, right? So you've adjusted for opportunity cost, too. Whether your five-year term was a bull market or a bear market, or had periods of both, the same conditions also prevailed for your benchmark index, so you've got it covered.

Blending benchmark indexes

If you're like most investors, your portfolio isn't extremely conservative or remarkably aggressive. It's somewhere in the middle. In the "Selecting and using a benchmark for comparison" section, earlier in this chapter, we tell you about the S&P 500 Stock Index and the Barclays Capital U.S. Aggregate Bond Index, which are useful for comparisons to portfolios that are very heavy on equities (aggressive) or loaded up with fixed income (conservative), respectively. But if your portfolio is somewhere in the middle, how do you choose between those two indexes? The answer: You don't have to choose. You just need to blend them together.

For example, if you have a conservative portfolio but not one that is almost exclusively dominated by fixed-income investments, then a very effective benchmark for comparison is a 70/30 blend of the Barclays Capital U.S. Aggregate Bond Index and the S&P 500 Stock Index. (You use 70 percent of the former and 30 percent of the latter.) If the Barclays benchmark return is 4 percent, and the S&P benchmark return is 10 percent, then a 70/30 blend would be 5.8 percent. (Here's the math: [0.04 × 0.70] + [0.10 × 0.30] = 0.028 + 0.03 = 0.058, or 5.8 percent.)

For a moderate portfolio, a reasonable benchmark would be a 50/50 (or equal) blend of the Barclays and S&P indexes; for an aggressive portfolio, a 30/70 blend (with the 70 percent weight going to the S&P).

Tracking Your Progress against Your Long-Term Plan

The fifth of the five key elements for understanding your investment results — and the only one we don't address elsewhere in this chapter — is *suitability*. The suitability of an investment relates to whether it helps you achieve your lifetime financial objectives, and we explain the ins and outs of suitability in this section.

Determining suitability with a little common sense

You can figure out whether an investment is suitable for you by simply thinking about where you are financially and applying a little common sense.

If you're long retired and you have little money coming in other than Social Security benefits and the investment income from your portfolio, then an investment that requires you to put a large share of your portfolio in a very risky venture with a high expected return but sizeable probability of losing your principal clearly isn't suitable for you. If the investment happens to do poorly early on, you don't have the luxury of a long investment horizon over which to wait for the investment to earn back its losses. This is true regardless of whether the investment beats its benchmark. If the return on your investment is negative, it's no comfort to you to know that its benchmark return was more negative still. A suitable investment? Not in our book.

At the other extreme, if you're in your early 30s and you have a good job with great prospects and the likelihood of several decades of high compensation, then putting whatever you don't spend in an extremely conservative investment with an expected return that may not beat inflation is probably not suitable for you. Given your long investment horizon, you have the advantage of not being too concerned with short-term volatility. Your main concern is making sure that your hard-earned savings do not get eroded by inflation. Therefore, a low-volatility investment, with its associated low expected return, doesn't jibe with your long-term financial plan, regardless of whether the investment outperforms its benchmark.

Determining suitability with a Lifetime Cash-flow Projection

If you want to figure out the suitability of an investment for you with the most accuracy, you need to use your Lifetime Cash-flow Projection (LCP). (You can read all about LCPs in Chapter 7.)

The LCP is a big "what if" scenario generator. If you plug an investment into your LCP and the results get better (the probability of your assets outliving you increases), then the investment is a suitable one for you. If your LCP results get worse, then that investment isn't suitable for you.

You can also use your LCP to gauge the ongoing performance of your portfolio. Each projected future year of your LCP contains an estimate of your portfolio balance at the end of that year. By comparing your actual portfolio balances against these projected balances each year, you can get a very good reading of how your investments are performing against your long-term plan, and whether you're truly making progress or losing ground. It's a customized, meaningful measure of how well your investments are doing for you.

If you haven't developed an effective LCP, flip back to Chapter 7 and read up on how to create one.

As an example, refer to Table 7-6. Say you're entering the second year since this LCP was completed. You would expect to begin Year 2 with approximately $203,300 in your taxable accounts and $588,500 in your tax-deferred accounts, or $791,800 in your combined invested accounts overall. If your actual account balances total that amount or more, you're doing fine against your long-term plan. If not, then you need to understand why. Did your living expenses go up more than you expected? Did your compensation not increase as you had hoped?

And here's the key question for this chapter: Did you achieve the investment returns you had anticipated? In particular, did you earn the assumed 7 percent per this example?

When you compare your actual investment returns against your LCP, use dollar-weighted returns.

Another name for dollar-weighted return is *internal rate of return* (IRR). IRR is pretty tiresome to calculate on your own, so we advise using a spreadsheet program like Microsoft Excel or a financial calculator to crunch the numbers for you. Simply enter the dates and amounts of your principal payments, the dates and amounts of your income, and the date and amount of the market value of your investment at the end of your term, and execute the IRR function in your spreadsheet or calculator. Your IRR pops out. Or, you could ask your financial advisor (see Chapter 16 if you need one) to do it for you.

If you fell short of your investment goals, per your LCP, in a given year, don't panic. **Remember:** The LCP takes a long-term average investment return and assumes that you'll get that return each and every year. In some years you'll do better than the long-term average, and in other years you'll do worse. Comparing your return against appropriate benchmark returns each year (as we do earlier in this chapter) can help you decide if this was just one of those to-be-expected occasional bad years or if you truly underperformed and should be concerned.

Part IV
Going beyond the Basics

"Eat your cereal. Your father's heavily invested in grain."

In this part . . .

We take your investing to the next level by exploring alternative investments and what they can do for your portfolio. We also show you how to gain the kind of tax knowledge that separates the experienced investor from the novice. You discover how to protect your hard-earned gains from taxation — it's easier than you may think. And, finally, we wrap it all up by providing guidelines for revisiting your asset allocation and finding the right expert help when you need it.

Chapter 13

Walking to the Beat of a Different Drum: Opting for Alternative Investments

In This Chapter

▶ Getting to know common alternative investments

▶ Understanding how alternatives can improve your portfolio

▶ Deciding if you're ready for alternatives

*F*illing your portfolio with traditional asset classes — cash (and cash equivalents), fixed income (bonds and bond funds), and equities (stocks and stock funds) is a good start, but it isn't enough. To truly protect your portfolio from downside harm and enhance its long-term performance you need to broaden your portfolio's horizons.

In Chapter 3, we introduce the so-called *alternative* asset class — assets other than cash, bonds, and stocks. In this chapter, we take a closer look at three popular subclasses — real estate, commodities, and hedge funds — and explore their pros and cons. We also touch on some more esoteric alternatives such as art and collectibles, financial derivatives, structured notes, limited partnerships, and private equity.

We let you know why adding alternative asset classes — in the right proportions — can improve the performance and minimize the risk of your portfolio by tapping the power of poor *correlation*. (Check out Chapter 4 for all you need to know about correlation.)

Finally, we give you some guidelines to consider when deciding whether you're ready to take the plunge into alternative investments. Alternatives aren't for the timid. But those investors who take the time to understand them, how they behave, and how they can transform a portfolio for the better, will find them, well, quite an asset, indeed.

We examine quite an array of alternative investments in this chapter. Some, like real estate and commodities, belong in most every portfolio, in our view. Others, like hedge funds, have become quite popular but should be approached with great skepticism. Yet others, including fine art and derivatives, should be left to the experts. Our aim in this chapter is to guide you through the jungle of nontraditional investments, to make you comfortable with some that may scare you away, and to warn you off the rest.

Identifying Investment Alternatives

In this section, we look at the pros and cons of three popular alternative asset classes: real estate, commodities, and hedge funds. We briefly expand our discussion to more exotic choices: art and collectibles, financial derivatives (forwards, futures, options, and swaps), structured notes, limited partnerships, and private equity, which are best suited for, and often restricted to, the sophisticated (and well-heeled) investor.

We calculate the statistics quoted in this section (returns, correlations, and so on) using Brinton Eaton Wealth Advisors analysis of data, compiled using Morningstar EnCorr.

Regarding real estate

Perhaps the most popular of the alternative investments is real estate. Almost all investors are familiar with this asset class to some degree — after all, you have to live somewhere — but investment opportunities in real estate are much more varied than the place you live in. If you're going to get involved in investment real estate, you need to understand your options and how you can get started with this promising asset class, which can yield attractive returns if managed correctly. As the saying goes, "Buy land — they're not making any more of it."

Residential versus commercial

Many investors with invested assets of any size already own a good chunk of real estate through the equity they've built up in their own homes. But your primary residence, regardless of how much you paid for it or how much equity you may have built up, isn't an investment in our view. It's a *use asset* — you're using it instead of holding it primarily for purposes of growth and/or income, as you do with a stock or a bond. A car is another common example of a use asset.

Outside of use assets, your portfolio can contain either residential or commercial real estate:

- ✔ **Residential real estate:** Residential investment properties include apartments, houses, and any other type of real estate that you own but someone else occupies. Residential real estate can be as simple as renting the room over your garage to your younger brother for a few months or as complex as a real estate investment trust (see the following section) that manages a few dozen apartment complexes across the country.

- ✔ **Commercial real estate:** Commercial real estate includes a wide variety of options, such as office buildings, warehouses, storage facilities, retail malls, and even empty lots.

If you choose to own real estate by buying it outright, be prepared for a lot of work — or having to pay for other people to do a lot of work. Being a landlord can soak up a lot of your time and money. Repairing roofs, plugging plumbing leaks, fixing furnaces — that's only for those with loads of time and a love for that kind of handiwork. Even if you hire it all out, you'll soon find yourself moonlighting as a general contractor, which isn't all that appealing if you're looking for low-maintenance investment opportunities.

Real estate investment trusts

So how can you invest in real estate but avoid all the hassles associated with being a landlord? You can invest in a *real-estate investment trust* (REIT).

REITs are companies that you can invest in that buy, own, and manage real-estate properties on behalf of their investors. Most REITs handle properties of the type we mention in the preceding section — apartment complexes, office buildings, warehouses, storage facilities, retail malls, and so on. Some REITs are mortgage REITs, which offer debt financing for residential or commercial properties through their investments in mortgages and mortgage-backed securities (MBSs). (Check out Chapter 3 for more on mortgage-backed securities.)

By law, REITs must invest at least 75 percent of their total assets in real estate, receive at least 75 percent of their income from the rent of real property, and distribute at least 90 percent of their taxable income annually to shareholders in the form of dividends.

You should consider REITs if you're seeking the following:

- ✔ Income and long-term growth.

- ✔ A significantly higher dividend yield than other equities.

- ✔ A predictable income stream. (Commercial tenants sign long-term leases that rarely default.)

✔ Share price appreciation that beats inflation.

✔ An attractive risk/reward balance.

Over the long term, if you lump all types of REITs together, they've delivered what investors like to call *equity-like returns* (total annual returns that average in excess of 10 percent). Those returns however, can be quite volatile year by year. For an example of REIT volatility, take a look at Figure 13-1.

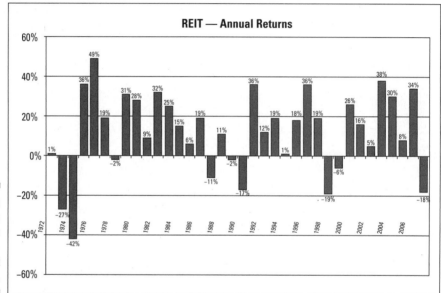

Figure 13-1:
Volatility in
real-estate
invest-
ment trust
returns.

Figure 13-1 shows the volatility of REITs using the National Association of Real Estate Investment Trust's (NAREIT) All REIT Index from the FTSE NAREIT Index Series. As you can see, in three of the last five years (2003, 2004, and 2006), the annual total return exceeded 30 percent! But in 2007, falling victim to the wide-ranging credit crisis that began that year, the return was seriously negative: –18 percent. Since NAREIT began compiling this index in 1972, the highest annual return was 49 percent (1976), and the lowest was –42 percent (1974). Since 1980, the situation has been a bit more stable: the highest return was 38 percent (2003), and the lowest was –19 percent (1998).

If that kind of volatility scares you, don't let it. Volatility in individual assets can be great for your portfolio as long as you maintain a low level of volatility at the portfolio level. As you can read in detail in Chapter 4, you want assets that have:

- **Healthy expected returns over the long haul:** Clearly, REITs qualify here.

- **Poor or even negative correlation with the other assets in your portfolio:** Although the correlation of REIT returns with equity returns has varied over the years from high (over 0.6) to reasonably low (under 0.25), their correlation with fixed income returns has always been low (usually below 0.2, and even negative over some periods). (To read all about correlation, check out Chapter 4.)

- **Sizeable volatilities:** REITs qualify here as well, as you can see in Figure 13-1.

Turn to Chapter 4 for a refresher on why this counterintuitive desire for high volatility makes sense. In brief, if an asset has the first two properties, then high volatility can work to your advantage at the portfolio level, giving you a portfolio that has a better expected return and lower volatility than a portfolio that lacks the asset. For these reasons, we like to see real estate (in the form of REITs) in virtually every portfolio.

If you're not comfortable picking individual REITs (which require just as much research and analysis as picking individual stocks), don't fret. There are a number of mutual funds and exchange-traded funds (ETFs) that package several individual REITs together, so you can get a nicely diversified exposure to REITs without too much hassle. You can get the scoop on ETFs in Chapter 2, but briefly, ETFs trade throughout the day like a stock and contain a basket of securities like a mutual fund.

A few popular REIT ETFs include iShares Dow Jones U.S. Real Estate Index Fund (symbol: IYR), Vanguard REIT ETF (symbol: VNQ), SPDR Dow Jones Wilshire REIT ETF (symbol: RWR), and SPDR Dow Jones Wilshire International Real Estate (symbol: RWX).

Harboring hard assets

Most of your portfolio will be made up of financial assets such as stocks and bonds, represented by pieces of paper of one sort or another. But your portfolio doesn't have to be limited to financial assets. There are other assets, called *hard assets* or *commodities,* which include such items as oil, gas, metals, textiles, foodstuffs, and livestock. These alternative investments can help to provide balance and variety in your portfolio, and in this section we let you know about some of the options and how you can capitalize on them.

Commodities

On their own, commodities are inappropriately risky investments for most investors. However, when you mix this asset class into your portfolio in the right proportion with your other assets, it tends to behave in a way that's *counter-cyclical* (meaning that commodities zig when other assets zag) to those other assets and produces a higher return with less risk over the long term. What's the right proportion for commodities? Turn back a few chapters to Chapter 8 for sample allocations that include commodities and vary depending on your style (aggressive or conservative) as an investor.

Commodities are generally a good thing to have in your portfolio because they have the three features (described in detail in Chapter 4) that you should seek out for all of your assets, as follows:

✔ **Healthy expected returns over the long haul:** Commodities provide attractive long-term return potential. They're like equities in that their total returns over many years (using the popular S&P GSCI), a commodity index) average above 10 percent per year. As you can see in Figure 13-2, the S&P GSCI return has exceeded 30 percent four times in the last nine years.

✔ **Poor or even negative correlation with the other assets in your portfolio:** For example, the correlation of the total return of the S&P GSCI with just about all the other common asset classes (bonds, stocks, real estate, and so on) has consistently been below 0.2, and has often been negative. (Read more about the important concept of correlation in Chapter 3.)

✔ **Sizeable volatilities:** Commodities have even more volatility than real estate (see "Regarding real estate" earlier in this chapter). Since the GSCI came into existence in 1970, its highest annual return was 75 percent (1973), and its lowest was –36 percent (1998). Even excluding those two extreme years, the range in annual returns was still quite wide, from –32 percent (2001) to 50 percent (2000).

Sizeable volatilities are desirable only if the asset has the first two features. (See "Real estate investment trusts," earlier in this chapter.)

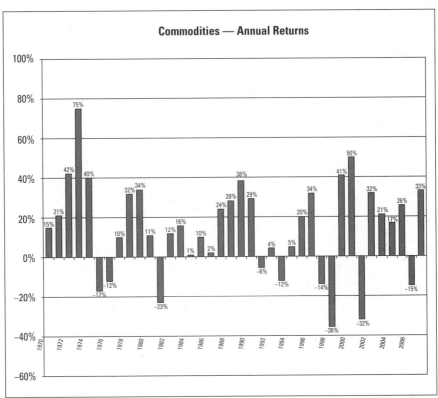

Figure 13-2: Commodity returns.

Commodity investment vehicles

Although, theoretically, you can own hard assets directly, doing so is problematic. As much as you may like to have your own 10,000-gallon gasoline tank in the backyard, gold bullion in your basement, or a herd of cattle grazing on the tomatoes in your garden, it probably isn't practical.

Many large investors own hard assets by purchasing *futures,* meaning that they agree to buy or sell the underlying assets at an agreed-upon date and price. (See Chapter 3 for more on futures.) Futures allow the investor's fortunes to rise and fall with the value of the hard asset, without taking possession of the asset itself.

As a practical matter, most individual investors don't own futures directly; they own mutual funds or ETFs or exchange-traded notes (ETNs) that, in turn, buy and sell these contracts. You can purchase these investments on stock exchanges just like stocks. They're an easy way for your portfolio to enjoy the fruits of a full basket of commodities. (See Chapter 9 for more information on ETFs and ETNs.)

Some funds are focused on a particular type of commodity, such as gold. Others correspond to a basket of commodities of various types.

Unless you're a commodities expert, you should focus on baskets of commodities if you want to incorporate hard assets in your portfolio.

Baskets of commodities are usually based on commodity indices that give weights to the different commodities in the index. Two popular commodity indices are the S&P GSCI and the Dow Jones–AIG (DJ-AIG) Commodity Index. The S&P GSCI has much more weight (over 70 percent in recent years) assigned to the energy subcategory (crude oil, natural gas, and so on). The DJ-AIG has no more than 33 percent weight assigned to any commodity subcategory, and is typically less volatile than the S&P GSCI. Investment vehicles that *track* the S&P GSCI (meaning that the vehicle moves in the same direction, by the same amount, at the same time, as the index) include

- ✔ Oppenheimer Commodity Strategy Total Return (symbol: QRAAX), a mutual fund
- ✔ iShares S&P GSCI Commodity-Indexed Trust (symbol: GSG), an ETF
- ✔ iPath S&P GSCI Total Return Index ETN (symbol: GSP), an ETN

The following investment vehicles track the DJ-AIG:

- ✔ PIMCO Commodity Real Return Strategy (symbol: PCRAX), a mutual fund
- ✔ iPath Dow Jones–AIG Commodity Index ETN (symbol: DJP), an ETN

Holding hedge funds

Hedge funds are private investment vehicles that engage in nontraditional strategies to enhance return or reduce risk, or both. (For more on hedge funds, check out Chapter 3.) Hedge funds continue to be lightly regulated compared to more traditional investments, given their history of catering to large and experienced investors who, presumably, can watch out for themselves. Their investors are generally required to meet minimum requirements regarding income level and net worth, and those minimums can be very high.

How big players use futures

How do large investors work with futures? Let's say an airline, concerned about the cost of jet fuel over the course of its fiscal year, is looking for a solution to price spikes. It fixes this cost at a constant value by entering into a futures contract, which guarantees delivery of a specified amount of oil, at a specified price, at a given time. The futures contract needs a *counterparty* (a party that participates on the other side of a financial transaction) to agree and make good on the guarantee. In this situation, an oil company that is equally concerned about the price of oil moving *in the other direction* may agree to be the counterparty. As a result, each party has hedged its risk.

A futures contract increases in value dollar for dollar if the price of oil increases. (Likewise, it falls dollar for dollar if oil prices decline.) By owning futures, an airline can hedge its exposure to oil prices. (By selling it, the oil company can as well.) Because it's impractical for counterparties to always find each other and agree on exact amounts to hedge each and every time they need to, a liquid futures market exists to facilitate this need. Structured notes serve the same purpose as futures contract (see ""Exploring more exotic choices," later in this chapter).

Although we encourage you to include real estate and commodities (we cover both earlier in this chapter) in your portfolio, we're less excited about hedge funds. They have their place, but you need to do some serious due diligence if you want to invest in one, and you need to be prepared to share a big piece of your wealth with the hedge-fund manager. For these reasons, and because hedge funds appear and disappear from the landscape with great frequency, we have no specific hedge funds to recommend.

So why cover hedge funds at all in this chapter? Because although you may not be ready to invest in hedge funds immediately, you'll certainly hear about them, and you may want to consider them as an option after you have a ton of investment experience under your belt. In this section, we walk you through some hedge-fund basics.

Hedge-fund strategies

There are a number of different types of hedge funds, categorized into various *strategies.* No standard terminology for these strategies exists, but here are some of the popular strategy terms:

- **Long/short equity:** This strategy is for investors who want to make simultaneous bets that certain stocks will go up in value and certain other stocks will go down. In the vernacular, they *go long* on the former and *go short* on the latter. Going long usually involves owning the stock or a call option on the stock. Going short often involves owning a put option on the stock or selling shares that you've borrowed from a broker and don't yet own. (We discuss options in the "Exploring more exotic choices" section, later in this chapter, and in more detail in Chapter 9.)

✔ **Global macro:** This strategy entails investing in vehicles that appreciate or depreciate depending on the performance of various country economies and inter-country currency exchange rates.

✔ **Event driven:**

• **Merger arbitrage:** In this strategy, the hedge fund capitalizes on the discrepancy between the market prices of two firms that are being merged, by simultaneously going long on the stock of the firm selling and going short on the firm buying.

• **Distressed securities:** The opportunities for this strategy occur when a company is undergoing, or expected to undergo, a bankruptcy or restructuring in an attempt to stay solvent. This strategy is usually very risky.

✔ **Relative value:**

• **Market neutral:** In this strategy, the hedge fund exploits perceived security pricing anomalies in an attempt to produce stable returns, regardless of the direction of the broad market.

• **Convertible arbitrage:** This strategy involves purchasing convertible securities (see Chapter 3) and then subsequently going short on the underlying stock (or vice versa).

How do you decide among the various hedge-fund strategies? We recommend you don't, unless you're an experienced investor. If you're relatively new to investing but still want to get in on some hedge funds, funds of funds could be a good option for you (see the following section).

Funds of funds

Some investors may want to spread their hedge-fund investments among a variety of different strategies. For most investors, this is difficult, given the hefty minimum investment that each hedge fund typically requires. Other investors may not feel comfortable enough in their investment expertise to pursue individual hedge-fund strategies. Luckily, there's another option that can solve both of those problems.

A *fund of funds* essentially invests in a variety of hedge-fund strategies on your behalf. Buying a share of a fund of funds gives you exposure to many different strategies at once, with only a single minimum investment. The choice of strategies within each fund of funds is outside of your control (a welcome feature for most investors), but different funds of funds offer different mixes of different underlying strategies, and you can choose the fund of funds that provides you a mix closest to the one you desire.

However, the constancy of this mix within the fund of funds over time is not always guaranteed, so you can start out with the type of mix you want — say, an emphasis on long/short equity and convertible arbitrage — and end up with a fund of funds that's loaded up with global macro.

Ask your broker or financial advisor for advice on how to go about investing in a fund of funds.

Hedge-fund fees

Hedge funds are generally quite expensive, and if you buy them you're often charged with two layers of fees:

- ✔ **A flat percentage of assets invested:** This percentage is typically 1.5 percent to 2.5 percent. And that's already on the high end of most mutual-fund fees.

- ✔ **A percentage of profits:** On top of the flat fee, you'll also typically be charged with a percentage of profits (20 percent is common). A hedge-fund fee schedule of 2 percent of assets and 20 percent of profits is referred to as *2 and 20.* The percentage of profits is usually levied on a *high-water mark basis,* meaning that, if the fund loses value, it must make up the loss first, before profits are calculated for purposes of fee determination.

With funds of funds (see the preceding section), there's yet another layer of fees on top of the two layers we just mentioned. This third layer is another percentage of assets levied to compensate the manager who selects and monitors the hedge-fund managers for each of the underlying strategies.

The hedge-fund industry has evolved quite a bit over the years. There has been explosive growth in the number of funds available, and the minimum required investment amounts have come down sharply, but they're still steep for most investors. Some funds of funds have now lowered — yes, *lowered* — their minimums to $25,000. More typical is a minimum of $500,000 to $1 million. Clearly, hedge funds aren't for the average novice investor.

The growth and increased availability of hedge funds is a natural response to higher demand, but the rising popularity has had troubling ramifications. It's now very easy for unsophisticated investors to venture into investments they don't fully understand, in an area that is still lightly regulated. More fundamentally, the substantial increase in the aggregate amounts invested in hedge funds means that there is a huge amount of money being spread over a limited amount of good ideas. This situation has inevitably led to more and more mediocre returns — but the fees have still remained high.

Not only do you need a hefty minimum to open a hedge-fund account, but the fund needs to consider you an *accredited investor* (a financially sophisticated investor who isn't required to receive certain securities filings on your investments). To be such an investor, as a rule of thumb, you need to earn more than $200,000 annually (or have a joint income of $300,000) and a net worth exceeding $1 million.

Although hedge funds are lightly regulated by the securities industry, there are rules and regulations to consider. You can jeopardize the tax-deferred status of your individual retirement account (IRA) by using assets from alternative investments. Check with your tax advisor before you make any decisions.

Exploring more exotic choices

If you want to expand beyond the three broad types of alternative investments (real estate, hard assets, and hedge funds), there are yet others to consider, though we don't recommend them for most portfolios. Like hedge funds (see the preceding section), we cover these exotic investment choices because there's a very good chance that you'll read and hear about them, and you need to understand the basics.

There's nothing that says you *can't* invest in them, if you have the means, investment experience, and expertise required.

Art and collectibles

Limited-edition oil paintings or collections of classic cars have value that isn't easily determined, and these types of holdings aren't very liquid — it's not easy to convert them to cash on short notice. You need a good amount of knowledge yourself to invest in such choices, or you need to work with a consultant who can provide reliable information.

Derivatives

Derivatives are securities that derive their value from another security. They include the following:

- ✔ **Forwards:** In a forward, two parties agree to sell and purchase a particular commodity at specific date in the future. Forwards are similar to a futures contract (we discuss futures in the "Commodity investment vehicles" section, earlier in this chapter), but they're not as easily transferred or cancelled.

- ✔ **Options contracts:** Options contracts allow you to *call* (buy) or *put* (sell) an asset at a fixed price until a specific date. To be successful, you have to be right about timing and the valuation of an underlying asset.

✔ **Swaps:** Swaps involve trading the income stream of one asset (such as a bond) for another. This type of derivative is for the ultra-sophisticated investor.

Structured notes

Structured notes are debt securities with special features. A structured note may be a bond that pays interest based on an index, such as the S&P 500 Stock Index, instead of paying typical interest payments.

Limited partnerships

A *limited partnership* is a group of investors in which one or more limited partners has a limited liability to the firm's creditors, meaning that they're liable only to the extent of their investments. The partnerships typically pursue unusual investments in the private equity markets (see the following section).

Private placements

Also known as *private equity,* a *private placement* occurs when an issue of debt or equity securities is sold to a single buyer, or a limited number of buyers, without a public offering. Generally an investment banker, who acts as an agent, brings together the buyer and the seller.

Tapping the Power of Investments That Zig when Others Zag

By themselves, real estate, commodities, and the other types of alternative investments that we explain in this chapter can scare the heck out of investors. But, paradoxically, when added to a portfolio in the right proportions (see Chapter 4 for the background information and Chapter 8 for some sample proportions), they can make a portfolio not only better, but safer. This is because these investments, although volatile, have a benign kind of volatility. They tend to zig when the more traditional investments zag.

For example, when stocks and bonds decline together, commodities tend to increase (and vice versa). But it isn't enough for an asset to exhibit counter-cyclical behavior; it must also be able to deliver healthy long-term returns in order for it to be worth adding to your portfolio.

As we discuss in detail in Chapter 4, finding assets with this kind of behavior is the holy grail of asset allocation. That's why enlightened investors (and we hope you'll join their ranks!) seek out these assets.

Savvy investors see the value that alternative assets can add to a portfolio — making it safer as well as better performing. Less-savvy investors may be scared away by the volatility of an alternative asset in isolation. Make sure you're in the former camp!

Take a quick look at Figure 13-3, which examines the combination of REITs and stocks. As we mention earlier in this chapter, these two assets are far from having perfect negative correlation. (See Chapter 4 for more on correlation.) In fact, they're positively correlated, but they aren't *perfectly* positively correlated, so they can actually work quite well together in your portfolio.

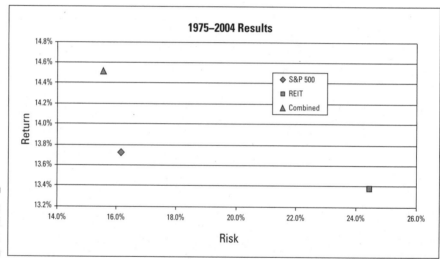

Figure 13-3:
How 2 + 2
can equal 5.

Stocks are represented in Figure 13-3 by the S&P 500 Stock Index, and real estate is represented by the NAREIT All-REIT Index from the FTSE NAREIT Index Series. Return is calculated as the 30-year compound annual growth rate (assuming reinvestment of dividends); risk is calculated as the annual standard deviation in the individual annual returns. (Chapter 2 is your source for all things risk and return.) The asset labeled "Combined" is a simple portfolio consisting of a 50/50 allocation to stocks and real estate, rebalanced annually. The figure plots each of these three assets on the risk/return map we introduce in Chapter 2.

The best assets are those farthest northwest on the map (the assets with high return and low risk).

As you can see in this figure, over this 30-year period, stocks achieve a return of 13.7 percent and a standard deviation of 16 percent. REITs deliver a 13.4 percent return and a standard deviation of 24.5 percent. The combination of the two results in a return of 14.5 percent and a standard deviation of just under 16 percent.

This simple example illustrates the phenomenon that there's magic in rebalancing. By combining assets with less-than-perfect positive correlation, you can get a portfolio with less risk than you would achieve with any one the assets alone. More remarkably, by combining these assets (and regularly rebalancing), you can get a return for the portfolio that is greater than the return for any asset within it! (See Chapter 5 for more on how to create such magic.)

Deciding When to Go Alternative

When should you consider adding alternative investments to your portfolio? When you determine you have the stomach to tolerate their unusual behavior and when you know you'll have the time to ride herd and pay attention to them. We discuss those requirements, in turn, in this section.

Hanging on for the alternative investment ride

The volatility of alternative investments isn't for the squeamish or faint of heart. It takes a certain internal constitution to dispassionately observe a substantial portion of your portfolio lose a significant part of its value, and to buy more of the culprit asset when that happens, anticipating that it'll rise again. But that's what it often takes for alternative investment strategies to work.

Paradoxically, your overall portfolio will be quite stable as the strategy plays out (if you have the right mix of assets), but the component pieces will bounce around erratically. You need to stay focused on the big picture and hang on for the ride — and maybe buy a couple of those big rolls of antacid tablets.

Paying enough attention to alternatives

If you're going to hold alternative investments, you have to be vigilant. The volatility of these assets presents opportunities to rebalance at unpredictable times. You need to be alert to these opportunities and be ready to jump on them when they arise, which requires virtually continual portfolio review.

The formula is to look frequently and act opportunistically (see Chapter 5). This activity can be quite a burden on the average investor, which is one reason why people hire advisors to do the heavy lifting. (For more information on how an advisor can help you, turn to Chapter 16.)

Chapter 14

Managing Your Taxes like a Pro

. . . .

. . . .

*I*t'd be a real shame if you did a great job creating a high-performance investment portfolio and ended up giving away a bigger-than-necessary chunk of it in income taxes. And it'd be an even bigger shame if you coughed up all those taxes for no other reason than poor planning!

Throughout the book, we give you information on the tax aspects of various investments and investment accounts, and specific advice on how to minimize the amount of income taxes you'll ultimately have to pay on your investments. In this chapter, we expand on all that good advice, give you some concrete examples, and help you develop a coordinated, coherent strategy to manage your investment-related taxes.

To do that, we look at several ways you can protect your portfolio from unnecessary and avoidable tax hits. First, we consider the income-tax implications of selling securities and tell you what you need to know to be tax-smart about the process. Then we delve into *asset location,* a strategy for matching the tax characteristics of your individual investments with the tax features of the investment accounts you place them in. Those are both great defensive maneuvers.

Then we tell you how to go on the offensive. We fill you in on tax-loss harvesting, which is a technique that many investors don't take full advantage of. You're bound to take losses as an investor, but understanding tax-loss harvesting will help you to take your losses when it makes the most sense for you. In other words, you can improve your portfolio by taking the lemons the market sometimes hands you and making lemonade.

We wrap up our chapter on taxes with a warning against going too far. Yes, you can get so carried away and enamored of being tax-smart that you make decisions based on tax considerations that are actually investment mistakes. *Remember:* Your true goal is not simply to minimize your taxes, but to maximize your after-tax results.

Throughout the chapter, we focus on federal income taxes. Many states have their own income-tax statutes, and these vary considerably from state to state. If you live or work in a state that levies income taxes, the strategies we outline in this chapter may also help you minimize those taxes as well.

In this chapter we give you effective strategies for protecting your assets from taxation while you're allocating them. If you're looking for a full tax guide, though, you'll want to check out *Taxes For Dummies,* by Eric Tyson, MBA; Margaret A. Munro, EA; and David J. Silverman, EA (Wiley). It's updated every year with the latest tax advice.

Playing It Smart When Selling Securities

Here's some good news: You have complete control over one of the most important events that contributes to the income taxes you pay on your portfolio. What are those events? The selling of securities.

You don't incur a tax when you buy a security. You're taxed to some extent on the income (interest and dividends) that your investments generate while you hold them, but you don't have much control over the amount and timing of that income. When it comes to selling, however, you're in the driver's seat. And just like any time you're behind the wheel, you want to be smart and alert. That's exactly what we help you to do in this section.

Note: We don't cover tax-advantaged accounts like your IRA or 401(k) in this section because nothing that goes on within those accounts — buying, selling, or receiving income — generates taxes. This section is devoted to taxable accounts, but we do cover tax-advantaged accounts later in this chapter, in the "Locating Your Assets Properly" section.

Identifying the information you need

Armed with the right information on your securities, you can minimize the tax impact of your selling decisions. There are two pieces of information about each security you own that you need to have available to make savvy selling decisions:

✔ Your cost basis

✔ Your purchase date

We discuss both cost basis and purchase date in this section.

Cost basis

Say what you like about the IRS and its minions, but one nice thing about them is that they try not to tax you on the same money twice (bless their hearts). The *cost basis* (sometimes called *tax basis*) of the security you're holding is the amount that the IRS assumes you've already paid taxes on. You don't have to pay taxes on that amount again. When you sell the security, you then get taxed on only the *realized gain,* which consists of your proceeds (the dollar amount you get from the buyer) less your cost basis.

Clearly the cost basis of your securities is very important in determining what you'll owe the tax man, so it's important that you know that information for every security you own. In some cases, that's relatively easy. If you buy shares of a stock for $20,000 and never buy any more, then your cost basis in that stock is forever $20,000. In other words, the IRS assumes that you already paid taxes on that $20,000 at some point. This remains your cost basis even if the stock splits while you hold it.

If the price per share of a stock gets high, the issuing company may declare a *stock split,* which increases the number of shares outstanding by some multiple and simultaneously decreases the share price by the same multiple. In the example earlier, if the stock splits two-for-one, you'll be holding twice the number of shares that you held before, at half the price per share on each of those shares, but your cost basis remains the same at $20,000.

Other cases can be a bit more complicated. For example, say you purchase a mutual fund for $10,000. The IRS assumes that you already paid taxes on that $10,000 at some point, and this becomes your cost basis. Now assume that you've arranged for the mutual fund to automatically reinvest any dividends and distributions back into the fund, which is common. After a while, the mutual fund pays you a dividend of $500. You owe income tax on the $500 that year, and your new cost basis in the fund becomes $10,500. (If you took the $500 dividend and spent it on a gigantic stuffed swordfish instead of reinvesting it, then you'd still owe tax on the money, but it wouldn't be added to your cost basis because it's no longer part of your investment.) Later, the mutual fund makes a capital-gain distribution of $1,000 (see Chapter 9 for a description of capital gain distributions — one of the features that distinguishes mutual funds from exchange-traded funds) and that gets reinvested, too. You owe income tax on the $1,000 that year, and now your cost basis increases to $11,500. Finally, you sell your shares in the mutual fund for $15,000. What is your gain? And what do you owe taxes on?

Here it's important to distinguish between your investment gain and your taxable gain. Your investment gain is simply how much money you made on your original outlay. You originally invested $10,000 in a mutual fund and sold it for $15,000, making your investment gain $5,000. Your taxable gain is how much of that gain you'll be paying taxes on. You already paid taxes on $11,500 of your investment. Therefore, your taxable gain will only be $3,500 ($15,000 proceeds less $11,500 cost basis). If you aren't paying attention to your cost basis and assumed it was just your initial investment of $10,000, then you'd be paying taxes on the entire $5,000 investment gain — and on the $1,500 piece of it twice!

Keeping track of the cost basis of every security can be quite tedious. Fortunately, most brokers do that for you, for the securities that you purchase with them. If you transfer securities from one broker to another, you need to make sure that the new broker records the correct cost basis for you.

Brokers can help with your record-keeping, but it's your responsibility to post the correct cost basis on your tax return in the year that you make the sale.

If you decide to do your own record-keeping on the cost bases of your investments, personal account management software such as Quicken and Microsoft Money can help you. These programs are particularly useful if you have multiple brokers or have changed brokers often.

Purchase date

It may sound simple, but knowing the date when you purchased a security is extremely important information. Here's why: The way the U.S. tax system is currently structured, gains on securities you hold for one year or less are considered short-term gains and get taxed at your marginal ordinary income-tax rate (the tax rate associated with your tax bracket), which can be fairly high. Securities that are held for one year plus one day get taxed at the long-term capital gains rate, which for most people is quite a bit lower.

As an example, you may have a security you'd like to sell that you happened to buy 11½ months ago when its market value was considerably lower. One simple strategy for reducing taxes is to hold onto that security a little while longer until it qualifies as being held long term. Doing this will likely result in materially lowering the amount you pay in taxes on the sale — perhaps by half or more, depending on your tax bracket. That's not chump change.

Keeping track of purchase dates can be tedious, just as keeping track of the cost basis of every security you own can be. Here again, most brokers can help with your record-keeping, as can the software applications we mention in the preceding section.

Figuring the tax implications of your transactions

If you know the cost basis and purchase date of your securities, you can determine how much income tax you'll be paying if you decide to sell. One area in which this is particularly useful is deciding which securities to sell when you rebalance your portfolio. (Rebalancing is a critical part of the asset allocation process, so if you need to brush up, turn to Chapters 5 and 11.)

For example, in Table 14-1, you can see three securities, their cost bases, their current values, and their purchase dates. (Each security is a representative of the energy equity sector.) Say that you own these securities, and when it comes time to rebalance your portfolio you figure out that you need to trim your energy holdings. Which security should you sell?

Table 14-1	The Tax Implications of Three Energy Securities			
Security	**Cost Basis**	**Current Value**	**Date of Purchase**	**Tax if Sold Now**
A	$10,000	$13,000	18 months ago	$450
B	$12,000	$10,000	2 months ago	$0
C	$10,000	$12,000	6 months ago	$500

Source: Brinton Eaton Wealth Advisors.

If you think all the securities in Table 14-1 are equally good investments with similar forecasts for future growth, then you should sell shares of security B. Because B's cost basis is greater than its current value, you'll have a tax loss, which you can later apply to your advantage. (Check out the "Harvesting Tax Losses" section in this chapter for all the details on how that works.)

What if you really weren't indifferent among all three securities? What if you really wanted to hold onto Security B, but you were willing to let go of Security A or Security C? Selling Security A would result in a gain of $3,000, while selling Security C would result in a gain of $2,000. You may think that selling Security C would, therefore, have the lower tax impact. However, note that Security C was bought only six months ago, so its gains would be taxed at your marginal ordinary income tax rate, which we assume is 25 percent in this example. The resulting tax would, therefore, be $500 (25 percent of your $2,000 gain). Security A was bought well over a year ago, so its gains would be taxed at the long-term capital gains rate of 15 percent; the resulting tax would be $450 (15 percent of $3,000). So, in this case, selling Security A is the better strategy. If your marginal ordinary income tax rate is greater than 25 percent, then the advantage is that much bigger.

It's not what you make, but what you keep that matters. By using the cost basis, date of purchase, and knowledge of your tax rates, you can execute trades that will accomplish your asset allocation goals while minimizing the tax impact. Doing so will save you some money in the short term and could save you quite a bit in the long term, if you're always mindful of it.

Locating Your Assets Properly

Of all the strategies at your disposal that can minimize taxes without sacrificing returns, locating your assets in the most appropriate accounts will have the longest-lasting impact. Other strategies that we discuss (such as the considerations for selling securities that we explain in the previous section) concern one-time events. However, if you buy an asset in a less-than-optimal account, you'll be paying extra taxes every year that you hold it. Asset location (see Chapter 10) can really help you hang onto your returns.

In this section, we fill you in on the details of asset location, and we illustrate its impact with a detailed example.

Understanding tax-advantaged accounts

There are two general types of accounts you can own: those that are tax advantaged and those that aren't. A tax-advantaged account is typically a retirement account such as a 401(k), IRA, or Roth IRA (see Chapter 10 for the tax features of these accounts). The beauty of these accounts is the *tax-deferred growth* they allow you. That means you don't pay any taxes on the growth or income you receive from the investments that are in these accounts (even if you sell securities at a gain), until you withdraw the money from the accounts. (With a Roth IRA, you don't pay taxes at withdrawal either!)

If an account isn't tax-advantaged, then you have to pay taxes every year on any income you receive from any investments that are housed in that account. If you sell a security at a gain, you owe taxes on that, too. With all these opportunities for the IRS to tax your investments, you can see how making clever choices about where you locate your money can help you greatly increase the amount you're able to keep. For a detailed example of what we're talking about, read on.

Considering an asset location example

Even with tax-advantaged accounts, you'll need to pay taxes on the growth of your investment eventually (when you withdraw it). So does it really matter if you pay those taxes every year versus only when you withdraw? You bet it does! To understand why, take a look at Tables 14-2 and 14-3.

Table 14-2	Investing in a Taxable Account				
Year	Beginning Balance	Investment Growth at 7%	Tax at 25%	Net Investment Growth	Ending Balance
1	$100,000	$7,000	$1,750	$5,250	$105,250
2	$105,250	$7,368	$1,842	$5,526	$110,776
3	$110,776	$7,754	$1,939	$5,816	$116,591
4	$116,591	$8,161	$2,040	$6,121	$122,712
5	$122,712	$8,590	$2,147	$6,442	$129,155
6	$129,155	$9,041	$2,260	$6,781	$135,935
7	$135,935	$9,515	$2,379	$7,137	$143,072
8	$143,072	$10,015	$2,504	$7,511	$150,583
9	$150,583	$10,541	$2,635	$7,906	$158,489
10	$158,489	$11,094	$2,774	$8,321	$166,810
11	$166,810	$11,677	$2,919	$8,758	$175,567
12	$175,567	$12,290	$3,072	$9,217	$184,784
13	$184,784	$12,935	$3,234	$9,701	$194,486
14	$194,486	$13,614	$3,403	$10,210	$204,696
15	$204,496	$14,329	$3,582	$10,747	$215,443
16	$215,443	$15,081	$3,770	$11,311	$226,753
17	$226,753	$15,873	$3,968	$11,905	$238,658
18	$238,658	$16,706	$4,177	$12,530	$251,187
19	$251,187	$17,583	$4,396	$13,187	$264,375
20	$264,375	$18,506	$4,627	$13,880	$278,254
				$178,254	

Source: Brinton Eaton Wealth Advisors.

The after-tax growth in Table 14-2 is $178,254.

Table 14-3		Investing in a Tax-Deferred Account	
Year	**Beginning Balance**	**Investment Growth at 7%**	**Ending Balance**
1	$100,000	$7,000	$107,000
2	$107,000	$7,490	$114,490
3	$114,490	$8,014	$122,504
4	$122,504	$8,575	$131,080
5	$131,080	$9,176	$140,255
6	$140,255	$9,818	$150,073
7	$150,073	$10,505	$160,578
8	$160,578	$11,240	$171,819
9	$171,819	$12,027	$183,846
10	$183,846	$12,869	$196,715
11	$196,715	$13,770	$210,485
12	$210,485	$14,734	$225,219
13	$225,219	$15,765	$240,985
14	$240,985	$16,869	$257,853
15	$257,853	$18,050	$275,903
16	$275,903	$19,313	$295,216
17	$295,216	$20,665	$315,882
18	$315,882	$22,112	$337,993
19	$337,993	$23,660	$361,653
20	$361,653	$25,316	$386,968
		$286,968	

Source: Brinton Eaton Wealth Advisors.

The pre-tax growth in Table 14-3 is $286,968. Upon withdrawal, the 25 percent tax would be $71,742, leaving an after-tax growth of $215,226. So, there is a $36,972 benefit to tax-deferred growth (the difference between $215,226 and $178,254).

To really grasp all the numbers in Tables 14-2 and 14-3, start by assuming that you want to invest $100,000 in real estate investment trusts (REITs), which are a great portfolio diversifier but a notoriously tax-inefficient invest-ment. (As we explain in Chapter 10, we consider REITs tax-inefficient because a REIT must distribute at least 90 percent of its income to shareholders, and this income is taxed at your marginal ordinary income tax rate.) Here are a few other assumptions you can make for the purposes of Tables 14-2 and 14-3, just to keep the example simple (all these assumptions are taken into account in the tables):

✔ Your marginal tax rate is 25 percent.

✔ The annual income from the REIT is 7 percent of its value at the beginning of each year.

✔ You reinvest this income (less the taxes you owe on that income) in that year.

✔ Your time horizon is 20 years.

In Table 14-2, the investment was made in a taxable account; in Table 14-3, the investment was made in an IRA, which is tax advantaged. After the 20-year period, we compare the after-tax amount of the growth of the portfolio (the final balance less the $100,000 initial investment) under both scenarios. In order to make a fair comparison, we assume that the amount of the growth in the IRA is completely withdrawn and so is decreased by your marginal tax rate.

As you can see, if you bought the REITs in your IRA instead of your taxable account, you'd have almost $37,000 extra in your pocket just because of that one-time decision you made 20 years earlier. And the difference could be even greater if your returns are higher, your marginal ordinary income tax bracket is higher, and your time horizon is longer. Capitalizing on tax-deferred growth really can help you hang onto thousands of dollars.

In addition to REITs, there are other tax-inefficient investments you should be aware of, including the following:

✔ **Commodity funds:** These can generate a lot of highly taxable income.

✔ **Mutual funds:** Mutual funds can create capital gains distributions; some of these distributions may be considered short term and, therefore, subject to your higher ordinary income tax rate. Furthermore, you have no control over the timing and may get a large distribution in a year when it's important for you to lower your taxable income.

✔ **Bonds and bond funds:** These allow you some flexibility. Their tax nature depends on what kind you buy. For example, in a tax-advantaged fund you can purchase highly taxable corporate bonds without tax concerns. If you want to hold bonds in a non-tax-advantaged account and you're in a high tax bracket, go for municipal bonds, which are tax-free.

Some assets actually have tax benefits that would be squandered in a tax-advantaged account. Here are a couple examples:

✔ **International stocks:** These stocks may cause you to pay a foreign tax, regardless of the type of account they're held in. This tax appears as a deduction on your account so you don't have to worry about filing foreign tax returns. If the international stock is housed in a non-tax-advantaged account, then you can claim the foreign tax you paid as a credit on your U.S. tax return. This credit is lost if you hold the stock in a tax-advantaged account.

> ✔ **Growth stocks:** When growth stocks do what you hope they'll do (grow in market value, without necessarily paying dividends), and then you sell them at least a year after you purchase them, the growth is taxed at the long-term capital-gains tax rate — if you hold the stocks in a taxable account. If you hold them in a tax-deferred account, then that growth will eventually be taxed at your marginal ordinary income tax rate, which can be double the long-term rate. This difference often outweighs the benefit of tax-deferred growth inside the tax-advantaged account. So, which account is the better home for a growth stock? It depends on how the stock grows and how often it's sold.

This doesn't imply that you should never hold growth stocks in an IRA or 401(k). But if you do have a choice, it's usually wise to push more of the growth stocks into the non-tax-advantaged accounts.

Harvesting Tax Losses

If you're faced with an investment that decreases in value, you can use that tax loss to your advantage. You just have to be alert to the opportunities. This is called *tax-loss harvesting*. We touch on this strategy in Chapter 11 and expand on it for you in this section. Here, we also show you how you can structure your portfolio to make these opportunities easier to exploit.

Tax losses are handy things. They can be used to offset any taxable capital gains you may have for the year on your other transactions. If your total tax losses are greater than your total taxable gains, then you can use up to $3,000 of your excess capital losses to offset ordinary income, such as your wages. And there's more: Any tax losses not used up in a given tax year can be carried forward, meaning that you can apply them against gains and (to an extent) income in future tax years. Tax losses are versatile and useful, so keep your eyes out for opportunities to snag them when you can.

Staying alert to tax-loss opportunities

Of course, the first step to taking advantage of losses is to notice that you have them. The market value of the securities in your accounts, and whether you have a gain or loss, should be available online daily through your broker. Checking for tax losses should be part of your regular investment mainte-nance routine and should be done frequently.

With tax-loss harvesting, be sure to keep the size of the loss in mind. You'll be paying two transaction costs when you harvest — one to sell the security and one to buy a replacement. Make sure that the loss is large enough to offer you a tax benefit that makes the transaction worthwhile. For example, the advisors at Brinton Eaton like to see a tax loss of at least $2,000 in a security before they consider harvesting.

Using exchange-traded fund swaps to harvest tax losses

Say you have an asset that you think has great long-term potential, but has temporarily decreased in value, to the point where its market value is now below its cost basis. In other words, it's sitting in an unrealized loss position. If it's in a taxable account, then it's possible to take (realize) the loss, get the tax benefit for it, and still get in on the future growth of the asset.

For example, suppose you have $100,000 invested in the healthcare equity sector, and your entire investment there is in a healthcare ETF offered by ETF Vendor A. But then the ETF's value drops to $95,000. You still think that healthcare is a great sector to be in with strong long-term potential for growth, so you don't really want to get out of the healthcare sector, but you'd like to take that $5,000 loss to offset other taxable gains you've realized during the year.

This situation is ripe for some tax-loss harvesting. How does it work? It's pretty simple, really: You sell your healthcare ETF, and then you get to claim the $5,000 loss on your tax return. You simultaneously buy another health-care ETF, one from ETF Vendor B. Each ETF tracks a different, but similar, healthcare sector index. As a result, the two ETFs behave almost identically, so from an asset allocation standpoint, you haven't changed a thing (but you have improved your situation for tax time).

In order to keep your asset allocation unchanged when tax-loss harvesting, it's important to buy a replacement security that's as similar as possible to the security you just sold. This is one benefit to mutual funds and ETFs over individual stocks. For each of the main asset classes, subclasses, and sectors we discuss in this book, there are several ETFs and mutual funds that behave practically identically. Finding a replacement can be much more difficult if the security is a stock because there's a lot of variation in how different stocks behave, even if the companies are in the same business. This is one reason that any sector you want to invest in should have a base or working layer of an ETF or mutual fund (see Chapter 11).

Keeping clean when it comes to wash sales

When you participate in tax-loss harvesting, be sure that you don't sell and buy back the same security within 30 days. This is called a *wash sale,* and tax losses that you rack up with wash sales aren't allowed on your tax return. So all the work you'd do to sell and buy those securities would be, well, a wash.

If you were to sell and then buy back the same healthcare ETF too soon, then that $5,000 loss we talked about earlier would be considered part of a wash sale and the loss wouldn't be allowed on your tax return. But the two ETFs we just described are considered distinct for tax purposes, so the transaction isn't considered a wash sale. This isn't an aggressive, underhanded bit of skullduggery either — the tax benefit of swapping ETFs in this manner is a feature touted quite publicly by ETF vendors, so don't feel bad about taking advantage of it.

Of course, you can always avoid a wash sale by waiting more than 30 days to buy back a security, but the ETF-swapping strategy we describe doesn't leave you light in that asset class for those 30 days.

Tax Sensitivity: Good in Small Doses

You can use several techniques to minimize the negative effects of taxes on your investments. But don't get carried away and find yourself making all your investment decisions based on tax ramifications. It may sound crazy, but each of the strategies we cover in this chapter should be disregarded if there are compelling investment reasons to do so.

Remind yourself often: "Don't let the tax tail wag the investment dog."

The only way to eliminate taxes completely is to not have any taxable income or gains. That's a steep price to pay just to frustrate the tax man. (The phrase *cutting off your nose to spite your face* comes to mind.)

When it comes to taxes, your goal is to maximize your after-tax return, not minimize your taxes.

For a basic example of what we mean, consider the case of municipal bonds (see Chapters 3 and 9). When it comes to taxes, municipal bonds are pretty appealing compared to other types of bonds, but their yields are also typically lower. Buying municipal bond funds may result in your not having to pay taxes on the interest income you make on the bonds, but is the lower yield worth it? In order to make that decision, you need to know how much you'd earn on the municipal bonds, how much you'd earn on alternative taxable bonds, and the tax rate you'd pay on the income from each of those bonds. You can't just see that the tax implications are lighter with munis and jump right in based on that criteria alone.

Generally, the lower yields on municipal bonds are more beneficial for investors in high tax brackets. If you're in a lower tax bracket, you may do better by buying taxable bonds and bond funds.

Want another example of how you need to consider a wide variety of factors — not just taxes — when making your investment decisions? Look back at Table 14-1 with the three energy securities, and at the example we go through in the "Figuring the tax implications of your transactions" section. What if you don't think that all three securities in the table have the same prospects? What if you think that Security C, which has the short-term gain, is on shaky ground? You've already owned the security for six months, so if you wanted to wait for it to become long term, you'd have to wait another six months — and in that time, the price may take a tumble or may not grow as fast as the rest of the sector. Better to take a short-term gain now than a long-term loss later!

Take care of your asset allocation first, and then figure out your asset location.

If your asset allocation calls for a certain dollar amount in REITs, commodity funds, or mutual funds (all of which are tax-inefficient investments), don't cut that amount short simply because your tax-advantaged accounts are too small to accommodate them all. As we detail in Chapter 10, fill your tax-advantaged accounts with these types of investments to the extent you can, and then put any excess in your taxable accounts. Likewise, there's no need to cut back on the amount of growth stocks or international stocks to fit the size of your taxable accounts.

By using the strategies we describe in this chapter — but not getting carried away with them — you'll minimize the income taxes you'll have to pay without damaging your investment performance. In other words, you'll maximize your after-tax results, and that'll leave you with a much more appealing return for all your hard work and careful planning.

Chapter 15

Knowing When to Revise Your Plan

In This Chapter

▶ Revisiting your asset allocation as you move through life

▶ Keeping tabs on the economy

*T*his book is all about determining and maintaining your long-term, strategic asset allocation. So after you've done all the work necessary to set up your asset allocation, why would you revise it? Simple: Things change. Inevitably, fundamental changes during your lifetime will require you to revisit the assumptions you made when you first set up your allocation.

Some of those changes are gradual and expected, such as aging. Others may be sudden and unexpected, such as job changes, divorce, or economic upheavals. Whatever the cause, sometimes prudence will demand that you take another look at your asset allocation. You may not revise it as a result — you may simply validate your earlier decisions — but it's healthy to periodically raise the question.

We're not talking about market timing here; we never recommend that dangerous investment method. The changes that should prompt you to review (and perhaps revise) your asset allocation have nothing to do with the state of the financial markets themselves. They represent either lasting changes to your lifestyle or fundamental shifts in the overall economy.

In this chapter, we take a look at some of the events that should trigger you to evaluate your asset allocation, so you'll know when it's time to review and decide if some changes are necessary. We also consider the changing investing lives of a fictional couple, the Does, for you to use as an example when you face similar circumstances in your own life.

Identifying Life Events That Should Trigger a Review

There are two general categories of changes that may prompt you to revisit your asset allocation plan: life events that are specific to you and your family (including gradual life changes and sudden life changes), and events that are tied to the economic environment around you. In this section, we cover the former. (For more on the latter, turn to "Keeping Your Eye on the Economy," later in this chapter.)

In each of these cases, the first step in revisiting your asset allocation is to go back to your Lifetime Cash-flow Projection (LCP), which we outline as part of the financial planning exercise in Chapter 7.

Gradual life changes

Some of life's changes are gradual and expected. Surprisingly, it can be easy to push these changes to the backburner because they happen so slowly, over time. Be sure that you don't let too much time go by before reviewing whether your asset allocation is still appropriate.

Aging

One thing we all have in common as long as we live is that we get older every day. Even though aging happens slowly, you need to think about this life change and how it relates to your asset allocation.

As we discuss in Chapters 6 and 8, the asset allocation for a 30-year-old should probably be different from an 80-year-old's. Why? For one thing, the 30-year-old's investment horizon is presumably much longer. If you're 30 years old now, you will (if you're lucky) eventually be an 80-year-old. If you never revisit your asset allocation in the interim, you'll likely end up with an inappropriate asset allocation in your old age. You need to revisit your asset allocation during that span — but how often, and when?

There aren't any hard and fast rules about when and how often you should revise your asset allocation as you age. But if more than four years go by without your reviewing your allocation, you're probably due.

Plan to revisit your asset allocation at least once every four years as you get older. If you need a way to help yourself remember, tie your allocation review to an event that takes place every four years, like the presidential election or the start of the Summer Olympic Games. When you make your quadrennial review, take the time to sit down and update the financial planning exercise we explain in Chapter 7.

You may have heard of the following rule of thumb: "The percentage of equities in your portfolio should equal 100 minus your age." As rules of thumb go, that's not a bad one. But just like all one-size-fits-all rules, it doesn't reflect your unique situation. There's really no substitute for periodically reviewing your own asset allocation strategy.

Changes to any of the parameters you set when you established your allocation (investment horizon, return objectives, risk tolerance, portfolio constraints, tax situation, or special considerations, which we outline in Chapter 6) should trigger an asset allocation review.

Deteriorating health

Another fact of life that we all encounter as time goes on is the continual wearing down of our bodies. Try as we might to slow down the process, we're ultimately no match for the forces of nature doing gradual damage to all our various moving parts. This has several implications for your financial planning and, thus, for your asset allocation.

Changes to your body and your physical situation mean changes to your lifestyle. And the cost of your lifestyle is probably the single most important element in the LCP that we outline in Chapter 7. (If you haven't checked out the LCP discussion, we highly recommend it!)

Declining health also increases the degree — and, therefore, the cost — of healthcare, medications, and preventive maintenance. Making matters worse is the fact that the cost of medical care tends to rise faster than the cost of just about anything else (see Chapter 7).

As you factor these changes into your LCP, you'll find out whether changes to your asset allocation are indicated.

Sudden life changes

You can see the gradual changes we describe earlier in this chapter coming from miles away, but other changes pop up and hit you when you may least expect it. We cover a few of these in this section. In each case, a return trip to your LCP is in order. And changes in your LCP may indicate changes in your asset allocation.

Birth

There's probably no event as profound and life-changing as the birth of a child. We're not just talking about diaper changes and 2 a.m. feedings. We're talking about the financial avalanche of costs, and the disruption in family dynamics that all come with the words "I'm pregnant!"

A new child, particularly a first child, requires a complete rethinking of the lifestyle you once lived. In addition to the direct costs of caring, feeding, and (eventually) educating, the blessed event may also necessitate a change in career for at least one of the parents. All this may shake your LCP to its very foundations — more than enough reason for a return visit to your LCP and asset allocation (maybe in the wee hours when you can't get back to sleep after making your third trip of the night to the crib).

It doesn't have to be your own child that generates this kind of reevaluation. A new grandchild (or even a niece or nephew) may also make you rethink who your nest egg is ultimately destined for — and that may influence your investment horizon, and, ultimately, your asset allocation as you reconsider the parameters we outline in Chapter 6.

Death

At the other end of life's continuum, the death of a loved one is a tragic event. The loss of a spouse can be especially life altering. The premature death of a bread-winning spouse can be devastating. Such events should prompt you to rethink your financial plan.

Unfortunately, the asset allocation review that should be triggered by a death comes at a time when you may be emotionally ill equipped to deal with it. And it's a sad fact that some unscrupulous vultures with financial credentials see an opportunity to prey on the vulnerable widow or widower in these situations. In such times, a trusted and sensitive advisor of long standing can be a valuable asset. Many families, particularly those in which the financially savvy family member has the shortest life expectancy, engage a financial advisor of the type we review in Chapter 16, in anticipation of the inevitable.

Sometimes death can result in a positive change to your financial well-being. You may be the beneficiary of an estate or a life-insurance policy. In any event, the passing of someone close to you should trigger a revisiting of the assumptions you made when you established your investment strategy.

Marriage

Love and marriage these days may not come with an old-fashioned horse and carriage, but a marriage certainly comes with a carriage full of costs and obligations. There are significant changes in lifestyle, of course (neighborhood barbecues instead of singles bars, for example). There's also a subtle, but very real, increase in investment horizon.

Looking into the perplexing world of probabilities

Take any two people. Assume for each of them that the probability of surviving past 90 is 10 percent. What's the probability that at least one of them will survive past 90? The answer is surprising. Why? First, consider that there are only four possibilities for the situation, as follows:

✔ Both people survive. The probability of this is 0.10×0.10, or 0.01 (1 percent).

✔ Person A survives, Person B doesn't. The probability of this is 0.10×0.90, or 0.09 (9 percent).

✔ Person B survives, Person A doesn't. The probability of this is the same as in the preceding situation (9 percent).

✔ Neither person survives. The probability of this is 0.90×0.90, or 0.81 (81 percent).

Even though it may not be obvious, the probability of at least one of the people surviving is the sum of the first three cases, or 19 percent.

There are two reasons for this lengthened horizon:

✔ If the probability of each of two people surviving past age 90 is 10 percent, the probability of *at least one of them* surviving past 90 is 19 percent. (We explain this surprising result in the nearby sidebar, "Looking into the perplexing world of probabilities.") It follows, then, that two people sharing an investment portfolio have a longer investment horizon than either one owning the portfolio alone.

✔ Some extra longevity in married couples is reported to be because of the nurturing effect of the other spouse.

Your own marriage is just the beginning. The marriage of your children should be an occasion you plan for financially well in advance, but it almost always seems to be more sudden and expensive than you were prepared for.

Divorce

On the flip side of marriage, divorce comes with its own set of baggage. Aside from the emotional stress, there's alimony, child support, and the equitable distribution of the assets that you've built up together — considerations no matter which side of the ledger you're on.

Divorced partners are also targets for the financial vultures we call your attention to in the "Death" section, earlier. And it doesn't have to be your own divorce that affects you. A divorced child of yours may end up coming back home to live with you for a time. What should you do if a divorce affects your life? You guessed it — reevaluate your LCP (and your asset allocation).

Sudden illness

Although the immediate and direct costs of an unexpected illness may be covered (at least in part) by health, disability, or long-term-care insurance, indirect costs and potentially long-lasting lifestyle changes can also befall you or your family. Your illness may not be life threatening, but it could permanently impair your ability to pursue the lifestyle you're accustomed to. If you're young, it could devastate your full earning potential. If you're married, the healthy spouse may have to devote substantial time to care-giving and make career sacrifices in the process.

It could be that the illness, while sudden and severe, is fleeting and fully insured. Well, you've dodged a bullet there, but it should still motivate you to review your financial plan if you haven't done so recently.

Job changes, unexpected dilemmas, and windfalls

Career paths are often full of road bumps. Job losses, career changes, corporate downsizings, company bankruptcies, and the like are part of the journey for many employees. Some employers may offer generous severance packages, and some states extend unemployment benefits, but these things are extras — not givens. But it's not all bad news. You may be the beneficiary of an unexpected promotion or a fantastic new job offer.

Outside of your job, you may face financial hardships such as uninsured damage to (or outright loss of) your home due to hurricane, earthquake, or another natural disaster. Or you may be the grand winner of your state's lottery. And, of course, there are myriad possibilities between these extremes.

In all these cases, remember to reconsider your overall financial plan, and, ultimately, your asset allocation.

Keeping Your Eye on the Economy

The second major category of change that may prompt you to revisit your asset allocation plan has less to do with your own personal situation and more to do with the economic environment around you. As we mention earlier, the first step in revisiting your asset allocation is to go back to your LCP, which we outline as part of the financial planning exercise in Chapter 7.

Recognizing major economic shifts

This isn't your grandfather's economy. For one thing, the economy is a lot more global than it used to be. The world is defined less by a series of isolated countries and more and more by an integrated network of international trading partners. This seems to be an irreversible trend, and there are several ramifications of this trend.

One consequence is that international equity markets are behaving more like the U.S. market. This is true of both developed countries and emerging markets. So international equities aren't the portfolio diversifier they used to be. In fact, investing internationally has become more of a play on currency exchange rates than anything. The only thing you get with foreign equities that you don't get with domestic equities is the opportunity to bet against the dollar. That's because, all else being equal, international investments will do better than their U.S. counterparts if the dollar weakens against those foreign currencies.

And that brings us to the second major effect of globalization. As emerging economies, such as China and India, continue to benefit from the energy and talent of their massive populations, their embracing of capitalist ideals, their own natural resources, and the free flow of information and education, they'll inevitably take a bigger role on the world stage. The reign of the United States as the world's leading economy isn't permanently guaranteed. Protecting yourself against a falling dollar over the long term in this environment seems sound, doesn't it? For this reason alone, your asset allocation should have some room for international investments.

You need to pay attention to the strength of the dollar whenever you revisit your asset allocation. If the dollar has consistently declined since your last review, and if most experts are calling for that trend to continue, then you should consider increasing your allocation to international investments.

Just as important as recognizing these fundamental economic shifts is the ability to discern the pseudo trends. For example, in the late 1990s, there was considerable talk of the "new economy," led by high-tech startups with no profits — no revenue, even — and no viable business model in any conventional sense. This eventually resulted in the irrational exuberance of the tech bubble. Those investors who bought into the vision of the new economy and adjusted their asset allocation to embrace a large dose of technology stocks ended up badly burned. When it comes to the things that you let shape your financial future, it's important to distinguish between the faddish and the fundamental.

Paying attention to the business cycle

On a less grandiose scale than long-term global economic change is the periodic cycling of the U.S. economy, as well as other countries' economies. Economies all around the world have alternating periods of expansion and contraction, recession and recovery, boom and bust.

Predicting the turning points of the business cycle (also called the *economic cycle*) is difficult, but you can pretty easily tell what phase of the cycle you're in when you're in it. For example, even though recessions aren't officially called by the government until a couple quarters after they've begun, you can tell what's going on just by paying attention to the news. If all you hear and read is about increasing unemployment, declining sales, company failures, government rescue efforts, and the like, then it's a good bet the economy is in its contraction phase, regardless of whether it's officially called a recession.

Investors have historically done well by tilting their asset allocation in recognition of the current phase of the business cycle, because different assets perform well at different points in the cycle. To better understand what we mean, have a look at Figure 15-1, which shows the cumulative total returns for a number of sectors over the time periods August 1990 through March 1991 and April 2001 through November 2001.

As you can see in Figure 15-1, equity industry sectors such as healthcare and consumer staples — the so-called *defensive sectors,* because they're well defended against economic downturns — tend to do well in recessionary economies. On the flip side, consumer discretionary and industrial sectors — the *cyclical sectors* — tend to benefit more than other sectors in periods of recovery. Because each phase of the business cycle can last for several years, the consideration of the phase we're in is a legitimate factor in reviewing and potentially revising your strategic asset allocation.

In Chapter 8, we discuss how the professional money managers develop their asset allocations. What they would do in the situation we describe here is to adjust their expected returns for the various industry sectors, in sync with the current economic phase. (This is just one input to the mathematical models they use to determine their asset allocations. We go through their analysis in more detail in Chapter 8.) But you don't have to be a pro, and imitate all their analyses, to be successful. You can do almost as well by making reasonable tweaks to your asset allocation directly, based on alertly reading the economic signs around you.

Don't rush to adjust your asset allocation every time some talking head on TV says that we're headed for the end of days. Instead, wait until reputable, even-handed news sources report substantive economic news in a factual and objective way.

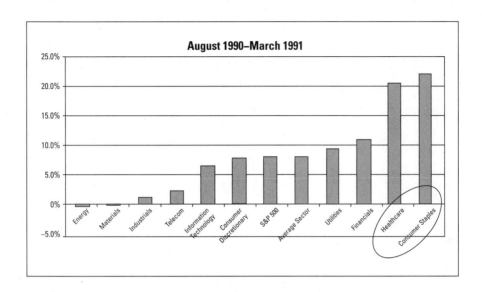

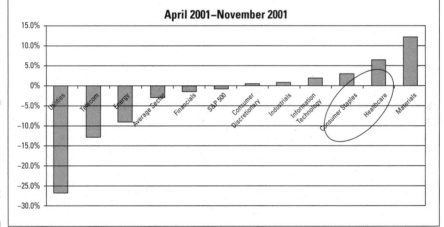

Figure 15-1:
Performance
of various
equity sec-
tors during
recent
recessions.

When you do get reliable news that we've entered a new phase of the business cycle, don't wreak havoc on your carefully planned asset alloca-tion. Don't, for example, decide to flee stocks and rush to bonds when the economy slows. Like all market-timing tactics, that's a loser's game. Instead, simply fine-tune your sub-allocations *within* your broad asset classes along the lines we describe earlier in this chapter. For example, you can tilt toward consumer staples and away from consumer discretionary for a year or so during contractions, while keeping your overall equity allocation intact.

Knowing the economic indicators

Federal agencies that track the economy periodically release updates on economic indicators, which are statistics that provide some insight to changes in various sectors of the economy. Here are a few of the most closely watched:

✔ **Gross domestic product (GDP):** The GDP is the widest measure on the state of the economy, sizing up all the goods and services produced in the economy within U.S. geographic borders in the previous quarter. Focus on the growth rate, which over long periods increases 2.5 percent to 3 percent per year. Growth above this range means that the economy is overheating, and the Fed will probably try to tamp it down by raising interest rates. Growth below this rate — and especially below zero — signals that the economy is slowing down, which can trigger more unemployment and less spending.

✔ **Consumer Price Index (CPI):** The CPI is the most widely used measure of inflation, and it measures the change in the cost of about 200 kinds of consumer goods and services and thousands of actual products. Social Security payments are adjusted annually as the CPI changes. (Make sure you read the report you want — there's one report for overall CPI data, and one for the "core" rate, which excludes food and energy prices. For more information, go to www.bls.gov/cpi.)

✔ **The Producer Price Index (PPI):** The PPI, the second most important indicator of inflation, measures the price of goods at the wholesale level. The PPI measures the cost of goods in three stages: crude (raw materials), intermediate (materials that are part of a larger product), and finished (goods sold to a reseller). The measure on finished goods is the most closely watched, because it reflects the actual price that consumers will pay.

✔ **Employment indicators:** These indicators calculate how much of the workforce is unemployed, how many new jobs were created, how many average hours were worked per week, and how much average hourly earnings added up to. In addition, there's also a weekly report on the number of people filing for unemployment benefits for the first time, which helps take the pulse of the job market.

✔ **Consumer Confidence Index (CCI):** How confident consumers feel directly influences the state of the economy and consumer spending power, which is why this monthly report of 5,000 households issued by the Conference Board is considered a leading indicator.

✔ **Beige Book:** Eight times a year, the Federal Open Market Committee (FOMC) of the Federal Reserve publishes its notorious little Beige Book, which is a summary of the economic conditions in each Fed region around the country. But the book's real value is as an indicator of how the Fed may act at its next meeting.

Financial news changes quickly. Don't overreact and adjust your portfolio's asset allocation every time headlines change.

You can also check out the economic indicators for yourself. Economic forecasters do, because they believe indicators change in advance of, at the same time as, or in the wake of important shifts in the economy. There are several popular indicators, and we summarize a few of the top ones in the "Knowing the economic indicators" sidebar in this chapter. We include these because you'll probably hear about them and you may want to know what they are. But don't try to use them to directly figure out what the markets will do. First, these are indicators of the *economy,* not the markets, and the markets don't move in lockstep with the economy. Second, even the professional economic forecasters get the forecasts wrong on a regular basis. (As the old joke goes: "Why did God create economists? To make weather forecasters look good." Of course, some of our good friends are economists, so we'll stop there.)

Considering a Lifetime's Worth of Examples

The best way to understand how the changes we discuss in this chapter can require a review of your asset allocation is to look at an example. In this section, we look in on the lives of fictional couple John and Jane Doe in stages, and describe the many changes in their lives and in the economy that trigger them to make modifications (or not) to their portfolio's asset allocation. You may find some of their responses to the changes we discuss earlier in this chapter insightful, as you consider the changes affecting your own situation.

When we look at the Does' asset allocation in Chapter 8, we actually catch them in midlife, in their late 40s. But in this chapter, we hit the Rewind button before showing you the home movie of their lives, back to when they first got serious about asset allocation.

Stage 1: Married 30-something parents

In the first stage of John and Jane Does' lives that we look at, the two of them are in their mid-30s. Both are in the early years of successful careers. The Does have only one child, Joanne, and she's in mid-adolescence. They decide to adopt an aggressive investment strategy, given their long investment horizon and desire to stay well ahead of inflation. (They had already pre-funded Joanne's college tuition through a separate 529 plan. The investments we talk about here constitute the rest of the family's invested assets.)

Their asset allocation at this point in their lives is shown as Stage 1 in Table 15-1, which shows you the asset allocations for all four stages of the Does' lives. (We get to the other stages in the following sections.)

Table 15-1	Revision to the Does' Asset Allocation over Time			
Major Asset Class	**Asset Allocation**			
	Stage 1	Stage 2	Stage 3	Stage 4
Fixed income	10%	15%	35%	10%
Equities	70%	60%	45%	70%
Alternatives	20%	25%	20%	20%
Total	100%	100%	100%	100%

Source: Brinton Eaton Wealth Advisors

The aggressiveness of the Does' portfolio in Table 15-1 is reflected in the heavy allocation to equities and the light allocation to fixed income. (We discuss this mix further in Chapter 8.)

Stage 2: Stay-at-home Jane and a hiccup in the economy

By the time we catch up with the Does about a dozen years later, several things have happened. Jane has decided to interrupt her career to stay at home and help Joanne through what turned out to be rough teenage years. Now in their late 40s, with a shorter investment horizon, only one income to rely on, and a more modest lifestyle, the Does decide to dial down the aggressiveness of their portfolio just a tad, to the moderate/aggressive levels we see in Stage 2 of Table 15-1. (This is, in fact, a summarized version of the asset allocation that we show for the Does in Chapter 8.)

In the period leading up to Stage 2, the economy suffered a major correction. (Some doomsayers on TV at the time were calling for the next Great Depression.) While their neighbors were pulling their money out of the markets and going to cash, the Does stayed with their aggressive investment strategy and did much better than anyone on their block.

Their subsequent decision to downshift to a moderate/aggressive posture at the beginning of Stage 2 was based purely on the changes to their personal situation, not on the doom-and-gloom reports they saw on TV.

Stage 3: Failing health and an unexpected windfall

In the third stage, the Does are in their mid-50s. Joanne has matured into a wonderful student, has graduated with high honors, and has now started a very promising career of her own. John and Jane never have to worry about supporting Joanne — in fact, Joanne thinks they've done more than enough for her already and never again wants to be a burden to her parents. (We should all be so lucky!)

Meanwhile, Jane decided to reenter the workforce, but not at her old job. She opted to pursue a passion of hers and start a new business, which took off immediately. She sold it at a huge profit just a few years later and started working as a consultant.

But not all is well in the family. John suffered a severely debilitating illness, and he's no longer able to work. Although his medical expenses are fully covered for the rest of his life, the Does' lifestyle was permanently curtailed — for example, they can't travel the way they used to. Because of these new circumstances, the Does decided to invest their portfolio, which now includes the windfall from Jane's business, in a portfolio that's much more conservative than they ever had before. After all, they've done well and accumulated abundant assets, and all of a sudden they're spending less than they expected to at this point in their lives. They figure, "Why take chances we don't need to take with our investments?"

This brings them to Stage 3 in Table 15-1. As you can see, the allocation to equities continues to get lighter, and the allocation to fixed income continues to get heavier.

Stage 4: A grand gesture for the grandchild

In Stage 4 of the Does' lives, John and Jane are in their mid-60s. John's condition hasn't improved, and Jane's health has deteriorated, but they still enjoy each other's company and their stay-at-home lifestyle immensely. Against all expectations, and after years of trying, Joanne and her husband (Did we forget to tell you she married and paid for her own wedding? What a kid!) had a child, Jonathan. The doctor called Jonathan a miracle, given Joanne's age at the time. Jonathan is clearly the only grandchild John and Jane will ever have.

Well, to say they were elated would be the understatement of the year. The Does make the decision that if they have anything to do with it, Jonathan will never want for a single thing. In fact, John and Jane have a serious talk, admit to each other for the first time that, although their life together was more than satisfying, their life expectancies may be shorter than their own parents' were, and they decide right then and there that they're going to focus their investments for their grandson. After all, they already have enough assets and insurance to cover their needs for the rest of their years. They call their advisor, tell her that their investment horizon has just lengthened by about 70 years, and have her switch their portfolio to aggressive. Stage 4 for the Does looks a lot like Stage 1 (refer to Table 15-1).

We don't describe every single detail in the lives of the Does, but rest assured that when they were faced with major life events, they took a good hard look at their LCP and asset allocation. Your situation probably isn't like the Does' in its details, but follow their lead, review your asset allocation when your life calls for it, and your portfolio (and your life) will be richer as a result.

Chapter 16

Finding Help When You Need It

. . . .

. . . .

Maybe you're overwhelmed at the thought of keeping up with your portfolio of investments on your own. Maybe you're afraid you'll make silly mistakes doing it all yourself. Or maybe you just want an expert to bounce ideas off of as you manage your assets. If you're thinking of hiring a professional advisor, you're not alone. The financial services industry is growing — fast! — because many people want the help of an expert.

Before you rush out and make an appointment with the first financial guru you find in the phonebook or your best friend's "money guy," you need to figure out what you're hoping to get out of your relationship with an advisor. There are good reasons and not-so-good reasons for hiring someone to help with your asset allocation, and you need to make sure you're doing it for the right reasons. The top reason for bringing on an advisor is to help you achieve your investment goals. (You can read more about goal setting and developing an investment plan in Chapters 6 and 7.)

When you're clear that your head is in the right place, you need to be able to wade through the dozens of financial certifications out there. Think we're exaggerating? Believe it or not, the Financial Industry Regulatory Authority (FINRA), a self-regulatory body for securities firms and registered securities representatives doing business in the United States, keeps track of this kind of stuff, and it has a database of over a hundred financial certifications!

So how are you supposed to know what all those acronyms mean? In this chapter, we fill you in on the kind of expertise you may need in an advisor, the handful of meaningful credentials you should look for (the rest you can ignore), and what kinds of questions to ask an advisor you're thinking of working with.

Finally, as with all experts, financial advisors come at a price. For many investors, the price is worth it, but in order to know whether that's true for you, you need to know the costs involved, and what you can expect to pay. We also tell you about other parties that may be paying your advisor and, therefore, competing with you for his allegiance.

Knowing the Right (and Wrong) Reasons to Hire an Advisor

If you're thinking about hiring an advisor to help you create, fine-tune, or implement your investment strategy, you're not alone. Many individuals seek the help of an investment specialist in hopes of getting the most possible bang for their buck.

Before you bring on an advisor, though, you need to make sure you have your priorities straight. There are good and bad reasons that drive people to hire advisors, and you need to be sure that you're looking for help for the right reasons.

In this section, we guide you through all the right reasons to hire an advisor, and alert you to a few of the wrong reasons that can do you more harm than good in the long run.

The right reasons

Before you begin shopping for an advisor, take a few minutes to think through your motivations for considering an advisor in the first place. Then, read the following sections to see how they match up with how you're feeling. If these reasons sound familiar to you, then you're on the right track and we can wholeheartedly support your search for an advisor's assistance.

To provide objective advice

Investing can be an emotional experience, and emotions sometimes lead investors astray, tempting them to act impulsively or even irrationally. Working with an advisor helps balance subjective behavior with objective advice. By taking as much emotion out of the process as possible and putting together an investment plan that suits your particular needs, you stand a good chance of avoiding the herd as it falls off a cliff every time the market runs into problems.

To avoid amateur mistakes

Amateur investors are often long on enthusiasm and optimism but short on expertise. A professional advisor can inject some know-how into your investment strategies and help you dodge the bullets that fell many new investors, such as buying tax-exempt bonds in a tax-deferred account (a major mistake) or misinterpreting a stock split.

To help you design and execute your written plan

You may know exactly what you want in a plan, but you're having trouble crunching the numbers or just getting it down in writing — a seasoned advisor can help you firm up and clarify your investment plan. Or you may know what you want to invest in but prefer a professional's help to buy and sell securities — to take care of the nuts and bolts of your transactions. Both are signs that you can wisely recognize your shortcomings and realize that you need professional help to bridge those gaps.

To put all the pieces together

Some individual investors have the time, interest, and know-how to handle their own taxes, their own investments, or even their own long-term financial planning. But very few can do it all and fully understand all the interactions among these varied activities. There are complex relationships between investing and income tax planning, for example, or asset management and estate-tax planning. Many people make bad decisions — despite their best intentions — when they have to do it all without the help of a professional who knows and understands all the moving parts.

The wrong reasons

Think you're considering calling on an advisor for help for all the right reasons? In this case, it's much better (and more profitable) to be safe than sorry, so consider the following lousy reasons to hire an advisor before making any decisions.

To "beat the market"

Most advisors who tout their stock-picking ability fail to beat the market averages over even the intermediate term. Those who outperform in a given year usually underperform in the years following. As the brochures are required to say, "Past performance is no guarantee of future results." Take that observation to heart, and don't hire an advisor just because he assures you that he's a market miracle maker.

A flip of the coin

One of our favorite stories, popularized by Warren Buffett, relates to a fictional National Coin Flipping Contest. According to one version of this story, 4 million people put up a dollar each to enter the contest. Each person flips a coin, calls heads or tails, and proceeds to the next round if the call was correct or goes home if it was not.

After the first round, approximately 2 million participants remain; after the second round, 1 million. After 20 rounds, the contest is over and the four remaining participants win $1 million each. And wouldn't you know it, three of them write books that explain how you can use their foolproof investing methods to turn $1 into $1 million. One of them lands a TV show dispensing her advice.

The moral? Don't be fooled by people who confuse dumb luck with real expertise.

To avoid making the important decisions yourself

It's okay to hand over the inner workings of managing your investment plan to an advisor, after you've done the important work of defining your goals and assessing your risk. But it's not okay to hand over the task — lock, stock, and barrel — to anyone.

If you want to reach retirement comfortably, you don't want an advisor who's going to gamble with your money and indulge in market timing, or put your money in risky investments. You can't always rely on the kindness of strangers — especially when it comes to your money.

Weighing Your Options for an Advisor

When you've decided that a financial advisor may be a good option for you, you're faced with a phone book full of people claiming to have the skills to do the job. How can you tell which person to trust? How do you know you won't be taken to the cleaners and hung out to dry?

You may be referred to an advisor by a friend, relative, colleague, or business acquaintance, or by a trusted expert in a related field, such as your estate attorney. Even in these cases, you need to be able to determine if the advisor is right for you.

Information is power, and in this section we help you build some serious strength. Here you find out which professional designations (the letters that appear after an advisor's name) really matter, and what kind of expertise you need in an advisor.

Making sense of all those letters after an advisor's name

When you're looking for a financial advisor, you'll come across a slew of acronyms after each advisor's name. Those acronyms stand for the qualifications and training an advisor has. You may be tempted to ignore the letters — or, worse, assume that the more letters, the better. But it's worth your time to pay attention to them and find out what they mean.

Today, brokerage firms and their staffs can offer investment advice to clients, but, strictly speaking, they aren't investment advisors. The government regulators in charge of investment advisors consider investment advice to be "incidental" to what these professionals do, which is mostly buying and selling securities. That doesn't mean that employees of brokerage firms operate unchecked — they are, indeed, regulated as securities personnel — but, technically, they aren't investment advisors.

Debates like these have been raging in Washington, D.C., for a while, and that isn't likely to change, but your task is clear: Figure out what kind of help you need, and choose the advisor with the proper designations to get the job done. To make that task easier, in this section we provide a list of the most important designations. And, because it's possible for unscrupulous individuals to claim designations that they haven't really earned, we also tell you how you can contact respected trade groups or regulatory bodies that can verify a person or firm's designations.

 You want an advisor who has the right licenses and registrations to meet your financial needs. Plus, the advisor's certifications must be current and valid, and he should have a clean disciplinary history. Don't just rely on the advisor's word — check for all that information with the issuing organization.

For help with taxes or financial planning

In this section, we tell you the major designations you should look for when you're searching for financial planning help, including tax planning.

CFP

For financial planning advice, the most widely regarded designation is Certified Financial Planner (CFP). In addition to satisfying demanding experience and education requirements, certificants must pass a 10-hour, 2-day exam, and complete 30 hours of continuing education every 2 years. To verify credentials, contact the Certified Financial Planner Board of Standards, 1425 K St. NW, Suite 500, Washington, DC 20005 (phone: 800-487-1497 or 202-379-2200; e-mail: mail@CFPBoard.org; Web: www.cfp.net/search).

There are two top financial planning membership organizations. Members of either organization hold the CFP designation, and you can contact these groups to find names of planners in your area.

- ✔ **Financial Planning Association (FPA):** You can write to the FPA at 4100 E. Mississippi Ave., Suite 400, Denver, CO 80246, or at 1600 K St. NW, Suite 201, Washington, DC 20006. For more information, visit www. fpanet.org or call 800-322-4237. You can e-mail the FPA by visiting the Web site and clicking the Contact Us link.

- ✔ **National Association of Personal Financial Advisors (NAPFA):** You can write to the NAPFA at 3250 N. Arlington Heights Rd., Suite 109, Arlington Heights, IL 60004. For more information, visit www.napfa.org, call 847-483-5400, or e-mail info@napfa.org.

CPA

If you need help with income or tax planning, you want a Certified Public Accountant (CPA). To check credentials and verify that an accountant is a CPA, contact the National Association of State Boards of Accountancy, which qualifies CPAs in the state in which they practice, or click on State Board Listing at www.nasba.org. You can write to them at 150 Fourth Ave. N., Suite 700, Nashville, TN 37219, call 615-880-4200, or e-mail communications@ nasba.org.

CPA/PFS

Another top choice for a planner is a CPA with a Personal Financial Specialist (PFS) designation. To gain this designation, a CPA must accumulate at least 1,400 hours of financial planning business experience and take continuing education courses. To search for a CPA/PFS near you, contact the American Institute of Certified Public Accountants, which issues the PFS designation, at 220 Leigh Farm Rd., Durham, NC 27707 (phone: 888-777-7077 or 919-402-4500; Web: http://pfp.aicpa.org).

For help with investments

There are three major sets of initials to be aware of when you're searching for investment help.

CFA

Wall Street securities analysts, as well as financial advisors, seek the top professional designation of Chartered Financial Analyst (CFA), widely considered to have the most rigorous qualification standards for investment advice. Candidates must have four years of professional experience making investment decisions, after passing three exams administered by the CFA Institute. To verify an advisor's CFA charter, check with the CFA Institute at 560 Ray C. Hunt Dr., Charlottesville, VA 22903 (phone: 800-247-8132 or 434-951-5499; e-mail: info@cfainstitute.org; Web: www.cfainstitute.org).

RIA

Although the term Registered Investment Advisor (RIA) can be bestowed on an individual, it is most often applied to an entire firm, and the appropriate professionals within the firm are referred to as Investment Advisor Representatives (IARs).

RIAs are regulated by the Investment Advisers Act of 1940, and those regulations are enforced by the Securities and Exchange Commission (SEC) or by the individual states. Advisors (whether individuals or firms) with assets under management of $25 million or greater must register with the SEC; those with assets less than $25 million have the option of registering with their state. In the registration process, passing the Series 65 exam administered by the North American Securities Administrators Association (NASAA) is required. This requirement can be waived if the advisor has one of the following designations: CFP, CFA, CPA/PFS, or Chartered Financial Consultant (ChFC).

By law, RIAs have a _fiduciary responsibility,_ meaning that they're legally required to act in your best interest.

To check that an RIA firm or advisor is properly registered, and for any disciplinary history, consult one of these two sources, depending on the size of the company:

- ✔ **For investment advisors and their firms with assets** _above_ **$25 million,** check with the SEC at 100 F St. NE, Washington, DC 20549 (phone: 202-942-7040; Web: www.sec.gov). The SEC is the federal agency that licenses securities professionals and enforces regulations for advisors and firms with more than $25 million in assets.

- ✔ **For investment advisors and their firms with assets** _under_ **$25 million,** consult NASAA at 750 First St. NE, Suite 1140, Washington, DC 20002 (phone: 202-737-0900; Web: www.nasaa.org). The NASAA is an organization of state securities regulators that supervises securities professionals and firms with assets under $25 million, in the state where the advisor has his principal place of business.

RR

You may also see the Registered Representative (RR) designation after an advisor's name. An RR is limited to buying and selling securities for a brokerage firm. In order to earn that designation, she must pass a securities exam. Sometimes these advisors are referred to informally as stockbrokers or Investment Advisor Representatives, and their firms as broker-dealers.

To verify an RR's credentials and disciplinary history, contact either:

- ✔ FINRA, 1735 K St., Washington, DC 20006 (phone: 301-590-6500; Web: www.finra.org)

> ✔ NASAA, 750 First St. NE, Suite 1140, Washington, DC 20002 (phone: 202-737-0900; Web: `www.nasaa.org`)

Use FINRA's BrokerCheck service to check records online (`www.finra.org/InvestorInformation/InvestorProtection/ChecktheBackgroundofYourInvestmentProfessional/index.htm`) or by phone at 800-289-9999. The information dates back only three years, so if you're interested in a more comprehensive look, contact NASAA.

Knowing what kind of expertise you need

Many financial planners can give you investment advice, but not all investment advisors can help you put together a detailed plan to reach your specific goals.

To figure out which type of advisor best suits your needs, consider the following questions:

> ✔ **Do you want someone to look over your shoulder and give advice about investments, but leave the task of managing your portfolio to you, or someone else?** If so, then you want a financial or investment advisor who charges by the hour or on a per-project basis. These experts may have the CFP, CPA/PFS, or CFA designation. (We decipher these designations and serve up a piping-hot bowl of advisor alphabet soup in the preceding section.)
>
> ✔ **Have you already received the advice you need, and do you have a specific, narrowly defined need to buy or sell securities?** If so, you're looking for a broker/dealer, stockbroker, or registered rep (RR).
>
> ✔ **Do you need help with your income-tax return, or ways to minimize your income taxes, gift taxes, or estate taxes?** If so, then a CPA is a good choice.
>
> ✔ **Do you have your investments and taxes under control, but you're looking for help in developing a comprehensive and detailed plan to reach multiple goals (such as buying a home, saving for your children's education, and planning for retirement)?** If so, you're seeking a comprehensive financial planner. Relevant designations here include CFP and CPA/PFS.
>
> ✔ **Do you want an advisor who can do all the above in an integrated way — in other words, to be your one-stop financial quarterback?** You need a full-service wealth-management firm. The firm should be an RIA; employ a collection of experts with qualifications such as CFP, CFA, and CPA/PFS; and have a contractual relationship with an asset custodian that employs RRs.

Fool me once, shame on me

The nice young insurance salesman seemed to have her best interests in mind. Before the free dinner seminar, he had the 71-year-old retiree fill out a detailed questionnaire and list her investments. That way, he said, he could give her the best advice possible on how to maximize her money.

His advice did maximize her money — for himself! He invested the retiree's life savings of $700,000 in two *annuities* (a type of investment that pays a stream of income in return for a premium payment). Annuities are popular choices with unsophisticated investors, and the equity-indexed annuities the salesman sold her had complicated conditions. She could earn big returns, as the salesman promised — but she could suffer big losses, because this type of annuity was tied to a volatile stock index.

Unless she was willing to pay a penalty of as much as $175,000, her money was locked up for 15 years before she could transfer to a more suitable investment. Sadly, too, the nice young man who had won her trust by introducing himself as a "Certified Senior Advisor" had a history of defrauding investors.

The vast majority of investments are held by those over 55, but there's a lesson for all investors in this financial tragedy: If this investor had read the prospectus, she would have learned that this type of annuity wasn't right for her at all; she could suffer double-digit losses, and pay a high penalty if she cancelled early. Had she done her homework, she would have known that there are more rigorous designations than "Certified Senior Advisor," which requires only a three-day, self-study course. Stiff education and examination requirements, strong ethical standards, and substantial continuing-education obligations distinguish the top designations. Also, if she had checked out the advisor's background, she would have learned that state and federal securities regulators had disciplined him and his firm several times for unethical behavior.

Regulators will pursue and penalize offenders, but they may be able to retrieve only part of what you invested, and the process may take years. To avoid becoming the next statistic among the thousands who get duped every year, learn how to protect yourself by choosing a reputable advisor.

Asking the Right Questions

After you come up with a list of potential investment advisors, you need to interview and evaluate them. Plan on meeting with several advisors (three is a good number; more can be confusing). If possible, meet with them face-to-face in their offices.

Before you go to the trouble of arranging meetings, check each advisor's history for any violations or disciplinary actions with the state and federal agencies or industry organizations that issue credentials and certifications. (See "Making sense of all those letters after an advisor's name," earlier in this chapter to read all about professional designations for investment advisors and where you can check up on an advisor's credentials and history.)

You may be tempted to skip the due diligence when selecting an investment advisor, but don't give in to temptation! Checking an advisor's record for any problems with regulators or other investors *before* doing business with that person is critically important. If you work with an unregistered securities broker or an unregistered firm that goes out of business, there may be little that regulators can do to recover your money.

If you're working with a brokerage firm or one of its stockbrokers (an RR), check with FINRA or the appropriate state regulator through the NASAA network. (Both are explained earlier, in the "RR" section.)

If the advisor or her firm is an RIA, get a copy of the advisor or firm's Form ADV, which qualifies the advisor to give investment advice. There are two parts to the Form ADV. Part I reveals whether the firm or any of its advisors has been fined for violating securities or other laws, and it's kept on file with the SEC (www.sec.gov). Part II discloses the advisor or firm's fees and any conflicts of interest the advisor may have. Part II is available from the advisory firm.

When you're reviewing Form ADVs, pay close attention to the following:

- ✔ Credentials
- ✔ Regulatory discipline
- ✔ Fee schedule
- ✔ Conflicts of interest

It's important to read both parts of the advisor's ADV. If you have any questions about what you see on the form, raise those questions during your meeting.

If you get a high-pressure sales pitch during your interview, or you feel uncomfortable for any reason, don't hesitate to thank the person for his time and get up and leave. You need a financial advisor who doesn't pressure you with "get-rich-quick" schemes, who respects you, and who is happy to answer your questions.

Here are the questions you should ask of every financial advisor you meet with:

- ✔ **Can you tell me about your experience as an advisor?** Find out where he's worked and for how long. You don't want a novice; you need someone who has worked with clients for at least three years.

✔ **What experience do you have working with an investor like me?** The advisor or her firm may have certain conditions that don't suit your needs. Some advisors, for example, may not be able to develop the comprehensive plan you're seeking. Others may prefer to offer advice only in specific areas, such as taxes or estate planning. Others may work only with certain types of clients, such as corporate executives or *high-net-worth clients* (those with assets of $1 million or more).

✔ **What are your qualifications and training?** You should already know the advisor's certifications (see the preceding sections). Your interview is an opportunity to have him expand on this information in person.

✔ **What services can you offer me?** Depending on what you need, the answer may be, "I can advise you about buying and selling stocks, bonds, and mutual funds," "We can buy and sell securities for you," "I can help you develop a financial plan for retirement and your children's education," "We can help you minimize your income or estate taxes," or "My firm can do it all for you."

A firm that can do it all is not necessarily better than an advisor who only handles certain tasks, as long as what the advisor handles is what you need.

✔ **Will you be handling my account?** You want to know who you'll be working with; your initial meeting at a large firm may be with a marketing representative you may never see again. Ask her to talk about and introduce you to everyone on the team who will handle your money and tell you how often you'll meet with each of these people.

✔ **Will the responsibility for implementing your advice be mine or yours?** Some firms only offer advice and leave the implementation to you. Some have *discretionary arrangements* (meaning, they'll implement buy and sell decisions on your behalf); this is much less work for you, of course, but you'll have to be comfortable delegating that level of control.

✔ **What kinds of reports will I receive, and how often?** You'll want to receive reports at least quarterly from any firm handling your investments. These reports should include the current market value of each holding in your portfolio, realized and unrealized taxable gains, and performance statistics, along with industry-wide benchmarks against which to compare your performance.

✔ **Will you put your services in writing?** Many firms never get asked this question, because they routinely put their agreements in writing, spelling out expectations and obligations of both parties. But you may have to ask. Either way, save this information in your files.

✔ **If I become a client, how long am I locked in? How easy is it to fire you?** You want to be able to fire your advisor at your pleasure and have the unearned portion of any prepaid fees returned to you. Be wary of contracts that obligate you to stay with, and pay, the advisor for some minimum period of time.

✔ **How are you paid? What are *all* your sources of income?** You want objective advice from an advisor, and knowing how an advisor's bread is buttered will disclose any potential conflicts of interest in recommending an investment or offering advice. Before hiring a financial advisor, understand how and by whom she is paid, and get the information in writing. (See the following section for more on how advisors are paid.)

✔ **Have you ever been disciplined for unethical or improper conduct? Have you ever been sued by a client?** Don't just take the advisor's word for it. Check with the licensing and regulatory bodies mentioned earlier in "Making sense of all those letters after an advisor's name" or your local Better Business Bureau (BBB; www.bbb.org) to find out if a client has sued the advisor.

✔ **What is your client-to-employee ratio?** In some firms, the ratio is several hundred to one. You could be lost in such a firm and may never meet the people actually making decisions that affect you. In other firms, the ratio is under 25 to 1. You need to decide how much personal care and attention is important to you.

✔ **Can I speak with some of your clients whose situations are similar to mine?** An advisor should be willing to provide you with at least a few references of current clients whose needs are similar to yours.

In addition to those general questions, which you should ask of any advisor you're considering, you may also want to ask the following questions, which are geared specifically toward gauging an advisor's investment expertise:

✔ **How did your clients do in the last down market?** "Everyone is a genius in a bull market" should probably be a bumper sticker for investors. You want your advisor to be able to protect your money in down markets, too.

✔ **Can you describe your investing approach for me?** Have the advisor clearly articulate the firm's investment philosophy. Are they stock pickers? Market timers? Long-term asset allocators? Are they dependent on one or a few individual "stars," or is their approach standardized, institutionalized, and capable of being reliably reproduced over many years? All are possibilities, and if you need clarification on the ins and outs of any of them, don't hesitate to ask the advisor to explain.

✔ **Are you sensitive to taxes when you do my investments?** Many investment advisors don't care. Their attitude is, "Our job is getting you a good return — taxes are your problem." You want an advisor who sees things more holistically and realistically, one who is sensitive to the taxes you pay. Keep in mind that it's not what you make, but what you keep, that counts!

✔ **What do you invest in?** Some firms may favor mutual funds. Others may like individual stocks, bonds, and exchange-traded funds (ETFs). Look for a firm that provides you the most choices and flexibility.

✔ **Where will my assets reside, and how are they protected?** Most firms house their clients' assets with a *custodian* (a large financial institution such as Charles Schwab, Fidelity, or TD Ameritrade). This is good for you and adds a layer of protection. Ask the firm if its custodian is a member of the Securities Investor Protection Corporation (SIPC), which provides limited protection for consumers if the custodian goes out of business. Also, ask if the firm and its custodian have other insurance, to provide additional protection.

Yes, these lists of questions are long, but you can get through them in an hour or so in an advisor's office. Commit to spending the time. The information you get will be key to choosing the best advisor for you.

If you don't think you can remember all the questions in this section, photocopy these pages and bring the questions along to your meeting. Remember to take notes at the meeting, too — they'll help you recall important information later, when you're having trouble keeping straight the advisors you've met with.

Don't settle on the first advisor you meet with. Meet with two or three before you decide. There are subtle and not-so-subtle differences that become clear when you can compare advisors to each other. Besides professional qualifications, be alert to more subjective considerations, such as:

✔ Do I feel I can really trust this person with my financial future?

✔ Am I comfortable sharing sensitive family information with him?

✔ Do I have good personal chemistry with her?

✔ Is this someone whom my spouse and children will be able to relate to and rely on when I'm no longer around?

✔ Did he spend more time talking or listening to my needs?

✔ How important will I be to her?

Embarrassed by the idea of asking a potential advisor so many questions? Don't be. Repeat after us: *It's my money.* The best advisors will welcome these questions, because they'll be proud to share their responses with you.

Understanding How Advisors Earn Their Income

Just like the type of training they have and the services they provide, advisors' fees vary greatly. Financial advice does come at a price, and the way that price is determined can also vary from advisor to advisor. Some may charge by the hour. Others may charge a project fee. And some may charge a fee that's a percentage of the assets you're investing.

Understanding how an advisor earns his money can give you a very useful clue to how he views his relationship with you. A stockbroker's income, for example, is often transaction-based, meaning that stockbrokers earn their money by selling clients a product. The more products the stockbroker sells, the better his chance for increased earnings. You can rest assured that the stockbroker will encourage you to consider more transactions, which can work out particularly well if you're knowledgeable about the stock market and can direct your stockbroker on the trades you want to make.

On the other hand, an RIA (see the "RIA" section, earlier in this chapter) is relationship-based, meaning that she earns her money solely from you. This type of advisor has a fiduciary responsibility that comes with the title, so she's legally required to keep your best interests front and center in her dealings with you. That doesn't necessarily mean that an RIA will always recommend investments that make you money, of course — no one's right all the time — but you can take comfort in the fact that any investments she recommends are, in her opinion, a wise choice for you.

Be sure to ask any potential investment advisor just how she earns her money, so that you can understand how she views your relationship and take that into account when working with her to make your investment decisions.

In the following sections, we cover the main ways in which advisors are typically compensated. Because they affect your bottom line — and the advisor's economic incentives — you need to make sure you understand how your advisor is making his money.

Fee

Advisors who work on a "fee-only" basis are paid solely by you and receive no compensation from third parties for selling a financial product. They get no commissions, no rebates, no awards, no finder's fees, no bonuses, and no other form of compensation.

The fee may range anywhere from a modest hourly fee (such as $50 per hour), to several thousand dollars for a comprehensive financial plan, to a percentage (typically 1 percent) of assets under management. (That may not sound like much, but remember that 1 percent can mean tens of thousands of dollars when an advisor is managing a multi-million-dollar investment portfolio.)

Members of NAPFA work strictly on a fee-only basis. Some FPA members are fee-only; others work for a combination of fee and commission (see the next two sections).

Commission

Financial advisors who work in the securities industry and insurance agents don't charge a fee that you can see. Instead, they're compensated by the commissions they earn for selling you an investment and/or insurance product. In these cases, the advisor is paid by the suppliers of the investment and/or insurance products, not by you.

Some FPA members work on a commission basis, and others work for a combination of commission and fee (see the following section).

Fee plus commission

Some financial advisors will charge you a fee to analyze your financial situation and make recommendations. In addition, they earn a commission on the sale of certain investment or insurance products. If the advisor doesn't disclose this information to you at the time of the sale, you'll have to ask.

This arrangement is sometimes called *fee-based compensation,* or, if the fee is reduced somewhat by all, or a part of, the commission received, *fee-offset* commission. Neither of these should be confused with fee-only compensation discussed in the "Fee" section earlier.

The commission you pay for an advisor's services is an important consideration, because commissions lower the total return your investment earns. (See Chapter 2 for a basic rundown of returns.)

Performance incentive

A *performance incentive* — where the advisor gets paid based on how well your investments perform (the more money you get, the more money the advisor gets) — is typical of hedge funds, which are usually only for sophisticated investors. Performance incentives typically accompany other forms of compensation.

Part V
The Part of Tens

In this part . . .

We follow hallowed *For Dummies* tradition and provide three short chapters of top-ten lists, all packed with easy-to-digest information. When you read these chapters — which include key historical data on ten important asset classes and ten popular asset allocation mistakes — you'll find yourself far ahead of most investors and well along the road to success. And that, we hope, will inspire you to revisit earlier chapters, as needed, to make sure you're always getting the most you can from this book — and from your investments!

Chapter 17

Ten Asset Classes and Subclasses and Their Historical Rates of Return

In This Chapter

▶ Reviewing 20 years of return data for selected asset classes

▶ Knowing what to do with this information

*T*his chapter is chock-full of raw data — but don't let that scare you! When it comes to investing, raw data is very useful stuff. In fact, it's critical when it comes time for you to make your investment plan and hammer out your asset allocation. Knowing how the various asset classes and subclasses behave over time will help you make informed decisions on the mix of assets that best suits your investment goals.

Use this chapter as a handy reference. Flip back here when you're reading (or rereading) about risk and return (Chapter 2), choosing asset classes and subclasses (Chapter 3), deciding on the right proportions among asset classes (Chapter 4), creating your allocation plan (Chapter 8), or buying securities (Chapter 9).

Before you check out the return data for each of the ten asset classes and subclasses covered in this chapter, have a look at Table 17-1, which lists all those categories and how they're related, as well as the indexes we use to measure the total returns for each class.

The figures in this chapter show the annual total returns for each of the ten selected assets in Table 17-1 over the 20-year period from 1988 through 2007. Looking at an asset's performance over time gives you a pretty good snapshot of the magnitude of the annual total returns themselves, as well as the annual volatility in those returns.

This chapter doesn't dwell on the specifics of the return magnitudes and volatilities in the charts. But we do spotlight some observations and explain why they're important for you to understand and how they can help you improve your asset allocation.

Table 17-1	Selected Asset Classes and Subclasses	
Asset Class	*Subclass*	*Index Used*
Cash	Cash equivalents	U.S. 30-Day Treasury Bill Index
Fixed income	Corporate bonds	Merrill Lynch Corporate Bond Index
	Treasury bonds	Barclays Capital U.S. Treasury Bond Index
	Municipal bonds	Barclays Capital Municipal Bond Index
Alternatives	Real estate	FTSE NAREIT All-REIT Index
	Commodities	S&P GSCI
Equities	U.S. large cap	S&P 500 Stock Index
	U.S. mid cap	S&P MidCap 400 Index
	U.S. small cap	S&P SmallCap 600 Index
	Emerging markets	MSCI Emerging Markets Index

Some of the assets have much higher volatilities than others, and in some cases, the resulting *risk drag* — which can weigh down returns (see Chapter 2) — is substantial. We point that out, where appropriate. In some cases, we refer to certain statistics that we introduce in Chapter 2 — such as simple average return, compound average return, range, and standard deviation — even though these numbers are not shown explicitly in the figures in this chapter.

The data in this chapter is useful, but don't make *any* decisions on the basis of this data alone. Make your investing and asset allocation plans only after you understand the bigger picture we paint throughout this book.

Cash

Cash is the most conservative asset. Figure 17-1 shows total returns for cash, which are based on the U.S. 30-Day Treasury Bill Index, a popular measure for this asset class. As you can see, these returns fall into a relatively narrow range. The range, and the standard deviation, of the returns for cash are by far the lowest of the ten asset classes covered in this chapter.

There's usually no free lunch (see Chapter 2), meaning that you generally don't get high returns without high risk. It should come as no surprise, then, that returns for cash are the lowest of the group of assets we present in this chapter, averaging about 4.5 percent annually. And cash is also the only asset of the group that didn't have a negative total return in *any* of the last 20 years.

Think of cash as a ballast that holds down your money and keeps it from floating away.

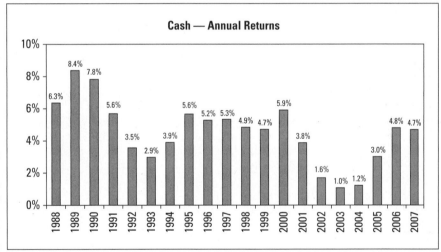

Figure 17-1:
Twenty years of total returns for cash.

Sources: The U.S. 30-Day Treasury Bill Index. Brinton Eaton Wealth Advisors analysis of data, compiled using Morningstar EnCorr.

Corporate Bonds

Corporate bonds are a subclass of the fixed-income asset class. Figure 17-2 provides return data for corporate bonds.

Corporate bonds, like the other fixed-income subclasses (see "Treasury Bonds" and "Municipal Bonds," in this chapter) have a range and standard deviation materially higher than those for cash, but substantially lower than the other asset classes in this chapter (alternatives and equities). Accordingly, their average returns fall between those for cash and the other classes. The average 20-year return for corporate bonds, at a little above 8 percent, is slightly higher than that for Treasury bonds, at about 7.5 percent, reflecting the compensation that the market demands for the generally lower creditworthiness of corporate bonds (see Chapter 3).

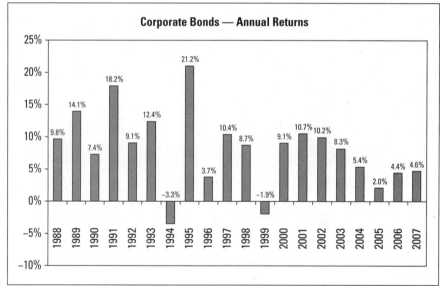

Figure 17-2:
Twenty
years of
total returns
for corpo-
rate bonds.

Sources: Merrill Lynch. Brinton Eaton Wealth Advisors analysis of data, compiled using Morningstar EnCorr.

Treasury Bonds

Treasury bonds are a subclass of the fixed-income asset class. Check out the total returns for Treasury bonds over the 20-year period from 1988 through 2007 in Figure 17-3. Note how the average return (7.5 percent) is just a little bit lower than the average return for corporate bonds during the same period (over 8 percent — see the preceding section).

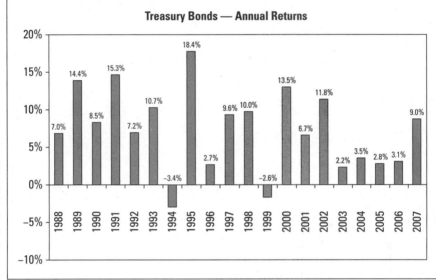

Figure 17-3:
Twenty years of total returns for Treasury bonds.

Sources: Barclays Capital U.S. Treasury Bond Index. © Barclays Capital, Inc. Used with permission. Brinton Eaton Wealth Advisors analysis of data, compiled using Morningstar EnCorr.

Municipal Bonds

Municipal bonds (or munis) are a subclass of the fixed-income asset class. The average return for municipal bonds is just under 7 percent (see Figure 17-4). As we discuss in Chapter 6, you expect munis to have lower returns because their returns are free of income taxes at the federal and state level (depending on where you live). So, on an after-tax basis, the returns on munis can be quite attractive to investors in high tax brackets.

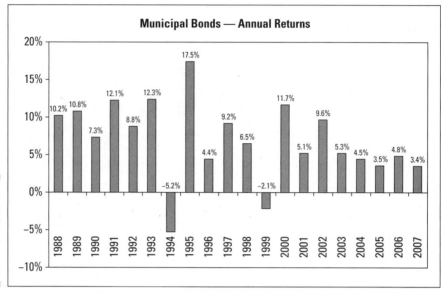

Sources: Barclays Capital Municipal Bond Index. © Barclays Capital, Inc. Used with permission. Brinton Eaton Wealth Advisors analysis of data, compiled using Morningstar EnCorr.

Figure 17-4: Twenty years of total returns for munici-pal bonds.

Real Estate

Real estate (other than the home you live in) is considered an alternative investment and is placed in the alternative asset class. In Figure 17-5, you can see the return history for real estate, as measured by the FTSE NAREIT All-REIT Index. (*REIT* stands for *real estate investment trust;* see Chapter 13 for more information on REITs.) Real estate has a range almost double, and a standard deviation more than triple, the corresponding measures for bonds over the same 20-year period. With this kind of volatility, you should expect a higher return, and real estate delivers. Its simple 20-year average return was 12.4 percent!

Real estate is the first asset we cover in this chapter where we make a dis-tinction between the simple and compound average return, because it's the first where the two are materially different — the 20-year compound aver-age return is 10.9 percent. The difference between the 12.4 percent simple average and the 10.9 percent compound average is due to risk drag, which you can read all about in Chapter 2 (and several other places throughout the book — it's an important concept!). But you can see that even the risk-dragged 10.9 percent is superior to the returns for cash and bonds.

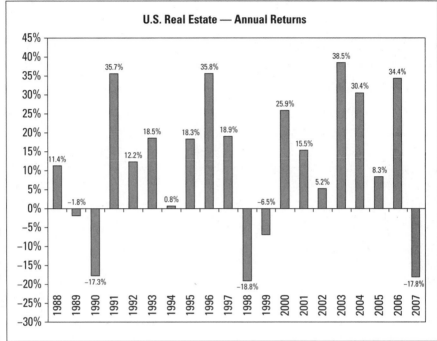

Figure 17-5:
Twenty
years of
total returns
for U.S. real
estate.

Commodities

Like real estate (see the preceding section), commodities fall in the alternative asset class. Figure 17-6 catalogs the returns over the last 20 years for the commodity basket represented by the S&P GSCI (a commodity index), the most popular index for this purpose. Commodities are very volatile, with a standard deviation much higher than that of any other asset in this chapter except emerging-market equities. But this volatility is benign; these returns tend to move in a direction counter to that of most other assets in your portfolio. (They're poorly correlated, as we discuss in Chapter 4.) The risk drag here is even more pronounced than with real estate; the 20-year simple average return is 13.1 percent, while the compound average is 10.2 percent.

But don't let this risk drag give you the creeps — you can eliminate quite a bit of the risk drag at the portfolio level by taking advantage of commodities' poor correlation. Mix them with other asset classes in the right proportions and diligently rebalance (as we explain in Chapters 4 and 5), and you'll end up very pleased with your portfolio's performance. As you can see, even a compound average return of 10.2 percent, weighed down as it is by substantial risk drag, is better than the returns of cash and bonds, and comparable to real estate.

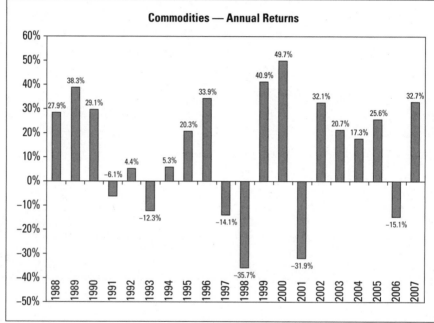

Figure 17-6: Twenty years of total returns for commodities.

Large-Cap Stocks

Large-cap stocks are a subclass of the equities asset class. Figure 17-7 displays the return data for large-cap stocks. You can see that large-cap stocks exhibit substantial volatility, but good-size returns, over the long term.

When it comes to equities, *cap* is shorthand for capitalization, which refers to a company's size. In this context, company sizes are determined by their share prices times the number of their outstanding shares. (For a detailed breakdown on company size, see Chapter 3.)

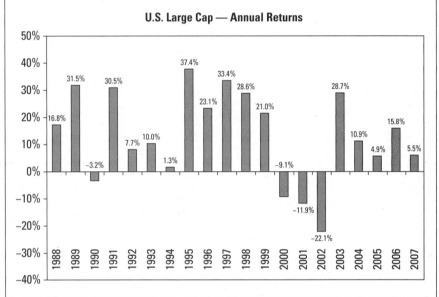

Figure 17-7:
Twenty years of total returns for U.S. large-cap stocks.

Sources: Standard & Poor's data. Standard & Poor's, S&P, S&P 500, and S&P GSCI are registered trademarks of the McGraw-Hill Companies, Inc. Used with permission of Standard & Poor's. Brinton Eaton Wealth Advisors analysis of data, compiled using Morningstar EnCorr.

Mid-Cap Stocks

Mid-cap stocks are a subclass of the equities asset class. Have a look at Figure 17-8 to see the return data for U.S. mid-cap stocks, for the 20-year period from 1988 through 2007. As with large-cap stocks (see the preceding section) and small-cap stocks (see the following section), mid-cap stocks involve substantial volatility but offer healthy long-term returns.

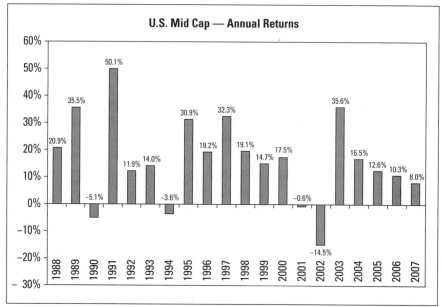

Sources: Standard & Poor's data. Standard & Poor's, S&P, S&P 500, and S&P GSCI are registered trademarks of the McGraw-Hill Companies, Inc. Used with permission of Standard & Poor's. Brinton Eaton Wealth Advisors analysis of data, compiled using Morningstar EnCorr.

Figure 17-8:
Twenty years of total returns for U.S. mid-cap stocks.

Small-Cap Stocks

Small-cap stocks are a subclass of the equities asset class. You can review the annual return data for small-cap stocks in the United States in Figure 17-9. Small-cap stocks, like mid-cap and large-cap stocks (see the two preceding sections) typically come with a good amount of volatility, but along with that volatility, you can count on solid returns over the long run.

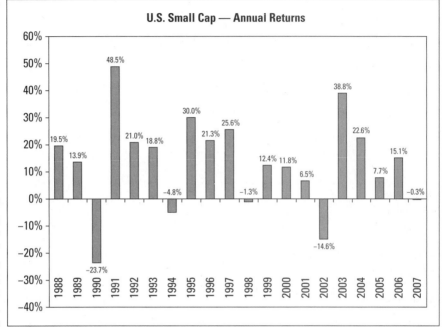

Figure 17-9:
Twenty
years of
total returns
for U.S.
small-cap
stocks.

Sources: Standard & Poor's data. Standard & Poor's, S&P, S&P 500, and S&P GSCI are registered trademarks of the McGraw-Hill Companies, Inc. Used with permission of Standard & Poor's. Brinton Eaton Wealth Advisors analysis of data, compiled using Morningstar EnCorr.

Emerging-Market Stocks

Emerging-market stocks, like the three preceding subclasses (large-, mid-, and small-cap stocks) fall in the equity asset class. You can see the annual return data for emerging-market stocks in Figure 17-10.

Emerging markets deserve special mention. They take the volatility prize for this chapter — their standard deviation is higher than that of even commodities, and roughly double that of the other equity subclasses. The expected return is high, but the risk drag is notable; the simple average return of 20.7 percent drops to 16.3 percent on a compound-average basis because of the effect of risk drag. Even so, this is the highest compound-average return we encounter in this chapter.

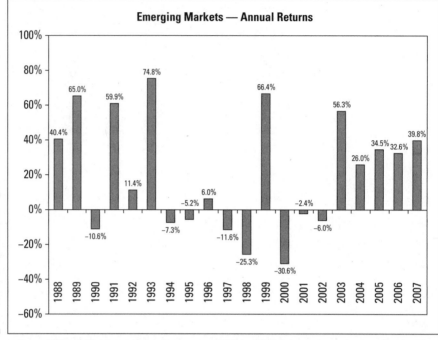

Sources: MSCI Barra. This information is the exclusive property of MSCI, Inc. (MSCI), and may not be reproduced or redisseminated in any form or used to create any financial products or indices without MSCI's prior written permission. This information is provided "as is" and none of MSCI, its affiliates, or any other person involved in or related to the compilation of this information (collectively, the MSCI Parties), makes any express or implied warranties or representations with respect to the information or the results to be obtained by the use thereof, and the MSCI Parties hereby expressly disclaim all implied warranties (including, without limitation, the implied warranties of merchant-ability and fitness for a particular purpose) with respect to this information. In no event shall any MSCI Party have any liability of any kind to any person or entity arising from or related to this information. Brinton Eaton Wealth Advisors analysis of data, compiled using Morningstar EnCorr.

Figure 17-10: Twenty years of total returns for emerging-market stocks.

The volatility of emerging-market stocks, like some of the other asset sub-classes we describe in this chapter, can be scary. You may be tempted to reject certain classes or subclasses from consideration for your portfolio because they look too volatile. Not so fast! You *need* some of that volatility in your portfolio. The correlation among these assets (a feature that cannot easily be shown in figures such as these) is at least as important as their expected returns and volatilities (see Chapter 4 for more on this). The figures in this chapter are informative, but they tell only *part* of the story.

Chapter 18

Ten Common Asset Allocation Mistakes

In This Chapter

▶ Identifying the mistakes many investors make

▶ Understanding how you can avoid them

*W*hat prevents success for most investors? Their own behavior.

Here's an example: Studies show that the average long-term return for equity mutual funds is in the neighborhood of 10 percent, but the average investor in those funds gets only 4 percent. Why? Problematic investor behavior.

In many cases, investors simply get in their own way. Whether it's letting emotions rule, paying too much attention to the talking heads on TV, chasing performance, or trying to time the markets, investors' bad behavior can destroy their best-laid plans and good intentions.

The good news: If you know what to look for, you can dodge these obvious mistakes. In this chapter, we outline ten common mistakes made by investors. If they sound just a little too familiar, don't sweat it! At the end of each section, we clue you in on how you can avoid the mistakes and nip the problematic behavior in the bud.

Ignoring Asset Allocation in the First Place

Asset allocation helps investors achieve success. In fact, it's the key driver of success (see Chapter 4). So why don't more investors use this strategy to their benefit? Why do they make the mistake of ignoring asset allocation?

A lack of information isn't the issue, so scratch that off the list. The Web sites of nearly every mutual fund and brokerage firm explain asset allocation. Bookstores have shelves full of good books on the subject that we can enthusiastically recommend — starting with this one!

A lack of interest isn't the reason either. Investors follow the news and go online daily to find out what's happening with their portfolios. They're keenly aware of the ups and downs of the market.

What may explain the less-than-universal adoption of asset allocation is this: Many investors aren't really investors at all. They're speculators. They find the pursuit of the undiscovered gem of an investment a sexy undertaking. They revel in the thought of making a killing, using market timing, or employing a similarly unreliable strategy.

Asset allocation, on the other hand, is methodical — a top-down, scientific approach. It's not sexy at all. In fact, some people even consider it boring. And most people don't like boring.

Don't fall victim to the mistake of shunning asset allocation as your principal investment strategy. Repeat after us: Boring is beautiful! You may need to rethink your idea of success when it comes to your money. Your aim should be to establish a long-term plan that will last and fulfill the financial goals you have in mind. Asset allocation should be the centerpiece of that plan. Embrace it!

Believing That Diversification Is Enough

Investors tend to confuse asset allocation with diversification. By diversifying their portfolio (making sure they're not overly concentrated in one or a few holdings), they believe they've achieved asset allocation. Not so!

Asset allocation requires you to be diversified, but that's not all there is to it. Diversification is an important step in asset allocation — but it's only one step. In Chapter 4, we tell you about an investor who owns a number of different energy stocks, as well as a commodity index fund. This investor is diversified (no single holding dominates his portfolio), but he has an extremely poor asset allocation, because his portfolio is excessively dependent on the price of oil.

Asset allocation goes beyond simple diversification; it involves picking asset classes that are poorly correlated with each other and then mixing them together in the right proportions to optimize the risk/return profile of your portfolio (see Chapters 4 and 8 for a more thorough explanation). After that, diversification comes into play again, because you want to make sure you have a proper spread of holdings *within* each asset class. Diversification is a good practice — but asset allocation is a full-blown, scientifically derived strategy, of which diversification is only one part.

Don't stop short and settle on simply diversifying your portfolio's holdings. Go the extra mile and develop a comprehensive asset allocation plan. You and your wallet will be glad you did.

Forgetting to Rebalance

Portfolios are like automobiles. If you want your car to perform over the long haul, you take care to practice regular maintenance. It's the same with your portfolio, and one of the most critical facets of regular portfolio maintenance is rebalancing.

Rebalancing wisely, and at the right time, is a great way to make sure you're getting the most out of your portfolio. (You can read all about the nuts and bolts of rebalancing in Chapter 5.)

The challenge of rebalancing, which is a key companion to asset allocation, is that it doesn't make sense to the uninitiated; it's counterintuitive. As markets shift gears, you buy and sell investments to bring your portfolio back to its target allocation. In the beginning, you may be very uncomfortable making these adjustments, because it requires that you sell assets that have gone up in value and buy others that are not performing so well. It'll be contrary to what your friends are doing and what the press is saying.

Don't be afraid to be a contrarian. When your portfolio tells you it's time, set it back to its target allocation. You'll improve its return without increasing its risk.

Not Having a Long-Term Plan

The steps you need to take to make sure you have a solid, long-term asset allocation plan can be many and varied, but we can't stress enough how important it is that you develop a sound plan. Without a plan, you'll be lost. To help you nail down your plan, make sure you're taking care of the following tasks:

✔ Think about your goals, and your sources of income and outgo, for the next 10, 20, and 30 years.

✔ Figure out how much risk you're comfortable taking.

- ✔ Understand various asset classes and subclasses, and how they behave.
- ✔ Decide what percentage of your total portfolio to devote to each of these asset classes and subclasses.
- ✔ Know how to track your performance and how to put it in the proper context.
- ✔ Document your plan.
- ✔ Stick to your plan!

Work like this is hard for those who prefer to make a quick buck, but if you take the time to work through the required steps, you'll end up with a winning, profitable plan.

Don't skip the work. No ifs, ands, or buts — this is work. But it's work that we guarantee will benefit you for years to come. When you're done developing a plan — aside from doing regular maintenance (rebalancing and making necessary changes as economic or life conditions require) — you're done. You're not at the mercy of the market, which is a lot more than many, many investors can say.

Indulging Your Emotions

Money represents an uncomfortable paradox for many people. They cringe when they think about it, yet that's all they think about much of the time.

If you don't have a reasoned, long-term investment plan in place, greed and anxiety can take over your thoughts. You may be tempted to hold onto your winners too long, or refuse to diversify out of your employer's stock. Without the right plan in place, your emotions can cause you to panic when the stock market dips — you may want to just sell out (quite possibly at a loss), and then sit on the sidelines until it feels safe to jump back in (usually when it's too late).

These types of emotions aren't the right guides for any life decision, particularly decisions involving money. Shooting from the hip may feel very exciting during the few situations when it actually works out in your favor, but it's not a strategy — it's gambling, and the opposite of a well-thought-out asset-allocation plan.

Don't let your emotions get the best of you. You may get lucky every once in a while, but you can't count on emotion to produce the results you want over the long haul.

Paying Too Much Attention to the Financial Media

If you're serious about investing, reading and listening to the financial news can be useful, but a 24/7 dose isn't healthy for anyone. The talking heads can blur your vision, batter your eardrums, and — if you listen too long — drive you nuts.

It's important that you know what's going on generally with the U.S. and global economies, of course, because the business cycle should influence your overall asset allocation and the periodic tweaks you make to it (see Chapter 15). But the news on any given day (or hour or minute) shouldn't dictate an abrupt or radical shift in your investing strategy. The truly meaningful economic news unfolds gradually.

You have to ignore "news" that isn't simply factual but offers to explain — or, worse, predict — the movements in the financial markets and what you should do about them. Don't buy into it! Ignoring these stories can be especially difficult when it's time for you to rebalance, because much of the media will be telling you to do the exact opposite of what you *should* be doing.

Don't turn to the financial media for investment advice. Instead, use the news to keep up on general economic trends.

Chasing Performance

In very small print at the bottom of every fund prospectus and advertisement, you'll read, "Past performance is no guarantee of future results." Yet many investors ignore these words and throw money at funds, sectors, or managers that are outperforming, hoping to catch some of the gold dust that fell on them over the past few years.

Chasing performance can be tempting, because it can make you feel smart — and, occasionally, you just may get lucky with it. But keep in mind that you'll still be chasing, not staying ahead of, the curve. Chasing performance, or buying the latest hot stock or sector, is like driving a car by looking in the rearview mirror. Results for a particular stock or sector may have been good for the past one, three, or five years — but there's no guarantee that they'll continue to outperform. In fact, if you rebalance as you should, you'll be lightening up on these hot performers as most everyone else is piling in.

Don't chase the hot stock, fund, or sector. Stick with your long-term investment plan, which is based on good, solid science, and rebalance regularly.

Thinking You Can Outsmart the Market

Active management — not to mention its evil cousin, market timing — is based on the premise that you can reliably do better than the market averages by knowing specifically what securities to invest in and when. Put simply, this is hogwash. Studies have consistently shown that such strategies underperform the market indexes over the long term, particularly after factoring in the relatively high costs of actively managed funds. Short-term exceptions to this rule are the result of luck, plain and simple.

The only reliable way to beat the market over the long term is through informed asset allocation and diligent rebalancing. And you can do this even if all you invest in is low-cost passive index funds. (Turn to Chapter 4 for more on how you can create a portfolio that produces more than the sum of its parts.)

Don't fall for active management or market timing. Don't bet your financial future on dumb luck. Stick with informed asset allocation and rebalancing instead.

Ignoring Taxes

We'd all like to ignore taxes, but let's face it: They're not going away. Perhaps in their wishful attempt to disregard the IRS, lots of investors fail to take advantage of simple and legal ways to avoid paying taxes they don't need to be paying.

Putting tax-inefficient investments like real estate investment trusts (REITs) in a taxable account is one of many common mistakes. Selling a holding at a taxable short-term gain weeks before it would qualify for lower taxes as a long-term gain is another. Failing to recognize the flexibility that a capital-loss carryover from a prior tax year gives you is yet another. And, perhaps the most common mistake (drum roll, please): failing to harvest tax losses throughout the year.

And those examples relate only to income taxes. Avoiding estate taxes can be even simpler. We offer numerous bits of advice on how to minimize the effect of taxes on your portfolio throughout this book; Chapter 14, in particular, is packed with good information on how to be a tax-aware investor and avoid taxes you shouldn't have to pay. We can't really offer a whole lot of help with death, but we're happy to take some of the bite out of taxes.

Don't forget to take a good long look at what you're losing in taxes, and what portion of that you could keep if you made a few tweaks to your portfolio. **Remember:** It's not what you make, but what you keep that really matters. Make sure you have the tax man in mind when making investment decisions. Don't let the tax tail wag the investment dog — but, at the same time, don't give away money needlessly because you weren't paying attention.

Disrespecting Inflation

Inflation is so pervasive, we tend to take it for granted. And yet some investors ignore inflation — at their peril. If your living expenses inflate at an average rate of 3.5 percent (not an unreasonable assumption, particularly when you factor in fast-rising medical costs), then what cost you $1,000 at age 65 will cost you roughly $2,000 at age 85. By then, you may have no other source of income but your investments, and, if you haven't factored in inflation in the meantime, your investments may not have lasted that long.

Some investors believe that they can best protect their nest egg by being as conservative as possible with their investments, loading up on cash equivalents and bonds (see Chapter 3 for more on these and other asset classes). But these low-risk investments are the ones most likely to underperform when compared to inflation over the long run. As we discuss throughout this book, you need to carefully consider the trade-off between capital preservation and inflation protection, and find the right balance for you.

Don't forget about inflation when creating your long-term investment plan. Recognize that wealth is only meaningful in terms of its purchasing power. And the purchasing power of a dollar declines over time with relentless regularity. Make sure (within your tolerance for risk) that you have a portfolio that generates a healthy long-term expected return in excess of inflation; the alternative is to get poorer — and we know you don't want that!

Chapter 19

Ten Questions to Test Your Asset Allocation Know-How

*Y*ou can't really learn unless you know what you don't know. In this chapter, we pose ten questions that test your knowledge of asset allocation. There's no special prize for acing these questions — other than the satisfaction that comes with knowing you've mastered important concepts that'll put you ahead of most investors.

If you don't know the answers, no problem — that's why you have this book! If you draw a blank on some of these questions, that'll tell you what you need to bone up on. We let you know where you can turn within this book to get the know-how you need.

Dive in, and good luck!

What's the Best Way to Get Consistently Good Investment Performance?

Is it by being a good stock-picker? Nope. Is it by timing the market? Of course, not!

The best, most reliable way to get consistently good investment performance is to determine an asset allocation mix that's right for you — and stick to it.

The performance of your investments will be determined mostly by your asset allocation. Your portfolio should include the fixed-income, equities, and alternatives asset classes (see Chapter 8).

Betting on your (or anyone else's) ability to pick stocks exposes you to a lot more risk. Why?

- ✔ Because you're investing from the bottom up, and you may end up with a portfolio that makes no strategic sense for you.

- ✔ Because, if you end up owning stocks that are concentrated in the same sector, they'll generally trend together — which can be a big problem. It's the opposite of proper diversification.

- ✔ Because individual stocks, including those of large, well-established companies, can be very volatile and can even become worthless.

- ✔ Because, by the time a "hot tip" makes it to the media, the stock has often reached a very high price, and it may not be a good deal anymore.

Relying on stock-picking can be the kiss of death when it comes to investing. But it's not the worst you can do. You could also engage in market timing — just saying the words sends chills down our spines. Aside from being unreliable, market timing is ultimately a losing strategy. Even the so-called experts who try to do it for a living generally end up worse off than the market averages over the long term.

Determining a good asset allocation mix and sticking to it lacks the drama and excitement of chasing hot stock tips or trying to outsmart the market. But it's likely to result in more money for you in the end. If drama and excitement are what you crave, take up skydiving.

What's Better: An 8 Percent Return or a 9 Percent Return?

A portfolio with a simple average return of 9 percent is the clear winner, *if* both portfolios have similar levels of volatility. However, if the portfolio with the 9 percent simple average return is a lot more volatile than the one with the 8 percent simple average return, all that extra volatility will create significant risk drag. If the volatility and resultant risk drag are severe enough, it could cause the portfolio with the higher simple average return to leave you with less money! For a more detailed explanation of this surprising phenomenon, turn to Chapter 2.

What's the Riskiest Kind of Portfolio?

Is it a portfolio with extremely high volatility? Not necessarily. The riskiest portfolio for you is one that has the lowest probability of meeting your overall long-term financial needs.

Throughout your life, you'll have numerous important goals, some of which are short term (such as funding education) and some of which are long term (such as living in retirement). Whatever financial goals you have, you want to make sure your portfolio helps you meet those goals.

To cover expenses that'll need to be paid soon, you want to minimize volatility in your assets. For expenses that are farther into the future, you'll be in a position to take a long view and tolerate the greater short-term volatility that comes with investing in assets that have higher expected returns. You'll, therefore, be better able to beat inflation. So risk and volatility aren't equivalent, and, depending on your situation, a high-volatility portfolio may actually be your lowest-risk alternative.

Your personal definition of risk will depend on your unique circumstances. Turn to Chapter 7 for details on how to figure out what kind of risk is right for you.

How Much Variety Should You Include in the Asset Classes You Choose?

It may be tempting to stick with what you know. On the other hand, it may be alluring to go after exotic investments that are put together by some really smart people. Neither is a winning strategy. Your best bet is to stick with a mix of fixed-income, equities, and alternative investments (like real estate and commodities).

If you limit yourself to investing only in what's familiar to you (bonds, for example), then your portfolio holdings will likely be concentrated in a couple of asset classes or subclasses. It'll lack needed diversification.

At the same time, you need to make sure you don't get excited about exotic-sounding investments and strategies that can have an even more disastrous effect on your portfolio. Many of these investments — hedge funds are one good example — are very risky and carry very high fees.

Instead of investing only in what's familiar, or investing in what's exotic but unknown, educate yourself on the building blocks of sound portfolios: fixed-income assets, equities, and alternatives. (You can read all about the breadth of asset-class choices in Chapter 3.)

Don't confuse diversification with asset allocation. Diversification is necessary, but not enough, to achieve true asset allocation. To get the full picture, check out Chapter 4.

What's the Best Way to Rebalance?

No, we're not talking about the rebalancing you can do to your car's tires, or the rebalancing you can do to your chi through yoga. We're talking about rebalancing your portfolio — and the best way to do that is to sell a piece of your winning assets and invest in your losing assets.

We know it can sound crazy to the novice investor, but rebalancing really works. Why? The only thing we can say for sure about the market is that, at different times, some asset classes will go up (or down) faster than others. Whatever is currently hot will eventually cool down. Whatever is cold will eventually heat up. If you account for this certainty by rebalancing — making trades when necessary to stick to your preferred asset allocation — you can keep a portfolio that stays warm all the time.

If you invest in assets with low correlation to each other and you diligently rebalance your portfolio, then you don't have to make bets on which way the different parts of the market are heading. By selling a part of whatever increases significantly, you won't lose as much money when it does finally decrease. By buying more of whatever has decreased significantly, you'll gain more money when it does finally rebound. Rebalancing forces you to buy low and sell high. Check out Chapter 5 for all the nuts and bolts of rebalancing.

It's important to distinguish between how you should treat individual stocks and how you should treat diversified assets. Although asset classes may go up and down and never go out of business, the same is not true for stocks. Companies, even household names, can go out of business, or their stock can decline dramatically and irreversibly. Before your portfolio suffers too much damage, it may be a good idea to either trim your holdings or get out of the stock altogether. No use in throwing good money after bad. However, this is no longer in the realm of asset allocation — it's about stock picking.

When Should You Rebalance Your Portfolio?

Every day? Every quarter? Every year? No, no, and no, again. You should rebalance when and only when your portfolio drifts significantly from your target allocation.

If you rebalance too often, you'll exit the winning assets too early, and the excess transaction costs from trading will eat away at your returns. If you wait too long, you may miss an opportunity to enhance your returns, as your winners become losers again. The best time to rebalance isn't on a fixed, regular schedule, but when your portfolio gets significantly out of balance. This may not happen for several months (or even more than a year, if the markets are tame), but in especially turbulent markets, you may get several rebalancing opportunities in a short period of time. (Flip to Chapters 5 and 11 for more on rebalancing.)

When Should You Revisit Your Asset Allocation Plan?

You should revisit your asset allocation plan at least every four years, or whenever you have a major life event. Asset allocation is for the long term, because most investment horizons are several years long. The only time you should consider revising your asset allocation plan is if there are material changes in your situation or if, through the passage of time, you're in a different stage of your life. (See Chapters 8 and 15 for all the relevant details.)

Should You Apply Your Asset Allocation Percentages to Each of Your Investment Accounts?

This one's a simple answer: No. You should apply your asset allocation percentages to the sum total of *all* your accounts. Doing so will help you keep more of the money that you make instead of paying it in fees and taxes.

For example, say you have two accounts: $1 million in taxable Account A and $100,000 in tax-deferred Account B. Let's also assume that your asset allocation plan calls for you to allocate 7 percent of your portfolio, or $77,000, to real estate (through real estate investment trusts, or REITs). If you decided to allocate on the account level, you'd invest $70,000 in Account A and $7,000 in Account B (7 percent of each account). If you were to allocate on the aggregate portfolio level, you might invest the entire $77,000 in tax-deferred Account B. There are several advantages to allocating on the portfolio level in this example:

- ✔ **Tax efficiency:** REITs are tax-inefficient, meaning that they generate income that is taxed at the highest (ordinary income) tax rates. In this example, the tax-inefficient REITs are better placed in the tax-deferred account, so you don't have to pay taxes at the higher ordinary income-tax rate every year on the income you get from the REIT.

- ✔ **Ease and cost of rebalancing:** When it comes time to rebalance, instead of having to do it twice (once for each account, in this example — more if you have more than two accounts), you can rebalance once across both accounts. This process is easier and also saves on transaction costs.

- ✔ **Meeting investment minimums:** Some mutual funds have separate share classes that require high minimum investments. These share classes offer investors lower fees. In other words, one $77,000 investment may cost you less to own than a $70,000 investment and a $7,000 investment.

The tactical placement of certain assets in certain accounts is called *asset location*. We touch on this in Chapter 6, and explore it in depth in Chapter 10.

How Do You Know How Well Your Investments Have Performed?

You can determine how well your investments have performed by calculating your time-weighted compound average return. The time-weighted return is a measure of how your *investments* did. For purposes of comparison to external market benchmark returns, this is superior to the dollar-weighted return, which is a measure of how well *you* did. What's the difference? The time-weighted return isn't affected by when you made deposits to or withdrawals from the account; the dollar-weighted return does. (If there are no deposits or withdrawals in an account, then the two will be the same.)

For example, say your portfolio returned –10 percent in the first half of the year and 20 percent in the second half of the year. Your time-weighted compound return would have been 8 percent for the year, regardless of what you may have deposited or withdrawn during the year (see Chapter 2 for how to calculate this). Your dollar-weighted return could be higher or lower than that, depending solely on the timing of your deposits and withdrawals, making meaningful external comparisons problematic.

Likewise, compound average returns are more useful than simple average returns. The compound average is the accurate and proper measure of multi-period returns. The simple average is a quick-and-dirty estimate for the compound average return. Specifically, the simple average doesn't take risk drag into account. For volatile investments, the difference between the simple return and the compound return can be significant.

We discuss these various measures of return in Chapter 2 and talk about making external comparisons in Chapter 12.

Where Can You Go for Help with Your Asset Allocation?

If you're interested in getting some help with your asset allocation plan, consult a qualified, proven professional. You need to be certain that the person has a designation that requires passing a rigorous exam, continuing education, and relevant work experience (see Chapter 16). And be sure that, above all, your advisor listens to your needs. Your financial advisor should focus on meeting your needs and not on pushing products, or her own special expertise, on you. Make sure you also know the handful of professional designations that are not only meaningful, but also appropriate to your goals.

Index

• F •

● *L* ●

• *P* •

BUSINESS, CAREERS & PERSONAL FINANCE

...ounting For Dummies, 4th Edition*
...-0-470-24600-9

...okkeeping Workbook For Dummies†
...-0-470-16983-4

...mmodities For Dummies
...-0-470-04928-0

...ing Business in China For Dummies
...-0-470-04929-7

E-Mail Marketing For Dummies
978-0-470-19087-6

Job Interviews For Dummies, 3rd Edition*†
978-0-470-17748-8

Personal Finance Workbook For Dummies*†
978-0-470-09933-9

Real Estate License Exams For Dummies
978-0-7645-7623-2

Six Sigma For Dummies
978-0-7645-6798-8

Small Business Kit For Dummies, 2nd Edition*†
978-0-7645-5984-6

Telephone Sales For Dummies
978-0-470-16836-3

BUSINESS PRODUCTIVITY & MICROSOFT OFFICE

...cess 2007 For Dummies
...-0-470-03649-5

...cel 2007 For Dummies
...-0-470-03737-9

...fice 2007 For Dummies
...-0-470-00923-9

...tlook 2007 For Dummies
...-0-470-03830-7

PowerPoint 2007 For Dummies
978-0-470-04059-1

Project 2007 For Dummies
978-0-470-03651-8

QuickBooks 2008 For Dummies
978-0-470-18470-7

Quicken 2008 For Dummies
978-0-470-17473-9

Salesforce.com For Dummies, 2nd Edition
978-0-470-04893-1

Word 2007 For Dummies
978-0-470-03658-7

EDUCATION, HISTORY, REFERENCE & TEST PREPARATION

...rican American History For Dummies
...-0-7645-5469-8

...gebra For Dummies
...-0-7645-5325-7

...gebra Workbook For Dummies
...-0-7645-8467-1

...t History For Dummies
...-0-470-09910-0

ASVAB For Dummies, 2nd Edition
978-0-470-10671-6

British Military History For Dummies
978-0-470-03213-8

Calculus For Dummies
978-0-7645-2498-1

Canadian History For Dummies, 2nd Edition
978-0-470-83656-9

Geometry Workbook For Dummies
978-0-471-79940-5

The SAT I For Dummies, 6th Edition
978-0-7645-7193-0

Series 7 Exam For Dummies
978-0-470-09932-2

World History For Dummies
978-0-7645-5242-7

FOOD, GARDEN, HOBBIES & HOME

...dge For Dummies, 2nd Edition
...-0-471-92426-5

...in Collecting For Dummies, 2nd Edition
...-0-470-22275-1

...oking Basics For Dummies, 3rd Edition
...-0-7645-7206-7

Drawing For Dummies
978-0-7645-5476-6

Etiquette For Dummies, 2nd Edition
978-0-470-10672-3

Gardening Basics For Dummies*†
978-0-470-03749-2

Knitting Patterns For Dummies
978-0-470-04556-5

Living Gluten-Free For Dummies†
978-0-471-77383-2

Painting Do-It-Yourself For Dummies
978-0-470-17533-0

HEALTH, SELF HELP, PARENTING & PETS

...ger Management For Dummies
...-0-470-03715-7

...xiety & Depression Workbook ...r Dummies
...-0-7645-9793-0

...eting For Dummies, 2nd Edition
...-0-7645-4149-0

...g Training For Dummies, 2nd Edition
...-0-7645-8418-3

Horseback Riding For Dummies
978-0-470-09719-9

Infertility For Dummies†
978-0-470-11518-3

Meditation For Dummies with CD-ROM, 2nd Edition
978-0-471-77774-8

Post-Traumatic Stress Disorder For Dummies
978-0-470-04922-8

Puppies For Dummies, 2nd Edition
978-0-470-03717-1

Thyroid For Dummies, 2nd Edition†
978-0-471-78755-6

Type 1 Diabetes For Dummies*†
978-0-470-17811-9

...eparate Canadian edition also available
...eparate U.K. edition also available

INTERNET & DIGITAL MEDIA

AdWords For Dummies
978-0-470-15252-2

Blogging For Dummies, 2nd Edition
978-0-470-23017-6

**Digital Photography All-in-One
Desk Reference For Dummies, 3rd Edition**
978-0-470-03743-0

Digital Photography For Dummies, 5th Edition
978-0-7645-9802-9

**Digital SLR Cameras & Photography
For Dummies, 2nd Edition**
978-0-470-14927-0

**eBay Business All-in-One Desk Reference
For Dummies**
978-0-7645-8438-1

eBay For Dummies, 5th Edition*
978-0-470-04529-9

eBay Listings That Sell For Dummies
978-0-471-78912-3

Facebook For Dummies
978-0-470-26273-3

The Internet For Dummies, 11th Edition
978-0-470-12174-0

Investing Online For Dummies, 5th Edition
978-0-7645-8456-5

iPod & iTunes For Dummies, 5th Editi
978-0-470-17474-6

MySpace For Dummies
978-0-470-09529-4

Podcasting For Dummies
978-0-471-74898-4

**Search Engine Optimization
For Dummies, 2nd Edition**
978-0-471-97998-2

Second Life For Dummies
978-0-470-18025-9

Starting an eBay Business For Dumm
3rd Edition†
978-0-470-14924-9

GRAPHICS, DESIGN & WEB DEVELOPMENT

**Adobe Creative Suite 3 Design Premium
All-in-One Desk Reference For Dummies**
978-0-470-11724-8

**Adobe Web Suite CS3 All-in-One Desk
Reference For Dummies**
978-0-470-12099-6

AutoCAD 2008 For Dummies
978-0-470-11650-0

**Building a Web Site For Dummies,
3rd Edition**
978-0-470-14928-7

**Creating Web Pages All-in-One Desk
Reference For Dummies, 3rd Edition**
978-0-470-09629-1

**Creating Web Pages For Dummies,
8th Edition**
978-0-470-08030-6

Dreamweaver CS3 For Dummies
978-0-470-11490-2

Flash CS3 For Dummies
978-0-470-12100-9

Google SketchUp For Dummies
978-0-470-13744-4

InDesign CS3 For Dummies
978-0-470-11865-8

**Photoshop CS3 All-in-One
Desk Reference For Dummies**
978-0-470-11195-6

Photoshop CS3 For Dummies
978-0-470-11193-2

Photoshop Elements 5 For Dummie
978-0-470-09810-3

SolidWorks For Dummies
978-0-7645-9555-4

Visio 2007 For Dummies
978-0-470-08983-5

Web Design For Dummies, 2nd Edit
978-0-471-78117-2

Web Sites Do-It-Yourself For Dumm
978-0-470-16903-2

Web Stores Do-It-Yourself For Dumm
978-0-470-17443-2

LANGUAGES, RELIGION & SPIRITUALITY

Arabic For Dummies
978-0-471-77270-5

Chinese For Dummies, Audio Set
978-0-470-12766-7

French For Dummies
978-0-7645-5193-2

German For Dummies
978-0-7645-5195-6

Hebrew For Dummies
978-0-7645-5489-6

Ingles Para Dummies
978-0-7645-5427-8

Italian For Dummies, Audio Set
978-0-470-09586-7

Italian Verbs For Dummies
978-0-471-77389-4

Japanese For Dummies
978-0-7645-5429-2

Latin For Dummies
978-0-7645-5431-5

Portuguese For Dummies
978-0-471-78738-9

Russian For Dummies
978-0-471-78001-4

Spanish Phrases For Dummies
978-0-7645-7204-3

Spanish For Dummies
978-0-7645-5194-9

Spanish For Dummies, Audio Set
978-0-470-09585-0

The Bible For Dummies
978-0-7645-5296-0

Catholicism For Dummies
978-0-7645-5391-2

The Historical Jesus For Dummies
978-0-470-16785-4

Islam For Dummies
978-0-7645-5503-9

**Spirituality For Dummies,
2nd Edition**
978-0-470-19142-2

NETWORKING AND PROGRAMMING

ASP.NET 3.5 For Dummies
978-0-470-19592-5

C# 2008 For Dummies
978-0-470-19109-5

Hacking For Dummies, 2nd Edition
978-0-470-05235-8

Home Networking For Dummies, 4th Edition
978-0-470-11806-1

Java For Dummies, 4th Edition
978-0-470-08716-9

**Microsoft® SQL Server™ 2008 All-in-One
Desk Reference For Dummies**
978-0-470-17954-3

**Networking All-in-One Desk Reference
For Dummies, 2nd Edition**
978-0-7645-9939-2

**Networking For Dummies,
8th Edition**
978-0-470-05620-2

SharePoint 2007 For Dummies
978-0-470-09941-4

**Wireless Home Networking
For Dummies, 2nd Edition**
978-0-471-74940-0